JUST WORDS

THE CHICAGO SERIES IN LAW AND SOCIETY
Edited by John M. Conley and Lynn Mather

Also in the series:

ADDITIONAL SERIES TITLES FOLLOW INDEX

JUST WORDS

Law, Language, and Power
Third Edition

JOHN M. CONLEY, WILLIAM M. O'BARR,
AND ROBIN CONLEY RINER

THE UNIVERSITY OF CHICAGO PRESS
CHICAGO AND LONDON

The University of Chicago Press, Chicago 60637
The University of Chicago Press, Ltd., London
© 1998, 2005, 2019 by The University of Chicago
Published 2019

28 27 26 25 24 23 22 21 20 19   1 2 3 4 5

ISBN-13: 978-0-226-48422-8 (cloth)
ISBN-13: 978-0-226-48436-5 (paper)
ISBN-13: 978-0-226-48453-2 (e-book)
DOI: https://doi.org/10.7208/chicago/9780226484532.001.0001

Library of Congress Cataloging-in-Publication Data

Names: Conley, John M., author. | O'Barr, William M., author. | Conley Riner, Robin, author.
Title: Just words : law, language, and power / John M. Conley, William M. O'Barr, and Robin
    Conley Riner.
Other titles: Chicago series in law and society.
Description: Third edition. | Chicago ; London : The University of Chicago Press, 2019. | Series:
    The Chicago series in law and society | Includes bibliographical references and index. |
    Originally published: Chicago : University of Chicago Press, 1998.
Identifiers: LCCN 2018030504 | ISBN 9780226484228 (cloth : alk. paper) |
    ISBN 9780226484365 (pbk. : alk. paper) | ISBN 9780226484532 (e-book)
Subjects: LCSH: Law — Language. | Equality before the law. | English language — Rhetoric — Sex
    differences. | Communication in law. | Sociological jurisprudence.
Classification: LCC K213 .C658 2019 | DDC 340/.14 — dc23
LC record available at https://lccn.loc.gov/2018030504

To Ernestine Friedl, who, seeing the promise of studying the language of the law, encouraged our original collaboration

and

To (in order of appearance) Mairead, Ronan, Cillian, and Tim. — JC

To my new family, Steve and Tim, and my parents, for your constant and invaluable support. — RCR

ACKNOWLEDGMENTS

Our primary debt is to those colleagues in the field of law and language whose hard work and critical insights are the subject of this book. The contributions of many of these scholars are specifically acknowledged as we discuss their work in the course of this book, but our thanks extend to all who do law and language research.

CONTENTS

PREFACE TO THE THIRD EDITION

Before his retirement from the University of Chicago Press in 2016, our long-time editor and good friend John Tryneski approached us (John Conley and Mack O'Barr) about a third edition of *Just Words*. John said that people continue to read and assign the book, but the 2005 second edition was becoming dated, in content as well as tone. We agreed, and the project was taken over by John's more-than-able successor at Chicago, Chuck Myers. While these discussions were going on, Mack decided to retire from teaching at Duke, and also from nuts-and-bolts work on the book. The three of us (Mack, John C., and Chuck) agreed that we needed to recruit a younger law-and-language scholar as a coauthor. We are joined in this third edition by Robin Conley Riner, a linguistic anthropologist who has worked extensively on law-related topics, including the death penalty in Texas, the treatment of transgender persons in US courts, and the training of soldiers to take others' lives. While Mack has continued to consult on big-picture questions, John and Robin have assumed responsibility for the writing of the new edition.

The mission of *Just Words* continues to be the one that John and Mack described in the original 1998 edition: to make an "argument about the importance of language and discourse in understanding law and legal processes." As in previous editions, we do so by presenting, topic by topic, research by ourselves and others that reveals the relationship between law, language, and power. The three of us continue to think of the book as a selective survey. Because of the depth in which we present the research we have chosen, our survey cannot be comprehensive; we have necessarily omitted more topics and researchers than we have included. We believe that each of the projects we have selected (1) focuses on a topic of significance, (2) clearly illustrates an important method, (3) links theoretical and real-world concerns in a compelling way, and (4) provides a model for other researchers.

In preparing this edition, we have added two new chapters on topics not covered in previous editions: nonverbal or "multimodal" communication in legal settings (chapter 9) and law, language, and race (chapter 10). To keep the book short (a virtue in the eyes of many teachers we have heard from over the years, and in our own), we decided to delete the original chapter 7, "The Discourses of Law in Historical Perspective." Something had to go, and John and Mack had long thought this chapter to be a bit of an outlier, since it analyzed the work of historians rather than sociolegal scholars.

We have also updated all of the existing chapters, adding more recent material, deleting some older work, and trying to give the book a more contemporary look and feel. Interestingly, though, when we went through the second edition in detail, we found that all of the principal research projects we had presented retained their saliency, so we have left them, with some updating of sources and style.

Finally, the first two editions contained a lot of prescriptive advice about the future of the field. As the reader will see, we have looked back on that advice with a critical eye. We are happy to say that, since 1998, the study of law and language has grown in a plethora of productive directions, some of which we advocated for and some of which we never thought of. We hope that our readers — especially teachers and their students — will continue to find *Just Words* to be a reliable and readable guide to this rapidly evolving field.

Chapel Hill, NC, and Huntington, WV
December 2017

PREFACE TO THE SECOND EDITION

The first edition of *Just Words* was intended as a thematic overview of the already vibrant interdisciplinary field of law and language studies. It was not our goal to write a comprehensive review of the expansive literature that comprised the field in 1998. Rather, we set out to highlight certain issues that lie at the heart of many investigations of the relation between language and law. We felt that we could do this best by following the themes of justice, equality, and fairness through the web of legal entanglements that real people encounter as they make their way through lawyers' offices, courts, and other legal venues. We tried to illuminate the role that language plays in the law's frequent failure to deliver on its basic promise of equal treatment. The single issue that emerged over and over was the centrality of language in the production, exercise, and subversion of legal power.

The reception of the first edition has gratified us, suggesting that others who read the book or use it in teaching share its underlying concerns. The study of law and language was not one of the foundational issues in the law and society movement, but it is now a major topic of books and journal articles and appears prominently in conference programs and course curricula. It is this very growth that has occasioned a second edition: more scholars exploring the law/language relationship in ever-more innovative and provocative ways.

This edition includes the original chapters plus two new ones. The new chapters focus on three developments in law and language scholarship that have become especially significant in the six years since we completed the first edition: the increasing attention to language ideology in legal contexts, the expansion of law and language research beyond the Anglo-American world, and the dramatic growth in the field of forensic linguistics.

Chapter 9 deals with the ideologies of language that permeate the law. It asks how the law itself and the actors within the legal system conceive of language and its instrumental role in law. We show how a body of newer research and writing has focused on language ideology to further our understanding of the ways in which the law's power plays itself out in practice. After explaining language ideology as a theoretical concept, we examine research that illuminates the role it plays in the American legal system. We then discuss a project that illustrates the use of language ideology to expose power relations in a very different cultural, linguistic, and legal setting.

Chapter 10 presents a survey and critique of the now large and rapidly growing field of forensic linguistics, defined as the use of linguistic expertise in legal proceedings. We assess the contributions that linguists are making to law and ask as well about the effect of their work on linguistics itself. While we applaud the role that linguists have often played in advancing the interests of justice, we ask whether forensic linguistics has become a discipline in which application drives theory rather than vice versa. We are particularly concerned about the diversion of scholarly time and energy away from fundamental critique of the law in favor of responding to an agenda that the law sets.

The emergence of such issues is evidence of health and vitality within the law and language community. There is productive debate over what the issues should be, how time should be allocated, what really matters, and the like. As members of the community we have our views about those topics. But as the debate unfolds, let us not lose sight of the goal of understanding how law works, how it often fails to deliver on its promises, and what we, as researchers and scholars, can do to illuminate its processes and thereby promote the values of democracy, open access, and fundamental fairness in an increasingly globalized world. To accomplish this we will need to move beyond our own societies, especially those of North America and Europe, into other areas of the world where other languages are spoken and where language itself may be understood in different ways. We must also be attentive to the political significance of the choices we make in allocating our time and selecting the questions that we study. The issues and the stakes are large, while the resources of our research community are finite.

Chapel Hill, NC
September 2004

PREFACE

Law and language emerged as a field of scholarship in the 1970s as sociolegal scholars incorporated the language of the law into their studies and as linguists began to concern themselves with language in legal arenas. Although there are now several edited volumes that focus on law and language (e.g., Levi and Walker 1990, Grimshaw 1990, Papke 1991), there is no book-length overview that attempts to assess the field and its contributions to sociolegal scholarship. What exists are primarily articles, book chapters, and monographs that take up one or another problem at the intersection of law and language.

The idea for a more comprehensive assessment of the field emerged from our teaching of general courses on law and social science and on legal anthropology, as well as more specialized topical seminars within these two fields. We have prominently featured law and language concerns in such courses because we believe that they make an important contribution to our understanding of the intersection of law and society, particularly of how law actually works in such everyday contexts as courtrooms, lawyers' offices, and even disputes outside specifically legal arenas. Moreover, law and language issues invariably generate a high level of student interest, whether the students are undergraduates, social science graduate students, or professional students in law or business. However, in bringing these materials into our teaching, we have often had to choose one monograph over another (because of issues of length, availability, and cost) and have seldom managed to cover as broad a set of law and language issues as we would have liked.

Another consequence of the scattered nature of publications about law and language has been the lack of an integrating perspective. In particular, there is no single source that canvasses a broad spectrum of the published research to develop a critical argument for the importance of studying the linguistic details of daily legal practice. We have tried to put that case forward here. In the pages that follow, we show how some of the most fundamental questions in sociolegal scholarship—issues such as unequal treatment by the law, the law's relationship to patriarchy, and gender discrimination within legal processes—play themselves out linguistically. Indeed, we argue, it is within the details of the talk that constitutes legal practice that discrimination occurs, that patriarchy manifests itself, and that the power of the law is realized. Thus, the microdynamics of the legal process and the broadest questions of justice are revealed to be two aspects of the same issue.

We hope this book will serve to encourage others to adopt the methods and perspectives of law and language. Much has been learned about law through studies of language and discourse. Language and law research has sometimes been able to clarify the details of thorny issues that have seemed resistant to other methods of analysis—questions such as what it is about rape trials that causes such great anguish for the victims, why women may not fare as well in divorce mediation as they do in adversarial litigation, and why the law accords some witnesses and litigants greater credence than others. Yet much more remains to be done, and we are hopeful that an assessment of what has been learned over the past two decades will be a stimulant to future work.

A Note about Authorship

This book is a joint project. We have always alternated priority of authorship in our publications in order to emphasize our common voice. We have brought different backgrounds and perspectives to this endeavor, and we believe that none of us would have conceived of or carried out the project singly in the manner that has emerged from our collaboration. We have worked together throughout and deserve jointly whatever blame or credit our readers accord.

NOTE ON TRANSCRIPT CONVENTIONS

We have made an effort in this book to standardize the linguistic texts we use as examples. We have drawn these texts from various sources, published and unpublished, including some of our own current and previously published work. We have found that the transcription conventions of different authors can be highly variable. Some try to approximate standard English; others attempt to render complex features of spoken language not noted in the conventions of standard orthography (pauses, coughs, overlapping speech, etc.). In devising a format for this book, we elected to simplify many of the transcripts. First, we have rendered most of the speech in standard English. For example, where an original transcript contains attempts at phonetic renderings such as *werenchu* and *you c'n get*, we have changed them to the standard *weren't you* and *you can get*. Second, we have eliminated many nonstandard-English features of the original transcripts that are not relevant to the issues that we are discussing. Thus, our texts do not note pause lengths except where that information is specifically relevant. We have taken these steps in order to make the texts accessible to readers with little or no background in linguistics or conversation analysis.

In simplifying and standardizing the texts in this book, we realize that we may be eliminating linguistic features that some readers may find useful in further analyses of the texts they might wish to undertake on their own. We refer such readers to the original sources (clearly referenced in each instance), where more detailed transcripts may be available. We believe that the inconvenience that may be caused to a few readers by this decision is outweighed by the argument for greater accessibility for all readers.

The following conventions are used in this book:

(2.5)	A silence whose length is specified in seconds (here 2.5 seconds)
CAPITALS	Loud speech
[ ]	Speech that overlaps with that of another speaker
Italics	Stressed words or phrases
— —	An interrupted utterance and its resumption, as in WITNESS: They did mention — LAWYER: Then did — WITNESS: — did mention that . . .
[*italicized words*]	Editorial comments
( )	The material contained within was not fully audible

CHAPTER ONE

The Politics of Law and
the Science of Talk

A lmost forty years have passed since we (O'Barr and Conley) began our own collaborative work at the intersection of law and language, and there is little in the field that is much older. The body of work that we consider here did not begin as the product of some theoretical master plan. Rather, it initially coalesced as scholars of diverse intellectual backgrounds arrived from many directions at the common realization that the language of the law is profoundly important. Some whose primary interest is the law have been struck by the centrality of language in almost every legal event, while others whose main interest is language have discovered the law as an extraordinary research setting. Collectively — if often unaware of each other — the members of this sometimes accidental alliance have produced the subject matter of this book.

When we first turned our attention to the subject in the mid-1970s, most scholarship that considered law and language focused on written legal language, especially the arcane language of statutes and legal documents. Although we found many articles and books that noted in passing the importance of the linguistic base of the law, we found only a single source that dealt with law and language in any real depth. This was David Mellinkoff's monumental *The Language of the Law* (1963), which analyzes the structure of written legal language and explains the Latin, French, and Anglo-Saxon origins of contemporary usages. It took a new generation of language-oriented fieldworkers with sociological, anthropological, and sociolinguistic backgrounds to initiate a broader study of the language of the law as it operates in the many venues of daily practice. Beginning in about 1970, this new generation of researchers went to the places where people actually talk about their troubles and express their claims and began to study what happens there. It is their scholarship that provides the foundation for our argument about the importance of language and discourse in understanding law and legal processes.

In the first edition of this book, we grouped those who have studied law and language in this latter way into three general categories. One group focused explicitly and self-consciously on language as the medium through which law does most of its work. Early research in this category was exemplified by Brenda Danet's (1980a) demonstration of the strategic significance of alternative ways of naming and categorizing objects and actions,[1] as well as by our own investigations of the practical legal consequences of differences in courtroom speech styles (Conley et al. 1978; O'Barr 1982). A second category consisted of people interested primarily in language itself who found that legal and quasi-legal settings are a rich linguistic resource. Important early examples included four ethnomethodologists: Gail Jefferson (1980, 1985, 1988), who began to study talk about troubles in everyday contexts as a part of a more general investigation of conversation; Anita Pomerantz (1978), some of whose early research focused on how blame is managed in conversation; and Max Atkinson and Paul Drew (1979), who studied English court proceedings as specialized exercises in the management of conversation. The third group comprised researchers who were less self-conscious in their focus on linguistic issues but ended up paying close attention to the language of legal processes in order to explain the workings of the legal system. For example, in Susan Silbey and Sally Merry's (1986) ethnographic study of community mediation, language emerged as a central issue even though the researchers themselves had little formal background in linguistics.

The particular body of work that is our focus here has introduced another important variable into the law-language equation: power. This research looks at the law's language in order to understand the law's power. Its premise is that power is not a distant abstraction but rather an everyday reality. For most people, the law's power manifests itself less in Supreme Court decisions and legislative pronouncements than in the details of legal practice, in the thousands of mini-dramas reenacted every day in lawyers' offices, police stations, and courthouses around the country — and, as we are becoming increasingly aware, in the streets, during traffic stops and other kinds of police-civilian interactions. Language is a critical element in almost every one of these mini-dramas, even those that escalate to violence. To the extent that power is realized, exercised, abused, or challenged in such events, the means are in large part linguistic. This book is a search for those linguistic means.

Focusing simultaneously on law, language, and power can give us new insight into what has been the fundamental question in American legal history: how a legal system that aspires to equality can produce such a pervasive sense of unfair treatment. In the one hundred fifty years since the ratification of the Fourteenth Amendment to the Constitution and its guarantee of equal protection, normative legal reform has succeeded, at least on some levels, in eradicating the most obvious forms of discrimination. The law permits all citizens to vote and hold public office. Federal and state laws prohibit employment discrimination on grounds of race, religion, gender, disability, age, and sometimes sexual orientation. No one may be excluded from public benefits for discriminatory reasons. In the courtroom, all criminal defendants are entitled to be represented by counsel. All citizens are eligible for jury duty, and lawyers may not rely on race or gender in selecting jurors for particular cases. Race is not a legitimate factor for judges to consider in sentencing.

Yet in the face of such undeniable progress in the law's ideals, there is still widespread unease about the fairness of the law's application. One can sense the problem just by spending time in a courthouse and paying attention to the daily routine. Listen to the way that police officers and judges speak to women seeking domestic violence restraining orders. Listen to the way that mediators interact with husbands and wives in divorce cases. Observe the reactions of judges and jurors to the testimony of different kinds of witnesses. Talk to small claims magistrates about what constitutes a persuasive case. Nobody is doing anything that the Supreme Court would condemn as a violation of equal protection. But it is hard to escape the feeling that the law's power is more accessible to some people than to others.

What is it that gives rise to this feeling? Why do many people continue to think that the law does not treat them fairly? The answer cannot be found just in the study of legal norms. The law no longer returns fugitive slaves, treats women as the property of their husbands, or excludes African American citizens from juries. If the law is failing to live up to its ideals, the failure must lie in the details of everyday legal practice — details that often consist of language.

In the chapters that follow, we take up a number of compelling instances in which linguistic analysis[2] has shed new light on the nature of the law's power and the inequality of its application. In chapter 2, we address the frequently asserted claim that rape trials revictimize women who attempt to prosecute their assailants. We argue that the feeling of revictimization has little to do with the rules about introducing the victim's prior sexual history, which so-called rape shield laws have attempted to reform. Rather, the reality of revictimization is to be found in the linguistic details of common cross-examination strategies that are taken for granted in the adversary system. Reformers, we conclude, have been looking in the wrong places, and the prospect for real improvement is uncertain.

In chapter 3, we focus not on a substantive area of the law (such as rape) but on a legal *process* that is brought to bear on a wide range of disputes: mediation. We look specifically at the current trend of resolving divorce cases through mediation rather than traditional adversary trials. According to the legal literature, this change is having two apparently contradictory effects: women tend to prefer mediation, but, from a financial standpoint, they do not do as well as they did under the adversary system. Collecting linguistic data from a variety of legal and social science sources, we attempt to discover the precise mechanisms through which these effects might be produced.

Building on the details of the previous two chapters, chapter 4 poses a more general question: Is there any linguistic substance to the claim that the law is fundamentally patriarchal? Legal writers often cite the revictimization phenomenon and the allegedly unfair treatment of women in divorce as evidence that the values of the legal system are the values of a historically male power structure; as a result, they argue, the law is insensitive to the social reality of women's lives. We assess this claim linguistically. Going beyond the examples of rape and divorce, we reanalyze some of our own earlier work to make the case that the law displays a deep gender bias in the way it performs such basic tasks as judging credibility and defining narrative coherence.

The subject of chapter 5 is the natural history of disputes. We draw on research about individual components of the disputing process, from initial injury to trial, to create a linguistic model of the evolution of a dispute. The theme of power emerges again, in a subtle yet significant way. As they progress from wrong to resolution, disputes undergo multiple transformations. Each transformation is interactive, the product of negotiation between a disputant and another person—the adversary, a friend, a lawyer, a court clerk, a judge. And every such negotiation is in large part a contest for power whose outcome will shape the rest of the dispute.

Chapter 6 extends the basic argument of the book across places and cultures. There we argue for the importance of a linguistic orientation in the comparative study of law. We introduce work in legal anthropology, both older and newer, to make the point that some of our most venerable assumptions about the law of non-Western societies may derive from inadequate attention to linguistic detail. In chapter 7, we consider the concept of language ideology, defined as shared beliefs about language and how it works. We analyze several studies that reveal how language ideologies (and their manipulation) can affect power relations in legal proceedings, with profound implications for access to justice. Chapter 8 reviews developments in forensic linguistics—broadly, the use of linguistic analysis in legal contexts. We assess the work of several linguists in court cases and reflect on the potential for linguists to influence law and the legal system.

Chapters 9 and 10 are new to this third edition. Chapter 9 examines the contemporary linguistic concept of "multimodality" in legal contexts. Linguists have come to realize that live communication involves more than the sounds being uttered. It also involves such elements as spatial and visual relations among the participants, including gesture and interactions with objects in the world. Chapter 9 explains the multimodal aspects of communication and illustrates their potential significance in legal environments. Chapter 10 considers the relationship between race and legal language, drawing on linguistic analyses of the murder trial that ensued after the tragic death of African American teenager Trayvon Martin. Finally, in chapter 11, we offer some thoughts about the past, present, and future of law and language scholarship.

Why We Wrote This Book

In the late 1990s, we were motivated to write the original edition of this book by a growing sense of need. We believed that the law and language field, as theoretically diverse as it was, was sending a coherent message about law, language, and power. But this message had to be dug out of individual books and articles scattered here and there across the scholarly spectrum. We decided that the time had come for a single accessible source that organized some of the most significant law and language research around a unifying theme.

There were at that time a number of useful review articles and collections. Brenda Danet (1980b) and Don Brenneis (1988) had written comprehensive review essays about law and language, but even then both were out of date; Elizabeth Mertz (1994) had done a more recent survey. Among the then-available anthologies, the most helpful were Allen Grimshaw's *Conflict Talk* (1990), Judith Levi and Anne Graffam Walker's *Language in the Judicial Process* (1990), and David Papke's *Narrative and the Legal Discourse* (1991). Grimshaw collects linguistic analyses of disputes and arguments from a variety of interesting cultural settings, including American and Italian nursery schools, psychiatric examinations, and labor-management negotiations. In Levi and Walker's book, a set of conference papers, the contributions all endeavor to show the value of linguistic methods in understanding the American legal process. In Papke's book, as its title indicates, the organizing theme is narrative, which the contributors study in contexts ranging from legal education to appellate opinions. None of these, however, is organized so as to tell what we believed to be the emerging theoretical story of the field.

The inadequacy of the late-1990s literature became especially evident in the dozens of courses that, between us, we had taught under the general rubric of law and society. In most instances, we brought together students from law schools and social science departments. Law and language was the exclusive topic of many of these courses; in the others, it was one of a few major topics. In both cases it was very difficult to find materials suitable for a class of students from varied disciplines. Much of the best work was in monograph form, substantial books devoted to a single, relatively narrow research project. (Moreover, some were available only at exorbitant cost.) The teacher thus faced a Hobson's choice: take an excerpt short enough to pass copyright clearance, which would probably be insufficient to convey the point of the book, or make the students buy the book and devote a major segment of the course to a single topic. In addition, much of the important writing in the field was highly technical. This slowed the progress of the course to a crawl, if it did not cause the students to give up entirely.

For reasons such as these, we had long felt a need for a book that lays out the major issues in the field in a readable form. Our objective in the first edition was — and still is, in this third edition — to capture the theoretical import of the work we discuss, while reducing the technical aspects to what is absolutely essential. We continue to strive for accessibility in every sense of the word, to create a readily available book of reasonable length that uses a minimum of jargon and makes few assumptions about the prior knowledge of readers. Our hope was, and remains, that the entire book can serve as the core of a law and language course, while individual chapters may prove useful as freestanding linguistic readings in broader law and society courses.

As we write this third edition, the problem of a scant literature has disappeared. Articles, monographs, and especially collections have proliferated. To mention just a few of the more recent collections, see Lawrence Solan and Peter Tiersma's *Oxford Handbook of Language and Law* (2012), a wide-ranging survey that covers such diverse topics as the history of legal language, the interpretation of statutes and other legal texts, courtroom discourse, and forensic linguistics; Deborah Tannen, Heidi Hamilton, and Deborah Schiffrin's *Handbook of Discourse Analysis* (2015), with a section devoted to legal, political, and institutional contexts; Chris Heffer, Frances Rock, and John Conley's *Legal-Lay Communication* (2013), with multiple chapters on courtroom interactions, police-citizen encounters, and written legal texts; and Susan Ehrlich, Diana Eades, and Janet Ainsworth's *Discursive Constructions of Consent in the Legal Process* (2016), which considers that fundamental concept across the spectrum of legal applications. But we still see a need for a book like this one, appropriately updated. The scholarly community has reinforced that judgment by continuing to buy and assign the earlier editions. The general purpose of the book remains what it has always been: to present to the reader a variety of specific research projects that illuminate the significant if subtle relationship among law, language, and power, and to do so in a way that can be understood by a broad legal and social science readership.

While updating the book, we have found that almost all of the research examples we discussed in the first edition remain relevant and illuminating. Though we may now know more about the issues being investigated, the original studies are still salient and vital to an understanding of their respective topics. So we have kept them, with updating comments as appropriate.

As we have considered more recent research for inclusion in this edition, three themes have emerged as particularly compelling and worthy of development. We hesitate to call these themes new, because they are not, but their significance can be fairly described as newly appreciated. The first is the central role of language, and communication generally, in the currently toxic political and legal climate. In a variety of contemporary controversies — ranging from the 2016 presidential campaign to violent encounters between police officers and civilians, from the fate of Confederate monuments to political activism by professional athletes — much of the public argument seems to be about actual and intended communication: What did people say (in the broad sense), and what did they mean to say? The second theme, closely related to the first, is that the details of language are especially important to understanding the dynamics of racial encounters, particularly in the realm of criminal justice. The third theme is the dramatic expansion in how linguistic scholars conceive of *language*. In earlier editions, our consideration was limited to spoken and written words. Now, consistent with the evolution of language research, we pay more attention to the visual, spatial, and tangible components of communication that are part of any live linguistic interaction. These three themes are prominent in the updating we have done throughout the book and are the subject of the two new chapters.

In explaining how we selected the research we have discussed in the three editions, it is important to be explicit about what this book is *not*. It is intended to be neither a textbook nor a comprehensive survey of the field. The fact that we do not mention some body of work does not mean that we do not think it is important. This is rather a book organized around what is, in our judgment, the most important theoretical issue in law and language: the use of linguistic methods to understand the nature of law and legal power. We chose the items that we have included primarily because each combines rich linguistic analysis with an interest in broader social issues. Taken together, they make the strongest possible case for the importance of law and language research to both the social sciences and the law.

In the remainder of this chapter, we introduce some background issues that are essential to an appreciation of the work that we discuss in the substantive chapters. First we examine three concepts that are at the core of law and language research: language, discourse, and power. We then review in some detail the intellectual traditions from which the field of law and language has emerged.

Basic Concepts: Language, Discourse, and Power

Many scholars still use the terms *language* and *discourse* without explaining what they mean by them. This can be confusing because these related terms have multiple meanings in the academic world; they are synonymous for some purposes but distinct in other significant ways. *Language* is the more straightforward of the two. Language includes sounds, units of meaning, and grammatical structures, as well as the contexts in which these occur. Language is also now understood to be inseparable from such multimodal aspects of communication as gaze, gesture, spatial relations, and speakers' interactions with their physical environment. Events that count as law in people's lives — making a will; getting a divorce; going to small claims court; serving as a juror, witness, or defendant — consist primarily of language. In a practical, everyday way, law is language, in either its spoken or written variety. Language is the stuff of contracts, statutes, judicial opinions, and other legal documents, as well as the essence of the daily dramas that unfold in trial courtrooms, lawyers' offices, and mediation centers.

The term *discourse* has two senses, one linguistic and one social. The former sense, which overlaps with *language*, is illustrated by phrases such as *everyday discourse* and *courtroom discourse*, the latter by phrases such as the *discourse of psychoanalysis* and the *discourse of human rights*. In the linguistic sense, discourse refers to connected segments of speech or writing, in fact to any chunk of speech or writing larger than a single utterance.[3] It thus includes conversations, sermons, stories, question-answer sequences, and so forth. Discourse analysis is the study of how such segments, or texts, are structured and how they are used in communication. In the context of law, discourse in the linguistic sense refers to the talk that constitutes courtroom testimony, closing arguments, lawyer-client interviews, arguments between disputants, mediation sessions, and the like. Over the last four decades, many researchers have turned their analytic attention to the linguistic structure of these events and have attempted to understand how such events accomplish the legal work that they do. In recent years there has been an increasing focus on the strategic aspects of these events and the implications for the exercise of legal, political, and economic power; this work is often referred to as *critical discourse analysis*. Discourse analysis scholarship forms the basis for many of the arguments that we make in this book.

The use of *discourse* to refer to more abstract social phenomena owes its currency to the influence of Michel Foucault. In *The Order of Things* (1970) and *The Archaeology of Knowledge and the Discourse of Language* (1972), Foucault lays out his notion of discourse as the broad range of discussion that takes place within a society about an issue or a set of issues. Examples include the *discourse of punishment* and the *discourse of sexuality*, which became, respectively, the subjects of two of his later works, *Discipline and Punish* (Foucault 1977) and *The History of Sexuality* (Foucault 1978, 1985a, 1985b). We will sometimes refer to discourse in the more abstract, Foucauldian sense as *macrodiscourse*, to distinguish it from discourse in the linguistic sense, which we will call *microdiscourse*.

Discourse in Foucault's sense is not simply talk itself but also the way that something gets talked about. Logically, the way that people talk about an issue is intimately related to the way that they think about it and ultimately act with respect to it. Discourse is thus a locus of power. Different discourses compete for ascendancy in the social world; one is dominant for a time and then may be challenged and perhaps replaced by another. The dominance of a particular discourse inevitably reflects the power structure of society. At the same time, however, the repeated playing out of the dominant discourse reinforces that structure. Discourse, as Foucault put it in *The History of Sexuality*, "can be both an instrument and an effect of power" (1978:101). In the end, though, because dominance is the product of competition and negotiation, dominant discourse plants the seeds of its own undoing. In effect, as people talk about an issue over and over again, they learn too much. Even as the participants in the social discussion are being constrained by the dominant framework, they are acquiring the resources to subvert it. In Foucault's words, "Discourse transmits and produces power; it reinforces it, but also undermines and exposes it, renders it fragile and makes it possible to thwart it" (1978:101).

Foucault's theory of discourse has shaped research in a variety of disciplines where scholars have come to share his concern with specific historical processes and the connection of discourse to power. Although Foucault does not present a unified theory of law, his concept of discourse has influenced contemporary legal scholarship profoundly. His principal contribution has been to emphasize the multiplicity and complexity of legal discourses (Hunt and Wickham 1994:39–49). Whereas traditional scholarship has tended to treat "the law" as a single, coherent entity, Foucault analyzes it as "a multiple and mobile field of force relations, wherein far-reaching, but never completely stable, effects of domination are produced" (1980:102). Law works both in opposition to and in concert with such "disciplines" as penology, psychology, and education, which operate "'on the underside of the law' to 'naturalize' the legal power to punish at the same time they 'legalize' the technical power to discipline" (Hunt and Wickham 1994:46, quoting Foucault 1977:223). Foucault thus encourages legal scholars to seek power in practice, to construct meaning from the bottom up rather than the top down.

As we have examined the varied uses of the term *discourse*, we have come to understand a fundamental relationship between its two principal meanings. We have become convinced that the linguistic and social notions of discourse are merely different aspects of one and the same process of expressing social power. In fact, the central argument of this book is that the concrete linguistic technique of discourse analysis is an indispensable tool for explaining discourse in the more abstract, sociological sense. For example, we argue in the pages that follow that the claim that the law is patriarchal—a statement about dominant legal discourse—can only be fully evaluated by examining the details of talk in the courtroom and other legal sites. Discourse at the macrolevel—discourse as Foucault understands it—must manifest itself at the microlevel, as talk. It is only through talk, after all, that dominance can be expressed, reproduced, and challenged. Seen from this perspective, the multiple meanings of discourse are quite natural, indeed inevitable, and a resource rather than a source of confusion.

Finally, *power* itself — although its meaning is in some respects self-evident — also requires some explanation. Harold Lasswell (1936) once defined politics as "who gets what, when, how." *Power* is the answer to the question of *why* some people get things, while others do not — why, in other words, the haves have what they do. Stated in this way, the study of power must deal with the fundamental issue of inequality, asking why it exists and how it is maintained. This sense of power is encompassed in the notion of *hegemony*, which means preponderant power in a political context, or the ability of some groups to subordinate others. We are concerned here with power in legal contexts. Legal power, like other forms of power, has an intimate relationship with inequality, but it is an ambiguous and sometimes ironic one. Throughout history, the power of the law has been a two-edged sword, simultaneously enabling some people to attack social inequalities and enabling others to defend them. People have used the law's resources in order to undermine a status quo that the same law has created and maintained. Thus, during the American civil rights struggle of the 1950s and 1960s, both opponents and defenders of segregation claimed the law's protection.

The work of Foucault is again helpful in sorting out the complex relationship between legal power and inequality. He reminds us that power involves more than the authority of the state. Indeed, the modern world is characterized by the importance of power exercised locally at myriad sites far removed from political centers (Hunt and Wickham 1994:16–17). Foucault (1977:12) emphasizes the need for attention to the mechanics or "microphysics" of this dispersed power. When we examine the exercise of power in detail, we discover that it not only excludes and prohibits but also produces: "it produces reality, it produces domains of objects and rituals of truth" (Foucault 1977:194). The very exercise of power thus reinforces it. Inevitably, however, power also produces resistance to itself. Power may exclude, but those who are excluded remain on the scene, ready to turn local-level episodes of oppression into moments of resistance. This resistance is not the large-scale revolution promoted by Karl Marx but rather the occasional yet still significant hijacking of local power by individuals who are usually on the receiving end. It is thus in the details of daily practice that the nature, the maintenance, and the subversion of power are all to be understood.

Foucault's ideas are especially relevant to the concept of legal power. Legal power occasionally manifests itself as the power of the state, as when Congress legislates or the Constitution is amended. But the manifestations of legal power that have the most direct impact on individuals are usually local: decisions by police officers to arrest and by prosecutors to bring charges, jury verdicts, sentences handed down by judges, and so on. In Foucauldian terms, the purpose of this book is to explore the microphysics of legal power by examining such events at the microlinguistic level.

The Origins of Law and Language Research

As we noted earlier, in the 1970s and 1980s the findings of a variety of re-searchers from different backgrounds began to converge in that area of schol-arship we term *law and language*. The resulting body of work has contrib-uted much to our understanding of the linguistic enactment of law's power. When we look back over more than four decades of research, two preexisting fields — sociolinguistics and law and society — stand out as having set the stage on which the joint study of law and language could proceed. Although each developed independently, their convergence helped produce the body of re-search on which this book is based. Sociolinguistics in its many forms taught us how to study the details of language, while law and society produced the critical perspective that this book employs. In terms of the three categories of our subtitle — law, language, and power — sociolinguistics gave us the tools for a deeper study of language, while law and society shaped our understanding of law and power. It is perhaps appropriate to consider each field individually before asking how their combined interests gave rise to our present concerns.

Sociolinguistics

Many contemporary linguists are concerned in one way or another with the fact that language is a social phenomenon. In contrast to earlier generations of linguists, they do not study the structure of language in isolation from society. Sentences do not exist in the abstract, they argue, nor are words usually spoken without a purpose. *Sociolinguistics* is the branch of linguistics that studies the relationship between language and its social context.[4]

It is perhaps not too great a simplification to say that the major impetus to the development of sociolinguistics was an effort to expand on the linguistics practiced in the 1950s. The primary concern of sociolinguistics has always been the integration of social variables into theories of language. Until the 1960s, it was common for theories of the structure of language to be based on ideal, perfectly formed utterances,[5] which typically existed only in the imaginations of linguists. The nonideal utterances[6] that real people actually speak (and write) were downplayed or ignored. Actual language is filled with sentences that seem to change their direction in the process of production and with variable forms of pronunciation and modes of expression. The very variation that was seen as a complicating factor in structural linguistics became the primary focus of sociolinguistics.

William Labov did some of the earliest significant work in sociolinguistics and remains one of the most prominent names in the field. He was able to show that social factors such as age, race, ethnicity, gender, and context are integral parts of language and its use. For example, he demonstrated that speech variations among New Yorkers correlate with class and social setting (Labov 1966). Although Labov's stated interest has always been in explaining how language works, rather than how society works, he has been convinced from the outset that social factors must play a central role in such explanations. This orientation has enabled Labov and others who share his vision to expand the understanding of language significantly beyond the limits of classical theory.

This concern of linguists with the language-society relationship has had parallels in other academic fields. For example, sociologist Erving Goffman (1959) initiated the study of how members of a society negotiate their way through everyday interactions — the field later named *ethnomethodology*. Some of Goffman's followers began to focus specifically on linguistic interactions, or conversations, and the field of *conversation analysis* developed. Its major premise is that, since conversation is one of the most basic human activities, the rules for organizing it must be among the most fundamental principles of social organization. Abjuring such abstract questions as why people *really* do things, conversation analysts search within the details of actual conversations for evidence of the rules that participants appear to "attend to" or "orient toward." We describe conversation analysis in considerable detail in chapter 2; we mention it here as a variant on the fundamental sociolinguistic concern with the concrete analysis of language in real-world contexts.

Similarly, in the 1960s, more and more anthropologists began to include language as a topic of study, rather than merely treating it as the medium through which culture can be studied. Dell Hymes captured this emerging concern in the phrase "the ethnography of speaking," which he defined as the concern with "the situations and uses, the patterns and functions, of speaking as an activity in its own right" (1968:101). Inspired by Hymes, anthropologists turned increasingly to questions of who speaks particular varieties of language when, where, and to whom.[7]

Legal anthropology in particular has become increasingly focused on the details of language. When we (Conley and O'Barr 1990) published our first collaborative book on the ethnography of legal language, the bibliography of comparable work on the law was relatively short. Such work has subsequently proliferated. In fact, in a current introduction to legal anthropology by Mark Goodale (2017), the first chapter is titled "Speaking the Law." Illustrative contemporary research cited by Goodale includes Larry Nesper's (2007) legal ethnographic work among the Ojibwe tribe, Justin Richland's (2008) ethnographic study of language ideologies employed in Hopi Tribal Court proceedings, and Elizabeth Mertz's (2007) multi-sited ethnography of US law schools.

But even as many legal anthropologists rapidly adopted a more explicitly linguistic orientation, linguistic anthropology — loosely defined as the study of language from a cultural perspective, and thus a form of sociolinguistics — has been slow to focus on law as an object of study. In a recent review chapter, one of us (J. Conley 2016:393) characterized linguistic anthropology as "a relative latecomer to the legal arena." Nonetheless, this situation is also showing signs of change, as illustrated by the recent work of Riner (chapter 9), Shonna Trinch (2013), and Hadi Deeb (2013).

Taken in conjunction with the new social orientation of many linguists, these developments mean that a great deal more attention has been paid to language in social contexts than previously had been the case. The pervasiveness of communication in social life meant that every discipline concerned with society would have to come to terms with language. As in the early days of cultural anthropology, there was a world of language use and variation to be documented and explained. But the very success of the sociolinguistic agenda gave rise to a new problem. As more and more observations were made about the social contexts of language, critics began to ask, So what?

Before we examine some of the answers that law and language researchers have given to this question, let us first consider some aspects of the parallel development of law and society scholarship from the 1960s.

Law and Society

Law and society is an interdisciplinary field that attempts to understand the connections between law and its social context. Researchers who identify themselves with this label come from a wide variety of fields — every one of the social sciences, many humanistic disciplines (especially history and philosophy), and academic law. Despite the diversity inherent in so broad a sweep of the academic world, law and society scholars seem united about their basic concern — showing how law really works in practice. For these scholars, deviation from the ideals of the law is the primary object of study, not something to be dismissed as mere noise in the system. Despite this shared interest in law in action, law and society is characterized more by a general research orientation than by a specific research agenda. In a 1994 collection of some of the most influential papers in the field, Roger Cotterrell makes a still-accurate observation:

> In legal studies in the English-speaking world "law and society" does not designate a unified field of scholarship, a distinct subject or an academic discipline. It is a label for very varied researches which need to be categorized in this special way only because of pervasive failures of imagination in traditional legal scholarship. (1994:xi)

Law and society researchers look skeptically on law's claim of equal treatment for all. They ask questions about who gets arrested and why (Black 1971). They seek to understand the gender biases that may result from the legal regulation of domestic and work relationships (Fineman 1991; McCann 1994; Edelman 2016). And they are interested in whether concerns about the process of making a legal decision can overshadow the outcome (Lind and Tyler 1988; Tyler

1990; Sunshine and Tyler 2003). Investigating these issues often means turning taken-for-granted assumptions on their heads in order to understand how law is complicated by the social context in which legal principles must be realized.

Like sociolinguistics, the law and society field developed its momentum in the 1960s, although skepticism about the law living up to its ideals dates back at least to the legal realist movement in the early decades of the twentieth century. Many of the founding members of the Law and Society Association were sociologists, but they were soon joined by anthropologists, historians, philosophers, political scientists, and some legal scholars. The association's journal, *Law & Society Review*, began publication in 1967. From the outset, law and society has not prescribed a particular theory, method, or application of its findings. Rather, the field has existed as an area of scholarship united by a concern with law and the complications caused by the social context in which law always exists.

More than five decades after the founding of the Law and Society Association and the *Review*, the field retains its interest in the law's failures to live up to its ideals. Law and society researchers are broadly empirical in their respective methods, and the articles published in the *Review* have always been preponderantly empirical. But qualitative, language-focused law and society research has been relatively rare. Anthropologists, linguistic and otherwise, have complained that recent editors of the *Review* have equated "empirical" with "quantitative" in their selection of reviewers and publication judgments.

Shortcomings of the Fields in Isolation

This section is carried forward from the previous editions. Readers will see that some of the criticisms we offered are out of date. But rather than updating it, we decided to reproduce it as it was and then comment on it in the conclusion that follows.

Despite the success of the research programs of both sociolinguistics and law and society, each field has, when working on its own, ultimately failed to address a fundamental issue. For sociolinguistics, the problem is this: after decades of empirical studies, it is now well known that language variation is not unsystematic, as some earlier linguists had assumed, but rather socially patterned. In fact, we now know a great deal about how social differences are encoded within language. What the field has often neglected to do is to connect the variation it has documented with broader issues. Much sociolinguistic research has failed to ask whether language variation is truly consequential in social life, as opposed to being merely an interesting curiosity. Some question how productive it is to continue to document instance after instance of socially patterned variation. Since the basic principle of sociolinguistics was established, many people outside the field (and even some within it) have felt that we have been learning more and more about less and less.

In conversation analysis in particular, researchers and theorists have frequently shied away from making a connection between conversational organization and the dynamics of power. The great strength of conversation analysis has been its attention to ordinary people speaking in everyday contexts: friends on the telephone, people around the dinner table, and the like. The product of this research — the preeminent achievement of conversation analysis — has been a grammar of conversational interaction. It is appropriate to call it a grammar because it explains the strategies that people employ in a conversation solely by reference to other events within the conversation. External factors, such as status inequalities or preexisting relationships among the parties, have rarely been taken into account.

But this focus on the ordinary, necessary as it was, has had a constraining effect. Most important, it has resulted in an overwhelming concentration on interactions between people who are (or are assumed to be) of roughly equal social status. To be fair, conversation analysts have not been unaware of such factors as status and power but have chosen not to consider anything external to the language of the conversation itself. Nonetheless, the fact is that there are few conversations in which status and power are not relevant; think, for example, of exchanges between parents and children, senior and junior coworkers, or even men and women. Far from being the norm, relationships of true equality are so rare as to be treasured. Although some recent work on gender issues in language has dealt with power and its consequences,[8] for most of its history conversation analysis has excluded this elemental issue from consideration. Even the research that has been done in institutional settings where power imbalances are explicit has been modest to the point of diffidence in dealing with the question.[9]

The problem with law and society scholarship is one of methods rather than goals. The primary objective of sociolegal scholars has been to document the law's failure to deliver on its biggest promises, especially the equal treatment of all citizens. Where the field has sometimes come up short is in its explanation of how such failures occur. For example, we have known for a long time that the haves come out ahead and that race and gender can make a difference in legal access and outcome. But law and society scholarship has been less successful in exposing the mechanisms that produce these inequalities. What is it exactly that the haves do for themselves or to others that results in their greater success before the law?[10] What happens to women and minorities in legal contexts that results in their positions being undervalued and underrewarded?

Conclusion: Combining Concerns

For more than four decades, it has been evident that the most effective way to overcome the weaknesses of the two fields is to merge their strengths. Sociolinguistics can benefit from law and society's focus on who gets what and when, whereas law and society can turn to sociolinguistics for a deeper understanding of how they get it. The two disciplines already share a common concern with social divisions along lines of class, race, ethnicity, and gender. Sociolinguistics explores how language variation correlates with these variables, while socio-legal scholarship argues that they influence access to justice. Nothing could be more logical than to investigate the places where language and justice converge. From a sociolinguistic perspective, the question is whether language variation has social consequences in legal settings. The sociolegal version of this question asks whether we can discover in language the precise mechanisms — Foucault's microphysics — through which injustice happens. Since law-in-action consists almost exclusively of linguistic events — trials, agreements, conferences with lawyers, and the like — the two disciplines have always had ample ground on which to meet.

The advocacy of this merger was a fundamental motivation for the original edition of this book. By analyzing a number of instances in which that merger had already occurred and greatly benefited our understanding of both language and law, we sought to make the case for even deeper collaboration in the future. Our objective was and remains to discover how the power of the law actually operates in everyday legal settings. Drawing on the work of an intellectually diverse group of law and language scholars, as well as some of our own research, we seek to identify the linguistic mechanisms through which power is realized, exercised, sometimes abused, and occasionally subverted. In the course of answering questions such as these, we also learn a great deal about the nature of power itself. We see, for example, how the linguistic details of particular legal events can simultaneously reflect and reinforce power relations that cut across society. We also discover the critical role of language in resisting and reforming existing power arrangements.

The increased collaboration we promoted in previous editions is, in significant respects, the current reality. Sociolinguists, without sacrificing the intensity of their focus on language itself, have paid more attention to questions of power, often under the rubric of critical discourse analysis. Legal anthropologists have made more and better use of linguistic evidence. More recently, some linguistic anthropologists have begun to see law and power as appropriate and important subjects for their method.

After twenty years of further research by ourselves and others, we reach the same conclusion that we had in 1998: language is not merely the vehicle through which legal power operates — in many vital respects, language *is* legal power. The abstraction we call *power* is at once the cause and the effect of countless linguistic interactions taking place every day at every level of the legal system. Power is thus determinative of and determined by the linguistic details of legal practice, and it is those details that are the subject of this book.

CHAPTER TWO

The Revictimization of Rape Victims

In this chapter, we begin the detailed examination of the linguistic mechanisms through which legal power is realized and reproduced. We focus on
the prosecution of the crime of rape and attempt to understand what it is
about rape trials that leads to claims that rape victims are revictimized by the
legal process. First we review the legal, political, and scholarly discourse about
rape, paying particular attention to the issues of power and domination. We then
examine the actual language of rape prosecutions in an effort to connect abstract
ideas about power with the day-to-day realities of courtroom practice. Here, as
in subsequent chapters, our objective is to understand how discourse practices
reflect, ratify, and sometimes challenge social hierarchies.

Rape and Power

Over the past forty-five years, few legal issues have been the focus of such
intense political, social, and scholarly debate as the crime of rape. This debate
has proceeded on several levels. Criminologists continue to argue about the incidence of the crime. In previous editions, we reported that whereas FBI reports
and other "official" statistics indicated that four or five women per one thousand
are raped each year (Koss 1994:161–63), a number of investigators had produced data indicating that rapes were at least ten times more common than that
(Koss 1994:163–72; Koss 1988; Russell 1984). In the face of an overall decline
in crime rates, current estimates of the incidence of rape and sexual assault
vary widely, depending on how the crimes are defined and how the statistics
are compiled (e.g., Morgan and Kena 2017; Federal Bureau of Investigation
2016; Rape, Abuse & Incest National Network 2018). Others debate the causes.
Explanations have ranged from pervasive male pathology (Koss 1994:19–34;

Koss 1988; Briere and Malamuth 1983) to the structure and values of society (MacKinnon 1989:182; Koss 1994:4–16).

Two aspects of the debate are particularly relevant to the concerns of this book. The first is its focus on rape as an exercise in *power*. At the physical level, this claim is obvious: rape is a crime in which one person overpowers another, using actual or threatened force to take sexual advantage of the other. But rape also involves power in other ways that are less obvious but equally significant. In particular, the abuse of power that occurs during the act of rape has been seen to reflect, indeed to be an instance of, broader abuses of power that society condones or even promotes (MacKinnon 1989:176).

Historical analyses, for example, have chronicled the changing definitions of the crime of rape. At any point in history, the definition of rape has included only a limited subset of all possible acts of nonconsensual sex. Forced sex with slaves, for example, did not constitute rape; and until fairly recently, married women could not complain of rape by their husbands.[1] The historical trend has been to expand the area defined as criminal (Koss 1994:158–59, 223–24; Spohn and Horney 1992; see, e.g., N.C. General Statutes §§14-27.3–14-27.10). Nonetheless, the fact that society has tolerated *any* forms of forced sex makes a statement about power relations and the sexualization of violence (MacKinnon 1989:145–46; Caputi and Russell 1992:18–19). If particular acts of nonconsensual sex have to be specially defined as criminal, then the unstated premise is that women are presumed to be subject to the power of men (MacKinnon 1989:169).

(As the previous sentence indicates, earlier editions of this chapter treated rape as being almost always a crime perpetrated by men against women. The legal, social science, and — as the MacKinnon citation reflects — feminist literatures of the time reflected the same assumption. This assumption embodied definitions of rape and gender that contemporary thinking rejects: in the former case as too narrow, and in the latter as too rigid. In light of this, we considered replacing the entire discussion of rape in this chapter. In the end, however, we decided that the scholarship we included in the earlier editions, and our commentary on it, has continuing value in a discussion of language and gender, so we have left it largely as is, with updated references to newer literature.)

The second and related point is that the power politics of rape do not end with the commission of the crime. Critics of the legal system point out that rape is grossly underreported (Rape, Abuse & Incest National Network 2018; Morgan and Kena 2017; Warshaw 1988; Russell 1984). When it is reported, they argue, it is not prosecuted vigorously, and convictions are rarely obtained (Matoesian 1993:14–15). All of this is particularly true with respect to acquaintance rape, which is said to be far more common than rape by strangers (Koss 1994:163–65; Estrich 1987) and is, in many states, defined as a less serious offense than stranger rape.[2]

The analysis of rape leads inevitably to an examination of the power relations between men and women. One problem that surfaces is the law itself. The elements of the crime are defined in male terms, it is argued, as is consent, which is the principal defense in acquaintance rape cases (Ehrlich 2016:66; Trinch 2013:288–89; MacKinnon 1989:169). The law, in other words, is patriarchal, because it is written and applied from a male point of view. It takes for granted the idea that women are subordinate to men. Because of the law's patriarchal perspective, the critics contend, a woman who did not actively, indeed aggressively, resist will be seen as having consented to sex. District attorneys look at the allegations from the same patriarchal perspective when deciding when to prosecute, as do jurors when judging guilt or innocence (Matoesian 1993:15, 1995:693–94). Thus, in the prosecution of rape — just as in the act itself — male domination is realized in social action.

Some of the strongest criticism of the system focuses on what happens when a rape case finally gets to the courtroom. What happens is commonly described as "revictimization" or "rape of the second kind" (Matoesian 1995:676). The victim is, of course, forced to relive the rape in her courtroom testimony and is revictimized in this literal sense. But all too often, it is argued, the courtroom reenactment results in the victim being blamed for the crime. Defense lawyers exploit male-biased legal definitions of consent to badger the victim about ambiguous signals she might have sent to the perpetrator (Estrich 1987:18). The vigor of her resistance will probably be questioned, again by male standards (Trinch 2013:303; Estrich 1987:65; MacKinnon 1989:177). Trivial inconsistencies in her testimony will be blown out of proportion to suggest a faulty memory, if not mendacity. She will also be attacked if any aspects of her post-rape behavior fail to conform to male notions of logical response to a crime — for example, if she did not flee the scene and report the crime as soon as physically possible.[3]

Perhaps the most controversial mechanism of revictimization is the common defense tactic of cross-examining the victim about her prior sexual history (Bohmer 1991:320–25; Spohn and Horney 1992:20–28; Allison and Wrightsman 1993). Previous sexual relations with the perpetrator will be highlighted to imply consent on the occasion in question. The defense lawyer may also draw on the victim's sexual experiences with others to portray her as a "loose woman," improving the odds for the consent defense.[4]

Efforts to reform rape prosecution have concentrated on these issues (Koss 1994:249–54). Some states, for example, have done away with requirements that the victim prove active physical resistance in order to defeat the consent defense (Bohmer 1991:323; Goldberg-Ambrose 1992). Units that have been specially trained to support and assist rape victims, often staffed by women, have become ubiquitous in police departments and district attorneys' offices.[5] Some jurisdictions have experimented with closing courtrooms and protecting the identities of rape victims from the press.[6] And in what is widely viewed as the most significant reform, many states have enacted "rape shield" laws, which prevent defense lawyers from putting the victim's prior sexual history before the jury.[7]

Despite the vigor with which these reforms were advocated, many scholars who have evaluated them have concluded that they are having little tangible impact on the incidence of rape, the rate of reporting, or the outcomes of rape prosecutions (Carimico, Huynh, and Wells 2016). In the words of anthropologist Shonna Trinch (2013:289), "critics argue that the last 30 years of work about and against rape has made little progress to erode the mythology that continues to surround rape and even less to eradicate it." Although newer laws appear to make a different ideological statement about gender relations than did their patriarchal predecessors, the realities of men's power over women seem little changed. Why?

One answer to this question has come from sociologist Gregory Matoesian. In his 1993 book, *Reproducing Rape*, Matoesian argues convincingly that rape reformers have been looking for solutions in the wrong places. The reformers, Matoesian contends, have assumed that the power imbalances inherent in rape prosecution derive from defects in the *structure* of the process — such things as evidentiary rules about what information can be used to attack the victim's credibility. Matoesian's essential point is that the realities of power are far more complex. Power is more than an abstraction that is made concrete through the operation of simple rules. Rather, the concepts of power and domination and their real-world manifestations are two sides of the same coin. On the one hand, *power* is an underlying reality that helps shape the rules by which those conflicts are waged and their outcomes determined: men are able to dominate rape prosecutions because they have power. On the other hand, *power* is the label we apply to the pattern we observe in the outcomes of innumerable daily social conflicts: men seem to dominate rape prosecutions, so they must have power. The thing we call power is thus both cause and effect. If this is true, then efforts to change the distribution of power by tinkering with the structures through which it is exercised are doomed to failure.

The key to unlocking the conundrum of power, according to Matoesian, is to understand the minute details, in particular the microlinguistic details, of the interactions in which power is exercised. It is widely accepted, for example, that defense lawyers revictimize rape victims through their cross-examination techniques. But just what is it that lawyers *do* that causes people to have this reaction? Is it something as simple as the power to mention the victim's prior sexual history? Or does the lawyer's apparent power over the victim depend on far subtler rules of interaction? Structural reforms, such as rape shield laws, assume the adequacy of the former class of explanations; their apparent inefficacy may be the best evidence that much more is going on.

Understanding the microlinguistics — the microphysics, to use Foucault's term — of power may lead to more-effective rape reform by exposing the futility of current efforts. Conversely, it may ultimately lead to the conclusion that the problem is too complicated for the law to solve. More important, Matoesian argues, linguistic analysis can help us to understand the nature of power itself. Language is the primary mechanism by which we act out the power relations in our society. It is also a means by which we reaffirm those power relations. Our shared understandings of power give meaning to the way we talk, but, at the same time, the way we talk helps to shape our understandings.

Another way to understand this linguistic approach to power is through the concept of *discourse*, which we introduced in chapter 1. To recapitulate, this multidimensional term has two meanings that are especially relevant here: *discourse* in the concrete linguistic sense of connected sequences of speech or writing, and *discourse* in the more abstract sense of "a way of talking about actions and relationships" (Merry 1990:9). Discourse at its various levels is not mere talk, however; it is intimately connected to both thought and action. A way of talking about something is also a way of thinking about it, since what we say both reflects what we think and helps to shape what we and others will think in the future. And by structuring the way that actions get talked and thought about, discourse ultimately suggests and limits the possibilities for future actions.

We can think of the law of rape together with the talk that occurs in and around the prosecution of rape cases as comprising a multilevel discourse. This discourse is the dominant discourse about rape in our society: the dominant way of talking, thinking, and acting with respect to those actions and relationships that rape implicates. Feminists and others who would reform rape law and its application contest this dominance and seek to substitute a discourse of their own. Both are discourses about power, specifically the power of men over women. The dominant discourse, its critics contend, both reflects and perpetuates that power, while the alternative seeks to reverse it.

Research such as Matoesian's seeks to connect the linguistic and the more abstract notions of discourse. It asks how the higher-order discourse about the power dynamics of rape is inscribed in the realities of day-to-day talk. In one sense, such work is a search for the mechanisms through which the power of the dominant discourse is exercised. But it is equally a search for the source of that power. The flow of influence is in both directions: higher-order discourse informs day-to-day talk, but the latter also shapes the former. And, significantly, changing daily discourse may be the most efficient way of subverting dominant ways of thinking. In the instance of rape, reform of normative legal rules seems to have had little impact on rape victims' experiences with the criminal justice system. Perhaps the answer lies in understanding the day-to-day talk that goes on in the courthouse.

To investigate the daily discourse of rape, Matoesian draws on the methods of *conversation analysis*. The original inspiration for this method was the work of sociologist Erving Goffman. In a series of works bearing such revealing titles as *The Presentation of Self in Everyday Life* (Goffman 1959; see also Goffman 1963, 1967), Goffman argues that sociology should pay less attention to searching for the grand "rules" that govern social behavior and more attention to understanding the logic of mundane social interactions. Society is, after all, the sum of a countless number of such interactions. Conversation analysts have taken Goffman's fundamental insight and applied it to a particular sort of social interaction: conversations that occur in everyday contexts. They have marveled at the orderliness of conversation that we, as members of society, take for granted, and have sought to discover the resources that we use to maintain that order. The essence of their technique is the fine-grained, qualitative analysis of everyday conversations.

Although he employs its method, Matoesian deviates from the conversation analysis tradition in two significant ways. First, he joins a growing number of conversation analysts who have studied conversations in institutional rather than everyday settings (e.g., Atkinson and Drew 1979; Maynard 1984; Heritage and Greatbatch 1986; Mertz 1996, n.d.; Philips 1990; O'Donnell 1990). Second, he seeks to do more than discover the logic of conversation itself. Most conversation analysts have limited themselves to the study of *how* people manage conversations, prescinding from such questions as *why* they do what they do (Atkinson and Drew 1979:20–21). The focus has been on the mechanics of conversation rather than on the social and political objectives the parties may be pursuing. Matoesian, however, studies courtroom conversation not as an end in itself but in order to understand the power dynamics of rape. (For a more recent example of a comparable approach, see Susan Ehrlich's [2016] work on the construction of consent in rape trials.)

In the rest of this chapter, we will examine and evaluate several of Matoesian's specific claims about the revictimization process, drawing on excerpts of trial transcripts published in *Reproducing Rape* and in Matoesian's (1995) article about the William Kennedy Smith trial. (Matoesian [2001] later expanded the article to a book-length analysis of the trial.) We will also introduce some additional issues that have arisen in our own study of that trial. To lay the groundwork for this material, in the next section we introduce some basic principles of conversation analysis that must be understood in order to follow the arguments.[8]

Principles of Conversation Analysis

Verbal interaction is the central and defining feature of human social life. Whether at home, at work, or at leisure, we spend an enormous amount of time talking to one another. Over the past five decades, conversation analysis has grown up around the study of this most human of activities. Its method is straightforward: record everyday conversations, transcribe them, and then dissect the transcripts in an effort to discern the resources that people employ to maintain order and coherence in social discourse. The most important discovery about talk in everyday contexts is its orderly and highly structured nature. Without external supervision or any conscious awareness of how they are doing it, participants in a conversation come to instantaneous tacit agreement on such complex questions as whose turn it is to speak and how long a speaking turn should last.

Conversation analysts tell us that conversations are governed by a structure that is as fundamental to talk as are the sounds of a language and its rules for constructing meaningful expressions. This structure is the grammar of turn-taking. We learn as children how to have orderly conversations, just as we learn how to construct meaningful utterances. Among other things, the grammar of conversation specifies the following:

- A person who is speaking can expect to finish a syntactically complete utterance before the issue arises of who gets to talk next. (For example, "I was getting ready to" is not syntactically complete, whereas "I was getting ready to leave" is.)
- A speaker who reaches a syntactically complete point in the utterance (or one that another speaker considers complete) must either relinquish the turn or attempt to continue speaking.
- A person who is speaking can influence who the next speaker will be. (For example, "What do you think, John?" attempts to select John to talk next, whereas "Do you know what I think?" is an attempt at self-selection.)
- When speaker overlaps do occur (usually at points when speaker change is relevant), one speaker normally continues as others drop out. The speaker who continues usually recycles what was uttered during the period of overlapping speech.[9]

Basic structural rules such as these allow us to communicate efficiently in everyday discourse. They enable ordinary conversations to take place with an alternation of speakers, with minimal gaps and overlaps, and without referees or advance plans that state who will talk, what will be said, and how long a conversation will last.

Institutional environments such as the courtroom employ these basic rules, but modify them in important ways. The special rules governing courtroom interactions specify, for example, that lawyers ask questions and that witnesses answer them. In addition, the courtroom environment has a distinctive feature not present in everyday conversations — namely a judge who acts as referee to oversee the system of turn-taking, monitor the substance of what is discussed, and resolve complex interactional problems when they arise.

The special rules of the courtroom are highly unusual from a conversational point of view. From an everyday perspective, it would be very peculiar to limit some speakers so that their only type of turn is asking questions, while restricting others to giving answers to whatever questions they are asked. Such institutional constraints introduce into courtroom interactions a degree of rigidity not found in everyday contexts and thereby help the court do its assigned task of trying cases. But, in addition, these courtroom-specific rules have the consequence of empowering lawyers linguistically over the witnesses they examine. For example, if a witness strays in answering a question, the lawyer has considerable leeway to interrupt and bring the witness back to the point of the question. And if the witness proves unresponsive despite such efforts, the lawyer may ask the judge to instruct the witness to answer the question. Witnesses, however, have no comparable power to demand that lawyers ask questions that they deem relevant to the issue at hand. From the outset, the structural arrangements for talking in court do not privilege all speakers in the same way.

This imbalance of power is present in all courtroom dialogue. However, its consequences are most extreme during cross-examination, when lawyers examine the opposition's witnesses. When lawyers question their own witnesses during direct examination, they typically do so in a supportive manner, allowing friendly witnesses leeway in the form and substance of their answers. By contrast, the cross-examination is a hostile environment for both the lawyer and the witness. The lawyer's objective is to discredit opposition witnesses and minimize the impact of their testimony. And it is in such contexts that lawyers make maximal use of the linguistic power accorded to them.

The Conversation Analysis of Rape Trials

We turn now to the linguistic features of the rape trial that may contribute to the process of revictimization. Using Matoesian's data from *Reproducing Rape*,[10] we examine five features that lawyers manipulate to control witnesses: silence, question form, topic management, evaluative commentary, and challenges to the witness's capacity for knowledge. We conclude, in agreement with Matoesian, that these five features are indeed important strategies whereby cross-examining lawyers can dominate witnesses. We question, however, whether we have learned anything specific to rape trials or rather something about the general nature of the adversary system. The answer lies in the interaction between the commonplace details of adversary discourse and the unique context of rape, and it is there that we discover the reality of revictimization.

Silence

One linguistic feature that lawyers manipulate to exert control over witnesses is *silence*. Although, as we shall see, witnesses are sometimes reticent in court, the use of silence for strategic purposes is almost exclusively in the hands of the lawyer. The examining lawyer has the power to decide when the witness's turn begins by simply ending a question. If the lawyer chooses to be silent before asking a question or to punctuate a question with an interval of silence, there is little the witness can do, since it is not the witness's turn to speak and any effort to seize the turn would be out of order. The witness has no comparable opportunities to use silence. He or she cannot, for example, use silence as an answer to a question. The lawyer can ask the judge to instruct the witness to answer, and the judge will usually do so. Alternatively, the lawyer can end the witness's silence by repeating or rephrasing the question or by asking a new one. In either case, the lawyer's action may have the effect of adverse commentary on the witness's failure to respond.

Lawyers' control over silence allows them to accomplish two important strategic objectives. First, they can manipulate the law's question-and-answer format in ways not usually permitted by the turn-taking rules of the courtroom. Second, they can comment critically on a witness's credibility, a practice nominally forbidden by the rules of evidence and procedure. Several excerpts from the cross-examinations of rape victims by defense lawyers illustrate these uses of silence.

The basic rules of courtroom turn-taking are these: the lawyer begins the dialogue by asking a question; when the question is complete, the witness answers; when the answer is syntactically complete, it is the lawyer's turn to ask a new question; and so on. However, silence on the part of the witness at any point before or during an answer may give the lawyer an opportunity to evade these normal rules of give and take. The cross-examining lawyer has almost unfettered power to declare particular silences appropriate or inappropriate and to respond accordingly. In everyday conversations, there are rules for interpreting and dealing with silences on the part of a speaker who holds a turn. For example, a person who has been asked a question has a brief but well-understood interval to begin answering before someone else will interpret the silence as a refusal to respond. And even if that happens, there will then be a limited range of things that are understood to be appropriate: in some contexts, the question will be repeated or rephrased; in others, someone will move the conversation on to a new topic.

Under similar circumstances in the courtroom, however, cross-examining lawyers can do essentially whatever they want. In Text 2.1, the witness does not respond immediately to the question. The lawyer cuts off the witness's silence after 2.5 seconds and repeats the end of his question, loudly. The silence, followed by the emphatic restatement of the question, suggests to the audience that the witness knows the answer but is unwilling to speak it.

TEXT 2.1 (Matoesian 1993:143)

> LAWYER: Then they're not in substantially the same condition, are they?
> (2.5)
> ARE THEY?

In Text 2.2, the lawyer allows the silence to continue for more than 6 seconds, finally resuming by disparaging the witness's apparent failure of memory.

TEXT 2.2 (Matoesian 1993:143)

> LAWYER: Well WHAT were the items that you hadn't remembered when you—remember as of Friday?
> (6.2)
> Or don't you remember that?

Finally, silence following an answer before a lawyer asks another question can serve as an all-but-explicit commentary by the lawyer on the credibility of preceding utterances—what several investigators have called the "pin-drop effect" (Matoesian 1993:144).

TEXT 2.3 (Matoesian 1993:145)

> LAWYER: Is it your sworn testimony (1.0) under sworn, SWORN oath (0.8) that in four hours at the Grainary you had only two drinks?
> (1.2)
> WITNESS: Yes.
> (45.0)
> LAWYER: Linda . . .

Note that the witness is powerless to resist this tactic. She has given an obviously complete yes/no answer, thus ending her turn. To begin speaking again would be to violate the lawyer's control over turn allocation and likely to earn a rebuke from the judge. The only constraint on the lawyer—and it is a minimal one—is the possibility that the judge may get irritated and tell him to get on with the cross-examination.

Thus, silence is a tool for lawyers in their management and control of courtroom discourse. It is available for them to use in the ways demonstrated here, with the consequences that witnesses are impugned and their credibility challenged. Witnesses lack any practical countervailing resource.

Question Form

Lawyers control not only the timing of questions but also their form. This is significant because the form of a question can limit the range of permissible answers available to the witness. Some kinds of questions can also serve as statements of blame that stand irrespective of the witness's answer.

Question forms differ radically in the extent to which they constrain the witness's answer. At the two ends of the continuum of control are the WH question and the tag question. The former is the open-ended why, where, when, which, who, what, how question. The latter consists of a statement followed by a question such as "isn't that true?" or "correct?" or "didn't you?"—as in "You drove the car into the parking lot, didn't you?" Among the numerous question forms available to a lawyer,[11] the WH question is the least controlling and coercive because it imposes no particular form on the answer, whereas the tag question, with its implicit insistence on a yes/no answer, is the most controlling.

All of this is common knowledge among trial lawyers. The techniques of question-form management are taught to law students in trial practice courses. As one widely used trial-advocacy text advises, "Open-ended questions are disastrous on cross-examinations. Hostile witnesses are always looking for an opening to slip in a damaging answer. Questions that ask 'what,' 'how,' or 'why' or elicit explanations of any kind invite disaster. These kinds of questions are best avoided altogether" (Mauet 1992:216).

The management of question form is illustrated by Text 2.4, in which a defense attorney initially uses WH questions to seek a definition of "partying" and then switches to tag questions to imply that the witness had an unhealthy interest in sex, drugs, and alcohol.

TEXT 2.4 (Matoesian 1993:151–52)

LAWYER: What's meant by partying? You, you're what? Nineteen? Were you nineteen at that time?
WITNESS: Yes.
LAWYER: What's meant among youthful people, people your age,
5   Brian's age, by partying?
WITNESS: Some take it just to go and, with some friends, people, and have a few drinks, and some do smoke, some do take the pills.
LAWYER: Partying.
10 WITNESS: (Drugs.)
LAWYER: Is it not true, partying among people your age, does not mean to go to a party?
WITNESS: That's true.

LAWYER: It implies to many people that, implies sexual activity,
15   doesn't it?

[An objection by prosecuting attorney at this point is overruled by judge.]

LAWYER: To many people your age that means sexual activity, does it not?

20   WITNESS: To some, yes, I guess.

LAWYER: And at the very least it means the use of intoxicants?

WITNESS: Yes.

LAWYER: So, when they suggested, who suggested that you go partying?

25   WITNESS: I don't know who first brought it up. They [did mention]—

LAWYER: [Then did—]

WITNESS: —did mention that, uh, there would be friends who had the apartment who would be having a party.

LAWYER: So the word partying, let's go party, some like that, (in

30   audible) not just go to a party?

WITNESS: Mmhmm.

LAWYER: Correct?

WITNESS: Mmhmm.

As is apparent from the question-and-answer sequences in lines 4–8 and 23–28, the WH form invites a narrative from the witness.[12] The tag form (lines 14–19)[13] demands a yes/no answer. But because each of the tag questions is preceded by a statement that is damaging to the witness, the answers are almost irrelevant. Even if the witness answers in the negative, the denial may be lost in the flow of the lawyer's polemic. By controlling question form, the lawyer is thus able to transform the cross-examination from dialogue into self-serving monologue.

Topic Management

Another linguistic resource available to a cross-examining lawyer is the ability to manage the topic under discussion. On the simplest level, this is an obvious consequence of the fact that lawyers ask questions and witnesses answer them. By posing a particular question, one might assume, the lawyer determines the topic of the answer.

The reality of topic management is a good deal more complex, however. A cross-examination is not simply a series of questions followed by topically parallel answers. Instead, a witness may employ a variety of strategies to evade the lawyer's preferred answer. The lawyer may then seek to regain control by repeating, rephrasing, or elaborating on questions that have failed to elicit the desired answers.

Text 2.4 illustrates these points. The lawyer moves the witness toward acquiescence in a definition of "partying" that includes consensual sex. As discussed above, the lawyer succeeds in part through his manipulation of question forms. But his ability to maintain topic control is equally important. He begins by asking for the witness's definition of partying; she volunteers the elements of alcohol and drugs (lines 6–8). The lawyer pursues the theme, pinning down the distinction between partying as understood by the witness and her peers and partying as understood by others — middle-aged jurors perhaps (lines 11–13). He then expands on the topic by suggesting that sex is another routine party activity (lines 14–19). When the witness's answer is mildly evasive (line 20), he returns to the intoxication theme (line 21). When the witness gives her unqualified assent to this proposition (line 22), the lawyer has closed the circle, linking the witness and her friends to a party scene that unequivocally includes drugs and alcohol, and very probably consensual sex as well.

The lawyer then executes a subtle and highly significant topic shift. Having defined the category "partying" to include drugs, alcohol, and sex, he moves to include within that category the behavior of the witness on the night of the alleged rape (lines 23–24). The witness is initially silent and then offers an answer that evades the full force of the question (note her phrase "having a party" rather than the lawyer's "go partying") (lines 25–28). The lawyer does not let the evasion stand, however. Instead, he presses the point in two final questions (lines 29–32), which insist that the night's activities came within the agreed-on definition of partying.

In the preceding example, the witness ultimately yields to the lawyer's topic-management strategy. Far from advancing her cause, she becomes an unwitting collaborator in defining her activities on the night in question in a way that undermines, perhaps fatally, her contention that she was raped. She, like other witnesses, is not entirely without resources to resist such linguistic domination, however. Witnesses often decline to provide the kind of answer that the question presupposes. For example, as the following text illustrates, a witness may refuse to give an expected yes/no answer, instead challenging the question by deviating from its specific topic.

TEXT 2.5 (Matoesian 1993:154)

LAWYER: You were attracted to Brian, weren't you?
WITNESS: I thought he was a nice clean-looking man.
LAWYER: He was attractive-looking, correct?
WITNESS: Yeah.
5   LAWYER: And basically when you left that parking lot all you knew about him was that he was a good-lookin' man, isn't that true?
WITNESS: Yeah.

As Text 2.5 also suggests, however, witness resistance is likely to be short-lived. When the witness sidesteps a pejorative question, the lawyer can use elements of the answer to frame another question that is almost equally damaging. In this instance, when the witness hears her own topic, and indeed her own key word (*looking*), in the follow-up question, she finally acquiesces in the lawyer's suggestion that she willingly went off with a man — the defendant — to whom she was attracted. The linguistic resources available to the lawyer are simply too many and those available to the witness too few.

Commentary

Another source of domination available to the cross-examining lawyer is the opportunity to make covert evaluative comments on the witness's behavior. Such comments may concern the witness's behavior during the trial (or other associated legal proceedings) or in the course of the events outside the trial that constitute the substance of the case. Such comments are not stated directly but are embedded in questions. This allows the lawyer to stay within the bounds of the courtroom's prescribed question-and-answer format. The following two questions are examples of such covert commentary.

TEXT **2.6** (Matoesian 1993:164)

> LAWYER: Isn't it true that on direct examination by Mrs. Roberts you never once answered a question with "I don't know" or "I don't remember"?

TEXT **2.7** (Matoesian 1993:164)

> LAWYER: Isn't it true that on cross-examination by Mr. Billings you, on numerous occasions, indicated you didn't know or didn't remember?

Although these utterances are couched in the required question form and do not constitute the sort of explicit commentary that is permitted only in closing argument,[14] they nonetheless contain clear negative evaluations of the witness's behavior. In each instance, the rhetorical force of the question is to comment critically on a discrepancy between what the witness now claims to remember and what she remembered during a previous examination. Significantly, the lawyer structures the question so as to both offer an evaluative comment and demand that the witness confirm his evaluation in her answer.

In another example, a lawyer expresses his contention that the witness planned, or even fabricated, her testimony in a way that she believed would enhance the probability of winning. What the lawyer's questioning strategy does in this instance is to raise, via implication, the issue of whether the witness is to be trusted.

TEXT 2.8 (Matoesian 1993:163–64)

> LAWYER: Did you ever say that three people got into your car?
> WITNESS: Yes, I did.
> LAWYER: How often did you say that?
> WITNESS: A few times.
> 5   LAWYER: Before you talked to the prosecutor in this case?
> WITNESS: Yes.
> LAWYER: Was that because you thought that made your story sound better?

The lawyer is not permitted to state directly that he suspects that the witness may have fabricated details of her story. However, when couched as a question, such an assessment may be made indirectly.

Although it is logical to assume that a witness might in turn offer parallel commentary on the questions asked (such as "I don't think that's an appropriate question," "You're trying to put words into my mouth," or "I don't see where you're going with that question"), such instances are rare in court. When a witness does not answer the question directly within the constraints imposed by the lawyer, the lawyer may object on the grounds that the answer is not responsive to the question. The fact that witnesses have no resource parallel to the objections permitted to lawyers further underscores the imbalance of power under which witnesses must face examination.[15]

Notwithstanding the resources that are disproportionately available to the lawyer, a witness will sometimes offer resistance to a lawyer's assessment of her conduct by *downgrading* it. In the example that follows, the general topic is crossing the border from Missouri to Illinois. In his first two questions, the lawyer attempts to impose a damaging assessment on the witness's border-crossing behavior: that she goes to Illinois in order to take advantage of the lower drinking age. In answering the second question, the witness attempts to downgrade the lawyer's original assessment ("That's not the sole purpose") and thereby to diminish the significance of her action. Because the lawyer can follow up with another question, the witness's downgrade does not stand. In framing his follow-up question, the lawyer upgrades the previous downgrade by insisting that alcohol consumption was at least a partial motive for crossing into Illinois, and the witness is compelled to assent. Once again, the structure of courtroom interaction gives the lawyer an insurmountable advantage.

TEXT 2.9 (Matoesian 1993:180–81)

> LAWYER: Can you drink over at Saint Louis?
> WITNESS: No.
> LAWYER: So you come over here so you can get some alcohol, is that correct?

5   WITNESS: That's not the sole purpose, no.
    LAWYER: That's one of the purposes, is it not?
    WITNESS: Yeah.

The Witness's Capacity for Knowledge

A final linguistic strategy used by cross-examining lawyers to achieve and maintain domination involves direct challenges to knowledge claimed by the witness. Matoesian calls these challenges "epistemological filters" (1993:184). Epistemology is the study of knowledge: how we acquire it and how we decide what is really known. The lawyers' challenges described below are epistemological in that they call into question not only the specific facts the witness claims to know but also the sources of the claimed knowledge, and ultimately whether the witness is capable of knowing anything at all.

In the cross-examination excerpt in Text 2.10, the subject is the location to which the defendant drove the alleged victim on the night of the rape. The witness has previously identified the place as Glen Carbon. The lawyer now probes the source of her knowledge (line 4), and the witness responds in a way that would certainly be adequate by the standards of everyday conversation (lines 5–7, identifying the inscription on the water tank). But the lawyer continues the challenge, deprecating the certainty of her knowledge (line 8) and then positing an alternative epistemological theory: that the police planted the idea in her head (line 17).

TEXT 2.10 (Matoesian 1993:184–85)

    LAWYER: You say that Brian's car led the way over to this Glen
    Carbon area?
    WITNESS: Mmhmm.
    LAWYER: How do you know that was Glen Carbon?
5   WITNESS: There's a water tank? Maybe? A big silver [bubble]—
    LAWYER: [(What?)]
    WITNESS: —thing that says Glen Carb–, Glen Carbon.
    LAWYER: (Okay) but you don't actually know whether or not you
    were in Glen Carbon, or had you been told you were in Glen
10 Carbon at that point in time?
    WITNESS: I was told that was a part of Glen Carbon.
    LAWYER: By the police officers?
    WITNESS: Mmhmm.
    LAWYER: (Okay), so you don't actually know it was Glen Carbon
15 of your own personal knowledge.
    WITNESS: No I assumed it when I'd seen [(that big)]—
    LAWYER: [And when] the police officers told you.

Two further aspects of this exchange are significant. First, because of the lawyer's control over turn-taking and question form, it is very difficult for the witness to contest the epistemological challenge. When the lawyer's "how" question elicits an ostensibly satisfactory response (lines 4–7), he pursues the point with a series of questions — in effect, statements — that exert progressively more control over the witness's response (lines 8–end). Because his final question (lines 14–15) calls for a yes/no answer, he is able to treat her initial "No" as a complete answer and cut off her developing explanation.[16] Despite the plausibility of that explanation (that she had seen the Glen Carbon water tank, assumed that was where she was, and then had her assumption verified by the police), the lawyer is able to interrupt it and conclude the exchange with a damaging evaluative comment.

Second, the genders of the lawyer and the witness seem highly relevant to the power dynamics of this exchange. The other methods of linguistic domination described thus far occur regularly in all kinds of cases and irrespective of the genders of the protagonists. As we shall see, the relationship between these devices and the politics of male domination is discoverable only at deeper levels of analysis. In the case of epistemological challenges, however, that relationship seems closer to the surface. Could a lawyer so readily challenge a *male* witness's ability to draw factual inferences from his observations? Or does the challenge depend on the cultural stereotype of women as being incapable of logical deduction and having diminished capacity for knowledge generally? We turn to these issues in the next section.

Is It Really about Rape?

In reviewing various linguistic strategies by which lawyers dominate witnesses, we have said very little about rape. In fact, until we reached the last of these strategies — epistemological challenge — we did not make a single argument that even depended on gender dynamics. On the contrary, anyone with any exposure to the adversary system will recognize that all but the last are staples of cross-examination, used without regard to the subject matter of the case or the genders of lawyer and witness. And with respect to the epistemological challenge, even if it is far more likely in the cross-examination of a female witness by a male lawyer, there is no reason to believe that its use is limited to rape trials or more prevalent there than in other contexts.

These unremarkable observations give rise to an important question: From a linguistic perspective, is there really anything unique about rape trials? Or does the revictimization process consist simply of generic cross-examination strategies?[17] Perhaps we think we see something unique because the adversarial treatment of rape victims is particularly offensive to our moral and political sensibilities.[18]

Matoesian has recognized the problem. In *Reproducing Rape*, he asks, "Could it not be that the relevant moral inferential work being transacted [in rape trials] represents instead mundane, gender-neutral categorizations: doing credible or incredible testimony; doing honesty or dishonesty; doing consistency or inconsistency, etc.?" (Matoesian 1993:163). In other words, is revictimization just ordinary cross-examination?

Matoesian's answer to this question seems oddly out of place in a work that aspires to rigorous linguistic empiricism. He acknowledges that the processes of reproducing rape are gender-neutral, "but only at a surface level!" (1993:163; exclamation his). "On a deeper level of social organization," he argues, ostensibly neutral linguistic practices are inseparably bound up with patriarchal values. Matoesian seems to be asking the reader to accept an argument about the meaning of linguistic behavior on the basis of an a priori assessment of the nature of society.

One need not rely on assumptions about social organization to demonstrate the uniqueness of rape trials, however. First, the appropriate background against which we should interpret the use of apparently generic cross-examination strategies is not some "deeper level of social organization" but the crime of rape itself. In judging a case of acquaintance rape, the jury's task is to assign social meaning to a commonplace behavior — sexual intercourse — that is in itself neither right nor wrong. In particular, the jury must decide whether the behavior in question was an act of *domination*. It is hard to think of another crime that has precisely these qualities. Although legal culpability may ultimately depend on the state of mind of the perpetrator, shooting another human being, hot-wiring someone else's car, and failing to file an income tax return are all presumptively pathological actions in and of themselves.[19]

With this point in mind, recall the various linguistic strategies we have reviewed: they are all strategies of domination. When used in a rape trial, they are strategies of domination employed in the service of one accused of domination. Thus, while these strategies may not be unique to rape trials, they have a poignancy in the rape context that is unmatched elsewhere. A woman telling a story of physical domination by one man is subjected to linguistic domination by another.[20] In this sense, revictimization is real, and its mechanism is linguistic.

There is also abundant direct evidence that rape trials are unique linguistic events. Matoesian (1995) develops some of this evidence in an article in which he analyzes the 1991 William Kennedy Smith rape trial. Smith is a nephew of the late Senator Edward Kennedy and a physician who has worked for many years on the rehabilitation of landmine victims. During his last year as a medical student, Smith was charged with raping a woman he had met at a Palm Beach bar while in the company of his cousin and Senator Kennedy. His trial and acquittal created a national media circus.

Matoesian discusses two linguistic phenomena that are of major strategic importance in rape trials and that would be inappropriate in any other context:

the "double bind" of sexual logic and the covert exploitation of the witness's prior sexual history (1995:686).

The Sexual Double Bind

The double bind is the dilemma that an acquaintance-rape victim finds herself in when she tries to explain her interaction with the defendant. In such cases, the victim is usually called on to explain how a normal social engagement evolved into a crime of violence. A critical element of the explanation is how the witness describes her state of mind at various points before and after the alleged rape. If she describes herself as having been emotional, the lawyer may play on the stereotype of the flighty woman to suggest that she is irrational and thus not credible, and perhaps now vengeful as well. If, on the other hand, she portrays herself as having been calm and in control, the lawyer may emphasize that she does *not* fit the stereotype, implying that an unusually logical woman would not have allowed herself to be dominated. When the defendant is a wealthy man like William Kennedy Smith, the calm, logical woman also becomes a target for accusations of gold-digging. The woman is thus in a double bind: she loses, whichever approach she takes.

In Text 2.11, Roy Black, Smith's defense lawyer, is cross-examining Patricia Bowman, the alleged victim. Black picks up on Bowman's evaluation of Smith's demeanor ("very smug") and upgrades it ("And arrogant?") in order to develop the theme of a woman scorned, perhaps driven to seek revenge by Smith's unwillingness to connect with her emotionally. Bowman falls into the trap: in denying the charge of anger, she admits to confusion.

TEXT 2.11 (Matoesian 1995:684)

> LAWYER: And he was sitting there, and I think you said, with his legs crossed?
> WITNESS: He had his ankle up on his knee.
> LAWYER: And you say that he was very calm at that time?
> 5   WITNESS: And very smug.
> LAWYER: And arrogant? Made you madder than you were?
> WITNESS: It didn't make me mad. It confused me.

Elsewhere in the cross-examination, Black does the same thing in a slightly different way. Once again, he exploits Bowman's characterizations of Smith to sharpen his portrait of her as a scorned woman whose emotionally charged story is not worthy of belief. He adopts Bowman's assessment of Smith ("indifference") and upgrades it ("cold and indifferent"). She acquiesces, accepting Black's now-enhanced description of her dismay at Smith's attitude.

TEXT 2.12 (Matoesian 1995:684)

LAWYER: He was calm and arrogant, you say?
WITNESS: Yes sir.
LAWYER: He was certainly not being very nice to you.
WITNESS: It was more an indifference.
5   LAWYER: He was cold and indifferent?
WITNESS: Yes sir.

Patricia Bowman and other rape victims cannot win. They are either too illogical or too logical. When Bowman elsewhere characterizes portions of her interaction with Smith as calm and rational, Black pursues the topic to suggest that she had a serious interest in him. The implication, of course, is that she was a calculating pursuer rather than a helpless victim.

TEXT 2.13 (Matoesian 1995:686)

LAWYER: He told you he was in medical school?
WITNESS: Yes he did.
LAWYER: Of course, that got you more interested in him, didn't it?
WITNESS: I was interested in any other outlooks he could have on
5   my daughter's problem . . .
LAWYER: And you talked to him about medical matters involving
your daughter, isn't that right?
WITNESS: Yes sir.
LAWYER: You became more interested in him as you found out that
10   he had this kind of background?
WITNESS: I became more interested in what he had to say.

Rape victims are not allowed to negotiate a middle course between emotion and reason. Defense lawyers push them to extremes. At one moment, the lawyer portrays the woman as so emotional that she probably consented to sex, regretted it, and then brought charges to get revenge; at the next, he depicts her as too rational and controlling to have been lured into domination by another. The woman is not permitted to be simultaneously competent and vulnerable. In Text 2.14, Bowman suggests that her initial feeling toward Smith was mild affection that stopped well short of sexual abandon. Black immediately challenges that possibility with negative assessments.

TEXT 2.14 (Matoesian 1995:680)

LAWYER: Yesterday you told us that when you arrived in the parking
lot in the car you kissed Will. Is that correct?

WITNESS: I testified that when we arrived at the estate, he gave me a goodnight peck.
5   . . .
LAWYER: That's all it was?
WITNESS: Yes sir.
LAWYER: Nothing of any — , nothing more than that?
WITNESS: No.

Sexual History

Rape victims are also subject to attack on the basis of their sexual history with men other than the defendants. Many states, including Florida, the site of the Smith trial, have enacted rape shield laws, which prohibit explicit questions about the victim's sexual history. Nonetheless, skillful defense lawyers can accomplish the same thing by innuendo. In Text 2.15, Black asks Bowman a series of apparently sympathetic questions about her meeting with Smith. But he subtly connects her to "the bar scene," with all its tawdry connotations, by suggesting that Smith rescued her from it. Then, by the device of abandoning his own question in midsentence ("You were no longer — "), Black implies that Smith's arrival interrupted the unspecified bar-scene activities in which she had been engaged. The rapist is thus transformed into a missionary to fallen women.

TEXT 2.15 (Matoesian 1995:679)

LAWYER: You had an engrossing conversation?
WITNESS: Yes sir.
LAWYER: You didn't have to be involved in the rest of the bar scene?
WITNESS: Yes sir.
5   LAWYER: You were happy to have found that?
WITNESS: It was nice.
LAWYER: You were no longer — , in fact you were with him almost exclusively?
WITNESS: I don't know.

In these examples from the William Kennedy Smith trial, the basic linguistic devices are not unique. On the contrary, Black accomplishes his objectives through such familiar devices as topic management, control over question form, and commentary disguised as questions. What is unique is the effect of these devices in the rape context. The double-bind strategy, for example, would have no saliency in other kinds of cases. One can imagine a lawyer suggesting that a woman who had witnessed an auto accident was emotional and flighty, but what sense would it make to imply in the next breath that she was too logical? Even more obviously, covert references to a woman's sexual history would be out of place in a case where her sexuality was not squarely before the jury.

It is also hard to imagine a man being subjected to this kind of cross-examination. On the one hand, imputing emotional instability to a man requires specific evidence, since it does not evoke a stereotype. On the other hand, what is to be gained by imputing a calculating, logical mindset to a man—even in matters of sexual conquest—since that is what everyone expects? The point is well illustrated by an excerpt from prosecutor Moira Lasch's cross-examination of Smith. When she accuses him of a lack of emotional involvement in the events of the evening, he simply acquiesces, and the attack goes nowhere.

Text 2.16 (Matoesian 1995:684)

> LAWYER: So you have this conversation—, well you had this act, then you ejaculate and then you say, "Well I'm going into the water and take a swim now."
> WITNESS: Yes.
> 5   LAWYER: That sounds not too romantic, Mr. Smith.
> WITNESS: I don't know how to respond to that.[21]

A final illustration of the uniqueness of rape trials comes from our own study of the Smith case. Here, Black cross-examines Bowman about her pantyhose, which she earlier testified she had removed at some point on the night of the rape.

Text 2.17 (Authors' transcription from videotape of trial)

> LAWYER: Did you take off your pantyhose at Au Bar?
> WITNESS: I don't remember doing that.
> LAWYER: Did you have your pantyhose on when you left the bar?
> WITNESS: I'm, I think I did.
> 5   LAWYER: Did you have your pantyhose on when you drove your car from Au Bar [*with Smith as her passenger*]?
> WITNESS: Yes.
> LAWYER: Did you have your pantyhose on when you got to the parking lot at the Kennedy home?
> 10   WITNESS: Yes.
> LAWYER: Did you have your pantyhose on in the car in the, in the parking lot?
> WITNESS: Yes.
> LAWYER: Did you have your pantyhose on when you got out of
> 15   your car?

WITNESS: I'm not sure.

LAWYER: Did you have your pantyhose on when you went into the house?

WITNESS: I'm not sure.

20 LAWYER: Did you have your pantyhose on in the kitchen?

WITNESS: I don't remember.

LAWYER: Did you have your pantyhose on when you walked through the house?

WITNESS: I don't remember.

25 LAWYER: Did you have your pantyhose on when you walked across the lawn?

WITNESS: I don't remember.

LAWYER: Did you have your pantyhose on going down the stairs?

WITNESS: I don't remember.

30 LAWYER: Did you have them on while you were standing on the beach?

WITNESS: I don't remember.

LAWYER: Did you have them on when you were going up the stairs?

WITNESS: I don't remember.

In this sequence, Black uses an ordinary cross-examination technique — the repetitive question form — to extraordinary effect. The form of the questions is within Black's exclusive control. The law of evidence does prohibit repetitive questioning, but Black skillfully avoids that prohibition by a subtle shift from question to question. Each question hammers home the identical point but in reference to a moment in time slightly later than that in the previous question.

In an effort to understand the effect, we have asked many of our students to analyze this testimony. The students continually focus on Black's ability to manipulate gender differences in the classification of clothing. From a male perspective, the students contend, there are two principal classes of clothing: clothes and underwear. Pantyhose constitute underwear because they are never fully exposed in public. One's underwear is exposed to the opposite sex only in circumstances of intimacy. "Decent" people do not lose track of their underwear when in mixed company. Patricia Bowman, by contrast, cannot remember what happened to her underwear during her evening with William Kennedy Smith. How, Black's questions imply, can a man be held responsible for his actions toward such a woman?

By contrast, the students argue, pantyhose are interstitial from a female perspective. They are underwear in the sense that they are worn beneath something else, but their removal does not always imply intimacy. Indeed, removing one's pantyhose in the dark before walking on the sandy beach is a perfectly ordinary act. From this perspective, the status of Bowman's pantyhose at various times during the evening is irrelevant to the issue of Bowman's consent to sex. Because of Black's control over the questions, however, this perspective is never expressed.

Conclusion: Rape and the Power of Discourse

The microdiscourse of the rape trial is a compelling example of how power is realized through linguistic practice. Rape victims are indeed revictimized, but not by any legal rules or practices peculiar to rape trials. Instead, it is the ordinary mechanics of cross-examination that, in this extraordinary context, simultaneously reflect and reaffirm men's power over women. The basic linguistic strategies of cross-examination are methods of domination and control. When used against the background of the rape victim's experience, they can bring about a subtle yet powerful reenactment of that experience.

The linguistic analysis of rape also yields convincing evidence of the inseparability of the multiple meanings of discourse. The discourse of rape is multifaceted; it consists, at a minimum, of the talk that transpires between rapist and victim, the statements contained in the law of rape, the largely linguistic practice of lawyers and witnesses involved in applying that law, and the cultural commentary on all of the foregoing. At every level of the discourse of rape, important social values concerning women, men, and their relationships are evident. The fine-grained analysis of the discourse of legal practice, however, affords insights that are not available at higher levels of abstraction. We see how the law translates social values into social action, as well as the role that the law can play in either strengthening or subverting those values. In the words of Alan Hunt and Gary Wickham, "Discourses have real effects; they are not just the ways that social issues get talked and thought about" (1994:8). Analysis such as this enables us to understand what those effects are and how they come about.

CHAPTER THREE

The Language of Mediation

In this chapter, we undertake another case study of the relationship between political claims about legal power and the linguistic means through which that power is exercised. Here, however, we focus not on a substantive area of the law (such as rape) but on a legal *process* that is brought to bear on a wide range of disputes: mediation. In general terms, mediation is any conciliatory, nonbinding process in which disputants, with the aid of a neutral facilitator, try to reach a mutually acceptable resolution of their problem (Hughes 1995:566). Mediation is conciliatory in the sense that the parties talk to each other in an effort to compromise, rather than presenting competing evidence as they would in a formal trial. It is nonbinding in that the facilitator has no power to enter a final judgment, as a judge or arbitrator can.

Mediation surged in popularity in the 1980s and 1990s (e.g., Grillo 1991: 1551–55). Many courts began to require it before certain kinds of cases could go to trial (e.g., Clarke et al. 1989). Community mediation centers have proliferated, and thousands of lawyers, social workers, businesspeople, and others are now holding themselves out as mediation professionals. Significantly, numerous published accounts report widespread consumer satisfaction with mediation as a less expensive, faster, and more satisfying alternative to litigation (see Hughes 1995:568–69; Bohmer and Ray 1994:224–25; Grillo 1991:1548–49; Clarke et al. 1989:53–66; Kelly 1989). The disputants' sense of control over the outcome seems to promote both satisfaction and compliance with mediated agreements (Garcia 1995:40). Even lawyers are reported to like mediation, despite the fact that it might be seen as a threat to their historical monopoly over dispute resolution.[1]

The reviews have not been uniformly positive, however. Critics charge that the very user-friendly qualities that have made mediation so popular also make it dangerous (e.g., Bryan 1992:453–54; Hughes 1995:573; Grillo 1991: 1601–5). That is, in the cooperative ambience of the mediation session, people with strong legal and moral claims may be induced to let down their guard and make concessions that are neither required by the law nor consistent with their interests. More recent critical analyses have also asked whether mediator neutrality is an illusion (e.g., Izumi 2010). Moreover, the critique continues, these effects are not randomly distributed but work almost invariably to support powerful interests and reinforce the political and economic status quo.

Our purpose in this chapter is to assess the mediation phenomenon from a microlinguistic perspective. What is it about the mediation process that prompts such strong reactions, both positive and negative? First we address the seemingly incontrovertible fact that mediation "works": by all accounts, it resolves many disputes in a way that is satisfactory to the disputants. How does it do so? What are the mechanisms through which angry people on the brink of litigation are led to talk to each other and agree on an outcome? Then we consider the practical consequences of mediation's apparent success in resolving disputes. We test the claim that mediation is subject to political manipulation by searching for the linguistic processes through which that might happen. Through the examination of microdiscourse, we seek to assess whether mediation reflects and reaffirms the dominant macrodiscourse. We begin with a brief overview of the mediation process.

What a Mediation Session Is Like

People often talk about mediation as though it were a unitary phenomenon. In fact, there are many kinds of mediation structures, and they differ from each other in significant ways.[2] Many community-based mediation centers, for example, have clients who seek mediation voluntarily, whereas court-annexed programs provide mandatory mediation for people who have been diverted from the judicial system. Some court-annexed programs offer mediation as an alternative to the formal prosecution of minor crimes, while others require that certain kinds of civil litigants (parties to divorce cases, for example) go through mediation before their cases can go to trial. Procedurally, some programs use a single mediator, and others have two or more; programs also vary in the amount of talk between the parties and in the way the interaction is structured. It is therefore difficult to describe mediation in terms of any universal features. Nonetheless, to set the stage for our discussion of how mediation works on a linguistic level, we offer the following description of mediation as it operates in a community mediation center where one of us (O'Barr) has worked as a mediator (compare Grillo 1991:1589; Hughes 1995:566–69).

Before a session begins, civil discourse between the parties has broken down. Something has happened; they have disagreed; perhaps the dispute has escalated to the point where they are not even speaking to one another. Mediation enters the picture as a possible mechanism for settling the conflict through talking things out. Some parties come to this community mediation center on their own. Others are referred by the local criminal court with the promise of having their cases dropped if working agreements can be reached. Although some are thus coerced into mediation by the threat of prosecution, many who enter mediation are voluntarily seeking a way to mend social relationships that have failed.

When the disputants arrive at the mediation center, they are often angry. They are ushered into separate rooms to wait for the session to begin. When they are called in by one of the two co-mediators, the first order of business is to lay out the rules that will be followed. Each side will present its version of the dispute, beginning with the complainant. There will be no interruptions. Each party will get to tell its story while the other listens. There will eventually be time for questions and discussion, but during the initial presentations they are to listen respectfully.

An unstated goal of the mediators is to work as impartial and supportive listeners, a technique in which they have been extensively trained. Ideally, this means that they will not take sides or show any partiality. Regardless of who is speaking, they should demonstrate through both gestures and linguistic behaviors that they are listening actively. They are encouraged, for example, to sit up in their chairs, to indicate understanding by nodding frequently, and to affirm the stories and positions of each side by repeating back what they have heard, using such introductory phrases as "What I hear you saying is . . . ," "Let me see if I understand you correctly," and "You seem to be saying that. . . ." In addition to providing support and encouragement to the speaker, these techniques have the important effect of making the mediators the addressees of each speaker's story, with the other party cast in the role of overhearer.

Beyond active listening, the mediators will work to structure the substance of the talk so as to promote the overriding goal of the mediation center: reaching an agreement that the parties can promise to follow. What this means in practice is that the mediators will help the parties separate the issues that seem amenable to some sort of resolution from those on which they are hopelessly deadlocked. If successful, the mediation session will result in a written agreement that both parties assent to and promise to follow. It will state in simple, everyday language what they have agreed to and what they will do to ensure that the terms work. It is supposed to be up to the parties to fashion the specific terms, with the mediators serving as nonjudgmental scribes and editors. This often results in agreements whose details might strike an observer (who incidentally would never be allowed in the room due to the mediation center's overriding concern with confidentiality) as odd ("X agrees not to let his dog out anymore at 3 a.m.," or "Y will pick up any garbage that spills on the walk in front of the apartment building where he lives"). But when the process works, the parties take a proprietary interest in the agreement and, for that reason, strive to live up to its terms. In the best of circumstances, the climate of civility that mediation fosters spills over into daily life, enabling the former adversaries to regenerate at least some of their social connections.

Restoring Civility

We turn next to the linguistic analysis of how mediation manages to restore communication and promote agreement between a pair of antagonists. The research of sociologist Angela Garcia is particularly helpful in understanding the microlinguistic phenomena that produce such effects. Using the methods of conversation analysis, Garcia (1991, 1995) focuses on the differences between mediation talk and everyday arguments. She points to details in the linguistic structure of mediation that serve to suppress some essential features of arguments. The result is the conciliatory environment that is the hallmark of mediation.

In her 1991 article, Garcia adheres to the traditions of conversation analysis, concerning herself with questions of *how* rather than *why*. She does not, for example, ask whether suppressing arguments is a good or a bad thing, nor does she assess the effects of doing so in particular contexts. Similarly, she is content to show how mediators acknowledge disputants' stories without addressing the issue of why they acknowledge them as they do. Nonetheless, her detailed data and fine-grained description allow her readers to extend the analysis to other, more explicitly political issues — as Garcia (1995) has done in her more recent work, and as we shall do later in this chapter.[3]

The Structure of Mediation

Accusations, counteraccusations, blamings, denials, raised voices, and hurt feelings make up the stuff of arguments in daily life. Once started, arguments easily escalate to a point where civility seems irretrievably lost. Driving this all-too-familiar pattern are the interactional mechanics of arguing.

Most arguments begin when one party accuses or blames another. The accused or blamed person retorts. There follows a counter-retort, and on it goes. Whether it is the you-did/no-I-didn't/yes-you-did of children's arguments or some more elaborate adult version, almost all arguments have this basic structure. Mediation alters the rules of conversational exchange in such a way as to mitigate argumentation and facilitate the regeneration of nonargumentative talk. A look into the linguistic details of mediation reveals just how this happens.

According to Garcia, two structural features are critical to the linguistic distinctiveness of mediation. First, mediation sessions usually allow each disputant to tell his or her story, while requiring the other to wait quietly for his or her turn to speak. In everyday conversation, by contrast — and especially in arguments — overlapping speech and competition for speaking turns are commonplace. Second, mediation sessions, unlike ordinary conversations, include a third party — the mediator — who is expressly empowered to enforce conversational etiquette and referee interactional disputes.

As a result of these structural features, Garcia contends, mediation suppresses arguments in several related ways. First, the accusations and denials/counter-accusations that occur in quick succession in everyday contexts are separated from one another temporally during mediation. This disrupts the back-and-forth rhythm of argument by imposing a cooling-off period before a retort can be issued. This decoupling can cause retorts to be less vehement, and in some cases to be omitted altogether. The fewer the contested accusations, the less there is to be resolved.

Second, accusations and denials between the disputing parties are addressed to the mediator rather than the other disputant. Instead of being confronted in the first person, the respondent is the subject of a less threatening third-person reference. Such an accusation is more easily ignored without loss of face. Finally, the normative order of mediation encourages mitigated rather than aggravated accusations and denials. This ethos of understatement prevents many of the escalations that occur in ordinary argument.

Garcia documents these processes with detailed examples drawn from mediation sessions. In Text 3.1, for example, the complainant accuses the respondent of verbally abusing her. We can readily imagine an everyday situation in which such an accusation, phrased in the confrontational second person, would elicit an immediate retort and continue to escalate. Here, however, the accusation is directed to the mediator and framed in the third person, and the respondent says nothing. Indeed, when the complainant solicits a minimal response (the final "you know?"), it is the mediator, not the respondent, who replies.

TEXT 3.1 (Garcia 1991:829)

> COMPLAINANT: The first knowledge I had of her dislike, aggravation
> with me, one time she, I was coming from the car, with my child
> who was about two at the time. And her daughter came up to me and
> said "Get her out of the way" or something and she said,
> 5   you know, she just hurled a lot of accusations. I don't know how
> much detail it's worth going into. But it was a lot of you know, rather
> vile obscenities that I only use if I'm furi–, you know?
> MEDIATOR: Um-hmh, yeah.

Contrast this with an instance in which the disputants violate mediation's special rules of turn-taking. Text 3.2 is taken from a child-custody mediation. The ex-husband is explaining why he is unwilling to give up visitation time. His ex-wife breaks two of the fundamental linguistic rules of mediation. First, she interrupts the ex-husband with a response and an accusation, rather than waiting her turn; and second, she addresses her remarks directly *to* her ex-husband (note her use of "you"), rather than speaking to the mediator *about* him. The exchange that ensues sounds like an everyday argument. It continues until the mediator loudly and forcefully reasserts control.

TEXT 3.2 (Garcia 1991:829)

> EX-HUSBAND: YEAH, I, you know? I still don't feel good about it,
> because like this is my flesh and blood! You know? And you know,
> uh, I['m yeah —]
> EX-WIFE: [But] *you* shouted abortion, for nine months [with
> 5 Sharon.]
> MEDIATOR: [Listen, we] are not —
> EX-HUSBAND: Hey —
> MEDIATOR: — talking a[bout] —
> EX-HUSBAND: — [WHO] had the abortion? Y[ou want to get]
> 10 SMART?
> MEDIATOR: [Wait a minute!]
> EX-HUSBAND: DIDN'T SH[E JUST] HAVE ONE?
> MEDIATOR: [Hey wait!] HOLD IT! WE'RE NOT IN HERE TO
> TALK ABOUT THAT. I DIDN'T TALK ABOUT MY PROBLEMS,
> 15 OR WHATEVER. WE'VE ALL GOT A STORY. That's no one's
> business.

The Moral Order of Mediation

In addition to these structural effects, the moral order of mediation sessions also facilitates agreement. By emphasizing at the outset the goals of compromise and noncompetitiveness, the mediator sets the stage for nonadversarial talk. Disputants' linguistic behavior appears to take the norms of mediation into account. They talk more about what happened than whose fault it is, and they employ linguistic devices that soften, or downgrade, the accusations that they make. For example, in Text 3.3, the complainant states the problem in a far less confrontational way than he might have in an everyday argument.

TEXT 3.3 (Garcia 1991:831)

> COMPLAINANT: A lot of the, uh, the la–, the labor that was, uh,
> conducted in the motor home was, was not done in a, in a
> professional, uh, way. I mean, basically, it wasn't completed
> professionally. It wasn't, it is my, uh, in my estimation, it wasn't,
> 5 uh, completed at all.

This complaint is constructed so as to focus on the problem rather than on the person accused of failing to complete the work. The talk is about *what* rather than *who*; the action is named but not the agent. Contrast this with another possible statement of the problem in which the complainant named the person he believed to be at fault, used pejorative adjectives to describe the person, and then linked that person with the problematic action — and in a raised voice. That kind of highly charged, accusatory statement of the problem is just what might occur in everyday argument. In mediation, Garcia argues, people rarely make direct accusations, instead mitigating them in a variety of ways, including, as here, by deleting the agent.[4]

Even when the accused party is named, the accuser may still downgrade the accusation by assuming some of the blame. For example, instead of saying simply that the other party has caused the problem, the accuser may use the inclusive pronoun *we* to describe what happened, as in Text 3.4.

Text 3.4 (Garcia 1991:832)

> COMPLAINANT: Since the beginning of this year, we've been harassing each other . . .

Such a statement seems calculated to promote conciliation rather than argumentation. By including himself as a causal agent, the speaker accepts a share of the blame for the problematic action, thus making a significant concession.

Finally, the accuser may downgrade the accusation itself. In Text 3.5, the complainant divides the problematic action into two components. Even though the mediator has explicitly asked for a statement of the *im*proper work, the complainant mentions first the component that was not blameworthy. This is indeed a gentle accusation.

Text 3.5 (Garcia 1991:832)

> MEDIATOR: Okay. Improper mechanical work?
> COMPLAINANT: Yeah, improper, uh, work completed by the
> mechanic. I would imagine part of it was done, uh okay, but
> there were two or three things that were, that weren't completed
> 5   properly.

Summary

Garcia's work presents a compelling linguistic picture of how mediation manages to move disputants toward agreement. By altering the conversational structure and moral environment of everyday argument, mediation defuses confrontation. Such devices as decoupling accusations and denials and forcing the parties to speak to the mediator rather than each other are the linguistic equivalent of a referee separating two boxers and sending them to their respective corners. And when the disputants do state their charges and countercharges, the normative order of the mediation session exerts a moderating influence on both the content and the tone of the accusations.

We thus begin to understand the linguistic processes through which mediation restructures communication, promotes agreement, and produces consumer satisfaction. The next question is whether the same kind of microlinguistic analysis can help us to evaluate the larger political claims that have been made about mediation. Can linguistics help us decide whether, as its proponents claim, mediation is a neutral and benign process or, as the critics assert, it is subject to subtle manipulation by the powerful? We must first review in greater detail just what the critics have said.

The Macrodiscourse of Mediation

The search for an answer to this question leads us once again to the concept of discourse. There is an extensive literature that treats mediation as a discourse in the sense of a way of talking about disputes. This body of work focuses on the ongoing contest between the discourses of mediation and adversarial adjudication for dominance in the field of dispute resolution. Since dominant discourses are translated into social action, this literature emphasizes, the outcome of the contest is not a mere theoretical concern. On the contrary, the ascendancy of one discourse over the other influences not only the process by which disputes are resolved but also who wins and who loses.

The idea of mediation as a way of talking about disputes has been perhaps best developed by feminist legal scholar Martha Albertson Fineman in her work on divorce, which remains highly influential. In a series of writings culminating in her book *The Illusion of Equality: The Rhetoric and Reality of Divorce Reform* (1991), Fineman characterizes the then-recent history of divorce law as a successful struggle by the "helping professions" (social workers and various kinds of therapists) to substitute their discourse for that of the law. Prior to the 1960s, divorce and custody cases turned on such traditional legal concepts as rights, responsibility, and fault (Fineman 1991:19). One spouse obtained a divorce by proving that the other had been at fault in destroying the marriage. The legal grounds for divorce were such things as adultery, desertion, nonsupport, and abuse; when husband and wife simply did not want to remain married, the conventional strategy was for the wife to complain of "mental cruelty" and for the husband not to contest the charge. Findings of fault influenced the distribution of property. Adulterous husbands could expect more onerous alimony assessments than those guilty only of unspecified mental cruelty. Fault, or its absence, was also an essential criterion in child-custody cases. Judges were supposed to decide custody disputes "in the best interests of the child." However, the law presumed that children of "tender years" belonged with their mothers. This presumption could be overcome only by a showing that the wife was an "unfit mother."

Divorce and custody law underwent radical change in the 1960s and 1970s. In pursuit of what Fineman calls "the equality ideal" (1991:20), liberal reformers attacked the existing regime as gender-biased. It presumed, they argued, that women were dependent on men and that women were inevitably homemakers, while men were breadwinners. "No fault" divorce was introduced, meaning that spouses could divorce by choice, without the need to persuade a court that one of them had done something wrong. (Note the revealing use of *divorce* as an intransitive verb: in the 1950s and 1960s, people said things like "A is divorcing B"; it is now much more common to hear "A and B are divorcing.") When the inquiry into fault was dispensed with, the old guidelines for distributing property and awarding custody became unworkable.

Under the newer law, which remains the norm, the starting point for adjudicating divorce and custody cases is Fineman's "illusion of equality." The law now presumes that men and women are equal: equal in their capacities to earn a living and to reconstruct their lives after the divorce, and in their willingness and ability to care for their children. This, of course, is fantasy. Despite a generation of gains in opportunity, women on average still earn less than comparably qualified men. Women remain far more likely than men to sacrifice career advancement to nurture children. And, with rare exceptions, mothers are more likely than fathers to sacrifice post-divorce autonomy in order to minimize the effect of the breakup on the children. Much research cited by Fineman indicated that, at least in economic terms, women and children were significantly worse off than before all of the "reform" began (Fineman 1991:36–38). A review of the more recent literature suggests that little has changed. As much as ever, divorce impoverishes women.

How did all this happen? Social conservatives blame the moral relativism of the sixties. Many feminists, Fineman (1991:26–28) included, point to their liberal forebears' exaltation of symbolic equality over economic reality. Almost everyone sees the law of unintended consequences at work.

Fineman's most original contribution is to identify the role of the helping professions. As the legal climate began to change, therapists presented the courts, state legislatures, and public with a discourse more in tune with the new environment. The adoption of this perspective in turn facilitated a change in divorce procedures. And the adoption of new procedures has had subtle yet significant effects on the social reality of divorce.

Originally, by Fineman's account, social workers and other helpers viewed divorce as pathological, something to be avoided if possible through counseling aimed at reconciliation. When divorce did occur, the helpers assisted the lawyers with expert advice on such issues as the best interests of the child. With the coming of no-fault divorce, the helping professions' attitude changed dramatically. Divorce came to be viewed not as the pathological termination of a marriage but rather as a "situational crisis" within the "family system" (Fineman 1991:152). Significantly, divorce did not end the former spouses' relationship; instead, it required the development of a new relationship as the family sought to establish a "post-dissolution organization." Where children were involved, the focus was no longer on a binary-choice custody decision. The new ideal was ongoing "co-parenting." Talk of "physical custody" and "visitation" gave way to a rhetoric of "shared parenting" and "periods of physical placement" (Fineman 1991:150).

This change in the helping professions' discourse about divorce itself was paralleled by the development of a new discourse about divorce procedure. In the early 1970s, social workers and therapists began to criticize the adversarial model of divorce and the lawyers who managed it. In the no-fault era, the legal aspects of the divorce were reduced to a mere formality. The critical task was managing the "emotional divorce," and this required the skills of the therapist, not the win-at-all-costs advocate (Fineman 1991:153). When the divorcing spouses fought over custody, the law's adversarial approach was worse than useless. All it could do was pick a winner. What was needed was a therapist who could make the parents realize that they were fighting over custody not to advance the child's best interests but rather to serve their own "profound psychological needs" (Fineman 1991:156).

To turn their theory into social reality, the helping professions offered the courts a procedural alternative to adversarial litigation—mediation, which would be directed not by lawyers and judges but by therapists. They backed up the offer with a pair of contrasting narratives about divorce. These narratives are pervasive in the literature and rhetoric of the helping professions. The first is the "horror story" of the adversarial divorce: both spouses employ lawyers who counsel them to fight over everything, there is a winner and a loser, and the children are deeply hurt by the specter of their parents' fighting and the reality of "losing" the parent who loses the custody dispute (Fineman 1991:159–60). The second narrative is the "fairy tale" of the mediated divorce: rather than the spouses taking sides, "the family" enters the divorce process as a unit; the spouses consult one mediator rather than two lawyers; the mediator leads them through a caring, cooperative, and nonadversarial process; and everyone lives happily ever after (and saves a lot of money, too) (Fineman 1991:160–61).

The process offered by the mediators has proved attractive to the legal system. Judges do not like to decide custody disputes. They are messy and time-consuming, particularly since the abolition of the old presumption in favor of the mother, and one party usually comes away embittered. Many divorce lawyers also find the new procedures attractive, as evidenced by the growing number of lawyers who commit themselves to nonadversarial "collaborative" divorce (e.g., Crawford 2017). They can escape their longtime image as the legal profession's bottom-feeders and hold themselves out as caring counselors.

As a result of all these factors, some kind of mediation is now the norm in most states, and the discourse of the helping professions is now the dominant discourse of divorce. Fineman (1991:144–69) argues persuasively that this has had disastrous consequences for women. The helpers are interested not in finding fault in past behavior but in shaping a workable relationship for the future. Everyone is presumed to be equally willing and able to share in that relationship. The problem is that the way people have acted in the past is often a good predictor of how they will behave in the future. Why should a father who defaulted on his parental obligations during the marriage suddenly be given equal standing with his ex-wife? Why should a woman be forced to continue a relationship with a man who has already shown himself to be an unfit partner?

The newly dominant discourse of divorce is one of neutrality. The helping professions talk of engaging in a process, of replacing confrontation with co-operation. Their rhetoric avoids mention of the power struggles between men and women, or of taking sides in those struggles. But, according to Fineman, that is exactly what they have done. By dispensing with the quest for fault and presuming both spouses to be equally fit to participate in family life, the helpers have denied women the moral high ground they formerly occupied in divorce litigation. Taking lawyers out of the process has also had a different impact on men and women: because women are typically less experienced in financial ne-gotiations, they need lawyers more. Finally, women may be more inclined than men to seek agreement for the sake of agreement, even if it is disadvantageous. As a result of culturally based gender differences in self-definition, a woman "may feel compelled to maintain her connection with the other, even to her own detriment" (Grillo 1991:1550).

Fineman thus tells a story of two narratives competing for dominance. When the new supplants the old, the result is a change in the generally accepted modes of talking and thinking about divorce. These new modes of talking and thinking are eventually, and very subtly, inscribed in social action, with important con-sequences for the power structures of our society. What remains to be uncov-ered is the mechanics of the inscription process, the specific ways in which the dominance that Fineman describes is realized in the day-to-day talk of divorce practice.

The Microdiscourse of Mediation

We begin the search for specifics with the work of the late law professor Trina Grillo (1991), who was also an experienced divorce mediator. Although her terminology differs, Grillo says many of the same things as Fineman about divorce mediation and its implications for the disempowerment of women. She argues that mandatory divorce mediation "can be destructive to many women and some men because it requires them to speak in a setting they have not chosen and often imposes a rigid orthodoxy as to how they should speak, make decisions, and be" (Grillo 1991:1550). The ascendancy of the narrative of mediated divorce over that of adversarial divorce is reproduced on the level of talk.

Drawing on her own mediation experience, Grillo (1991:1556) provides several instances of how this process works. For example, under the norms of mediation, a "good" woman is one who is ready to cooperate, is rational, and does not wish to hurt her spouse. Her "bad" counterpart is bitter, vengeful, and irrationally angry. How do mediators enforce these norms? By their responses to what they hear: they may criticize a woman for not putting her children first or instruct her to stay away from a particular topic. Though these "punishments" might seem trivial, they are, in Grillo's experience, quite powerful. Women hear them clearly and reform their own behavior accordingly.

The sanctioning of particular topics is not random, Grillo argues. On the contrary, it is often done in ways that directly disempower women. Thus, mediators typically make accusations about past behavior off-limits; the effect is often to deprive a woman's argument of its primary moral force (Grillo 1991:1563). Mediators are similarly dismissive of women's expressions of anger. Although they are trained to let the parties "vent," mediators do not listen for long. They denigrate the anger as counterproductive squabbling and insist that the parties move on to a more rational search for solutions. By refusing to take anger seriously, Grillo contends (1991:1574–75), mediators may demoralize women whose anger is righteous, perhaps born of a history of abuse. Such women may conclude that the process is hopelessly stacked against them and acquiesce in an unfair agreement just to be done with it.

A final example is the tendency of mediators to deflect talk about individual rights, insisting instead on "the language of interdependent relationships" (Grillo 1991:1560). Many women are culturally more comfortable with the language of relationships. For such women, discovering that they may have rights and bringing themselves to claim them may be a long, difficult, but ultimately empowering process. That power is tenuously held, however, and even a mild expression of disapproval by a mediator can prove devastating.

Through examples such as these, Grillo moves us closer to an understanding of how the power of the macrodiscourses of divorce is realized or inhibited in the microlinguistics of mediation practice. But can we find detailed real-life examples of precisely how the biases of which Grillo complains intrude into the mediation process?

Additional evidence from the research of Angela Garcia (1995) can help us to understand bias as a linguistic process. As we noted earlier, mediators are trained in "active listening." That is, they not only listen when someone is speaking but also say things to the speaker to indicate that they are hearing and understanding what is being said. From time to time, they also summarize the parties' remarks, using such prefatory phrases as "what I hear you saying is. . . ." Garcia calls this latter tactic "mediator representation," meaning that the mediator is speaking for, or representing, one of the parties (1995:31). She argues that representation is often more than a verbatim playback: instead, the mediator may alter or extend what the party has said in subtle but potentially significant ways.

Text 3.6 illustrates the representation process. The ex-husband in a custody mediation offers a compromise solution, and the mediator later "repeats" the offer to the ex-wife.

TEXT 3.6 (Garcia 1995:32)

EX-HUSBAND: The twins said, "Well what happened to Thursdays?" They, you know they, you know they specifically brought that up to me and I said, "Well, it looks like Mom wants to spend more time with you two. So if you know you want to do Thursday, Friday one
5   week, and then just a Friday the next week, that's compromising a little bit . . ."
[*A few minutes pass.*]
MEDIATOR: And then what I hear, is the last month or so, it's been every other Thursday, and then the next week is uh for the Friday,
10   and you're not willing—
EX-WIFE: Uh—
MEDIATOR: —to he's willing to relinquish! He used the word. Uh one of those Fridays.
EX-HUSBAND: No—
15   MEDIATOR: Instead of making it cons[iste]nt I MEAN THURSDAYS!
EX-HUSBAND: [No] Thursdays right.
MEDIATOR: Instead of [mak]ing it I just
EX-HUSBAND: [I]
EX-HUSBAND: I'm willing to go along with the schedule that she said
20   just to keep the status quo and keep her happy that she's you know,
MEDIATOR: Um hmh. He's offering the two Thursday night.

Garcia notes two important ways in which the mediator's representation of the ex-husband differs from the latter's earlier representation of himself. First, she states his position directly to the ex-wife (e.g., "you're not willing"), whereas he had spoken to the mediator and had referred to the ex-wife only in the third person. Second, the mediator significantly upgrades the characterization of the ex-husband's offer. He had described himself as "compromising," but the mediator describes him as "willing to relinquish," implying an outright concession. (She emphasizes the point in an ironic way by saying, "He used the word" *relinquish*, even though he did not.) Clearly attentive to the mediator's tactics, the respondent seizes the opportunity to inject a self-serving statement of his motivation ("to . . . keep her happy"). The net effect of the mediator's representation would seem to be to make the offer far more difficult to refuse.

This effect is realized a few minutes later, in Text 3.7, when the mediator restates the offer in yet another way and the ex-wife acquiesces.

TEXT 3.7 (Garcia 1995:33)

> MEDIATOR: And he is willing to give up two of those Thursdays.
> EX-WIFE: I know.
> MEDIATOR: Number one I heard it to make it consistent for the children, and that that would please you!
> 5   EX-WIFE: I'll just do it, just to meet him half way, . . .

At times, a mediator may go beyond simply restating or paraphrasing a disputant's position and actually develop new arguments in favor of one of the parties. In Text 3.8, for example, drawn from the same custody dispute, the ex-wife argues that the children should spend more time at her house because they are spending too much time away from the "home base." The ex-husband attempts to interrupt to argue the point. The mediator silences him but then goes on to make an argument on his behalf.

TEXT 3.8 (Garcia 1995:34)

> EX-WIFE: That I got the base, the home, family, and I feel that Thursday, Friday, and Saturday without them being, consistently at home, is too much. I feel that it's too much. Even though you don't get to see them, they're not at home, and they're at school, and they're on
> 5   the road, —
> EX-HUSBAND: They're home seventy five percent of the time.
> MEDIATOR: Stan wait.
> EX-HUSBAND: Okay.
> MEDIATOR: That's your feeling.
> 10   EX-WIFE: Right.
> MEDIATOR: And you have every right to that. That is not his feeling, a[nd that's] not how he sees his home base.
> EX-WIFE: [I know] I know.
> MEDIATOR: You know he sees it very loving, very whole, very
> 15   consistent, very disciplined.
> EX-WIFE: I know!

MEDIATOR: Okay. For him that's what he sees and what we have to
discuss.

EX-WIFE: I know.

20   MEDIATOR: And he's fifty percent a parent, and you're fifty percent a
parent.

Significantly, Garcia points out, the "home base" argument that the mediator
makes on behalf of the ex-husband is one that he has never made for himself.
Likewise, the laudatory characterization of his home as "very loving, very
whole, very consistent" is the mediator's, not his.[5] The mediator's words are
"fair" in the sense that they are consistent with the ex-husband's position. But
the mediator's strategy of extending and elaborating on his position surely has
consequences for the balance of power in this mediation session. To prove the
point, we need look no further than the ex-wife's litany of resigned *I know*s.

In a final example from Garcia's work, two mediators take the even more
radical step of "replacing" a disputant. Rather than merely restating or extending
arguments in ways that are consistent with positions already stated, in Text 3.9
the mediators negotiate instead of the disputants. When the respondent in a property dispute proposes that the complainant compensate him for benefits that he
has conferred on the complainant's property, both mediators attack the proposal
in a way that has nothing to do with what the complainant has actually said.

TEXT 3.9 (Garcia 1995:36)

RESPONDENT: Damned for my troubles that I went through, and the
money that I paid the county to improve his property and getting the
base rock fill, and everything else, that he should compensate me for
part of my expenses.

5   MEDIATOR B: Let's try to understand one thing, Mister Cartel, the
work and the money that you expended in putting in this culvert, and
actually rescuing this property from destruction, you did it, for your
sake.

RESPONDENT: I went for a compromise with the county.

10   MEDIATOR A: Yes.

MEDIATOR B: Yes.

RESPONDENT: That I would take my fences and they would accept
the —

MEDIATOR A: You went with the compromise with the county, not

15   these folks. *You* went there. *You* did it.

RESPONDENT: They wouldn't have done it —

MEDIATOR A: *You* decided it was worth it to you to do it, otherwise
you wouldn't [have] —

RESPONDENT: [It's not] only to my advantage, though I'm protecting
20   my neighbor's advantage also.
MEDIATOR A: THAT is something you were giving your neighbors
unwittingly. You were between a rock and a hard place. I will agree!
But you can not, you could not have committed them to something
they didn't agree to. Now, if you feel that equity is on
25   your side. Then you can after the fact sue them for their share. If you
feel that you want to do arbitration on that you can do that. But we're
talking about something else here. Remember we defined the area.
You put five thousand dollars in there but that wasn't his statement
of the problem.

Note carefully how this interaction develops. The respondent opens with a proposal. Mediator B, without any prompting from the other party, attacks the logic of the proposal (*Why should he pay when you did it for yourself?*) and, at least by implication, the credibility of the respondent (*It's not really true that you did it for your neighbor's benefit.*). When the respondent tries to fight back, mediator A jumps in and joins the attack. In his final statement, mediator A summarizes the argument and concludes with a new point: that the respondent's claim is out of order procedurally. As if to underscore how far he has strayed from the role of neutral conciliator, mediator A says, "I will agree!"—agreeing is the job of the parties, not the mediators. Text 3.9 looks less like a cooperative, conciliatory mediation session than some kind of tag-team cross-examination.

Garcia's observations are corroborated by those of David Greatbatch and Robert Dingwall (1989), who have studied the strategies that British divorce mediators may use to favor one party's interests over the other's. They frame their research as an empirical assessment of the claim by mediation critics "that the process may be used to press weaker parties into accepting less than they could have expected had their case gone through traditional adversarial channels" (Greatbatch and Dingwall 1989:613). Using conversation analysis, they, like Garcia, find that a number of linguistic techniques employed by mediators have the effect of facilitating the presentation and discussion of one side's interests while minimizing parallel consideration of the other side's position.

In a case that Greatbatch and Dingwall examine at great length, a husband and wife are discussing possible ways to divide their common property. Because he would prefer having cash, the husband proposes to sell the two houses that the couple now owns and divide the proceeds. The wife prefers to keep the house she is presently living in and to let the husband have the other. What happens in the session is that the mediator's management strategies operate to maximize discussion of the wife's position and minimize the attention given to the husband's proposal. The mediator does this in a variety of ways: by selecting the wife's plan for full discussion when the two possibilities are first introduced, by moving away from full consideration of the husband's plan when it is reintroduced, and by reintroducing and recycling the wife's plan for further consideration.

The alliance of the mediator with the wife's plan is seen in a number of specific ways. In Text 3.10, for example, the mediator focuses on the wife's plan as a possible solution to the couple's dilemma. The husband is objecting on the grounds that the second house is presently occupied by tenants. The mediator and the wife repeatedly urge the husband to consider possible ways around the problem.

TEXT 3.10 (Greatbatch and Dingwall 1989:621–22)

> MEDIATOR: You can't live in the house in Britvale?
> HUSBAND: Er, no it's let. Um, well there is one room, one vacant at the minute and um . . .
> MEDIATOR: You can't get them to leave then?
> 5   HUSBAND: No, it's tenanted. It's difficult to get the tenants out.
> WIFE: Well, I'm [not sure] if we really wanted to before.
> HUSBAND: [It was never—] set up to, to, sort of, it was set up to produce money for insurances for the next twenty years and that's exactly what it's doing, basically.
> 10   WIFE: It's very underlet.
> HUSBAND: It's underlet. It's not managed properly, or hasn't been for a number of years. [And it needs some work done on it.]
> MEDIATOR: [You're sure you couldn't get the] tenant, tenancy back? I mean if you needed it as your home.
> 15   HUSBAND: That was one possibility that did crop up. Um, you can apply to evict somebody if you require it as a home.
> MEDIATOR: That's right. It's what I thought.

This attention to the wife's proposal is one-sided: there is no comparable exploration of the husband's preference for selling the houses and dividing the proceeds. On the contrary, as in Text 3.11, when the husband tries to assert his concerns, the mediator responds by reasserting the wife's plan as a solution.

TEXT 3.11 (Greatbatch and Dingwall 1989:634–35)

> HUSBAND: But it's a question of point of view, but it's traumatic from my point of view. I've got nowhere to live.
> MEDIATOR: W[ell, can you] —
> WIFE: [No.]
> 5   HUSBAND: Really, I mean I have got my sister's place to live, I've got a [room] —

MEDIATOR: [Yes.]
HUSBAND: — but I've nowhere that's mine to live. If I wanted some-
where to live [right now] —
10   MEDIATOR: [Yes.]
HUSBAND: — I mean I'm —
WIFE: But you say you wouldn't want to live on your own anyway,
so —
HUSBAND: (Laughs.) A general hobo, running around.
15   MEDIATOR: Well I must say if, er, it seems to me worth trying the, the
Britvale property once again.
HUSBAND: Mhm.
MEDIATOR: Seeing how, uh, as like Hazel, um, my understanding is
that if you needed it for yourself [you] —
20   HUSBAND: [Yeah.]
MEDIATOR: — have a far better chance of regaining possession. And
you have every reason to say "I need it as my home."

The most important implication of such texts is, once again, that the ostensible neutrality of mediators may disappear when their behavior is subjected
to detailed linguistic scrutiny. There is probably nothing in these texts, or in
Garcia's, that a lawyer would point to as evidence of overt bias. The mediator
lets both parties speak, she speaks respectfully to both, and she neither praises
nor criticizes either party on a personal level. The parties themselves provide
no evidence that they are aware of any bias on the mediator's part. But the texts
leave us with little doubt that the mediator is subtly yet effectively steering the
talk toward a preferred outcome.

By showing how mediators can covertly influence outcomes, researchers
such as Garcia and Greatbatch and Dingwall demonstrate the plausibility of the
claim that mediation can systematically disadvantage one side or the other. But
do they shed significant light on the truth of the claim that mediation works to
the disadvantage of women?

Conclusion: Is Mediator Bias Systematic?

We have now seen in very concrete terms that the neutrality of mediators is
sometimes more of an ideal than a reality. Mediators can and do employ a
variety of language strategies to shape both the process and the outcome of
mediation sessions. Significantly, these strategies seem transparent to all but the
most intensive kinds of scrutiny. The final question is whether these strategies
have political consequences. That is, are mediators indulging their biases in
purely idiosyncratic ways, or is there something systematic in the way that
mediators employ their subtle power?

Both Garcia and Greatbatch and Dingwall claim to have proved conclusively the possibility of mediator bias by discovering some of its linguistic pathways. Neither project, however, claims to prove whether mediator bias is exercised in any consistent way.[6] Indeed, a comparison of the two demonstrates the extraordinary difficulty of using microlinguistic analysis to address such a question. Garcia's published examples tend to illustrate mediator activism working to the disadvantage of women, but in Greatbatch and Dingwall's extended single case it is the husband, not the wife, who is the victim of the mediator's power.

In theory, what is needed is a broader sampling of how potentially biasing linguistic tactics are distributed. This is much easier said than done, however. In the first place, it is difficult to get statistically meaningful samples when doing intensive linguistic research. As we know from firsthand experience, access to mediation sessions is hard to get. Many mediation centers will not let researchers in the door because of confidentiality concerns; even when general permission is given, the specific consent of all parties to a mediation must be obtained. As a result, randomization is all but impossible. In addition, it takes an enormous amount of time to watch, record, transcribe, and analyze even a single mediation session — in our experience, a single hour of field observation requires dozens of hours of data preparation and study. To do quantitatively significant amounts of the kind of analysis that, for example, Garcia has done would be a superhuman task.

The second problem is one of principle rather than logistics. The work that conversation analysts do is interpretive and necessarily judgmental. We may find their interpretations and judgments highly persuasive, but conversation analysis will never be experimental physics. As the work discussed in this chapter and in chapter 2 illustrates, some of the most insightful interpretations are also the subtlest. Is it appropriate to reduce these insights to coding conventions that are both simple enough and absolute enough to feed into a formula? We suspect that in many cases this would imply a degree of precision that is not there and thus would mislead more than it would inform.[7]

At this point, we believe that it will be all but impossible to establish exactly how mediator biasing tactics are distributed. Nonetheless, there are a number of independent reasons to believe that mediator bias systematically disadvantages women and that the most important mechanisms of such bias are linguistic.

First, there is some empirical evidence — albeit equivocal — that women in fact do less well in divorce mediation than in divorce litigation. A two-state study of divorce mediation by Carol Bohmer and Marilyn L. Ray (1994) yielded complex and inconsistent findings. In New York, they found that mediation significantly disadvantages women with respect to child support and the burden of child caretaking, but in Georgia, they concluded that "the well-being of women, and the children for whom they care, is not adversely affected by the method they select for resolving their dispute" (Bohmer and Ray 1994:232, 245). More recent studies have been similarly mixed in their findings.

Other researchers advance reasons why women are *likely* to be disadvantaged in mediation. Penelope Bryan (1992), for example, argues that men usually come to divorce mediation with a set of resources that their wives often lack. In the economic sphere, "the husband's greater tangible resources will grant him the lion's share of power in divorce negotiations, particularly over critical financial issues" (Bryan 1992:456). Men also control such intangible resources as status, self-esteem, dominance, and higher aspirations, all of which are logical correlates of success in mediation.

In an elegant case study, Scott Hughes (1995) illustrates these and other prejudicial factors at work in a divorce mediation. He puts particular emphasis on the tendency to be competitive versus a propensity for cooperation: in mediation, "[t]he unconditionally cooperative bargainer will cooperate at every turn, even if this results in her own destruction. She will collapse in the face of a competitive bargainer" (Hughes 1995:583). Competitiveness and cooperativeness do not seem to be randomly distributed. In Grillo's apt phrasing, "[I]t is clear that those who operate in a 'female mode' — whether biologically male or female — will respond more 'selflessly' to the demands of mediation" (1991:1602). In litigation, such people have their positions argued — competitively — by their lawyers. But in mediation, where there are no lawyers and cooperation is the highest normative value, they may be especially vulnerable.

Substantial linguistic evidence corroborates this suspicion. Research on gender differences in language socialization has shown that women are more likely than men to do the work of facilitating communication, of engaging in supportive listening, and of actively seeking consensus.[8] These behaviors converge with the demands of mediation. Therefore, this reasoning suggests, women, simply by virtue of the way they are socialized to talk, may be more likely than men to pursue agreement as an end in itself. Consequently, they may not do as well (in tangible terms) as they might have if their cases had been handled by aggressive lawyers in an adversarial context.

We thus have a convergence of circumstantial evidence in support of the claim that mediation disadvantages women. Conversation analysis has demonstrated the existence of linguistic strategies through which ostensibly neutral mediators can exert subtle but significant influence on the process. We cannot say with certainty that this influence works against women in a systematic way, but this is a plausible suspicion. A number of things we know about gender differences in social behavior suggest that women are more likely than men to compromise for the sake of compromise, often in ways that are adverse to their material interests. Since the mediator strategies that the conversation analysts have identified can all be categorized as devices calculated to facilitate compromise, it is reasonable to suppose that, more often than not, their effects are felt by women.

We have moved in this chapter from the examination of mediation as a neutral process to an assessment of the charge that it is in fact a tool for oppressing women. On the basis of linguistic and other evidence, we have concluded that the charge, if not proved, is at least one that should be taken seriously. If we ultimately decide that the feminist critique of mediation is accurate, we will be faced with a wrenching irony: a process advocated largely because of its solicitude for women's sensibilities has become a weapon used against them. We may also find some compelling analogies between the mediation process and the rape trial.

Grillo comments that "[w]omen who have been through mandatory mediation often describe it as an experience of sexual domination, comparing mandatory mediation to rape" (1991:1605). This feeling may derive from the similar ways in which power is exercised in the two settings. In rape trials, we observed in chapter 2, the language strategies used in cross-examining the victim (some generic, some unique to rape cases) both reflect and reinforce men's power to dominate women. The same may be true in mediation. The language strategies of mediators may be effective precisely because they take advantage of certain social tendencies that contribute to women's relative powerlessness. As mediation becomes more and more entrenched—as it is increasingly perceived to "work"—the result will be to reinforce that powerlessness. Once again, the pattern is one of simultaneous reflection and reproduction of society's power dynamics. And, once again, it will be the detailed analysis of microdiscourse that reveals the working of power in the macrodiscourse of the legal process.

CHAPTER FOUR

Speaking of Patriarchy

T he claim that the law is patriarchal has become so widely accepted in legal scholarship that its validity now goes almost without saying. Specifically, the claim is that "law and legal institutions in a number of cultures (if not all) have played a significant role in maintaining systems that subordinate and oppress female human beings, and the law continues to do so" (Henderson 1991:411). The patriarchy of the law is seen as working on multiple levels. In the most direct sense, law is patriarchal because it is powerful and men control it. Law has been described as the means for deciding "who does what to whom and gets away with it" (MacKinnon 1989:139). In every society, men have largely controlled this decision-making mechanism and, for the most part, still do. Thus, men get to decide who gets away with what. Historically, they have exercised this power to further their own interests at the expense of women. Even in the liberal democracies of the West, men denied women the right to vote until the first quarter of the twentieth century. The subordination of women is also evident in the history of marriage and property law (Henderson 1991:411–12). Male control over divorce trapped women in abusive marriages, while married women surrendered control over their property and were not allowed to enter into contracts.

Legal reform movements have eradicated the most overt sources of patriarchal power. In 1920, the Nineteenth Amendment to the Constitution finally enfranchised American women. Title VII of the Civil Rights Act of 1964 prohibits employment discrimination on the basis of sex; the Equal Employment Opportunity Commission and the courts have gradually expanded its reach to prohibit such forms of sexual harassment as the maintenance of a hostile environment in the workplace (Henderson 1991:413–14). Twentieth-century changes in family law — no-fault divorce in particular — have made divorce more readily available to women (although, as we discussed in chapter 3, some feminists contend that these "reforms" have done more harm than good) (Bartlett 1994).

Gender and Equality

The elimination of discriminatory legal rules may not have changed the law's essentially patriarchal character, however. The reason, it is argued, is that laws that appear to be evenhanded still embody a distinctively male point of view. To begin with, the very notion of evenhandedness is a male concept (MacKinnon 1989:40–43; Bartlett 1994:1261–62). To the law, "equality" traditionally has meant allowing everyone to assert rights without regard to race, sex, religion, or other status markers. For this concept of equality to work, "rights" must mean the same thing to different kinds of people. That is, the rights that the law protects must be recognized as significant all across society. In addition, people in all elements of society must have a realistic opportunity to assert those rights.

Many feminists, however, drawing on the work of Carol Gilligan (1982), have pointed out that the rights the law recognizes are, for the most part, rights to be separated from other human beings (West 1988:4–7; Bartlett 1994:1260–61). A quick look at the Bill of Rights confirms this insight. The First Amendment, for example, protects freedom of speech and of the press. Free-speech claims usually involve people who are asserting the right to offend someone: neo-Nazis who want to march through a predominantly Jewish town, "adult" bookstore owners who are contemptuous of community moral standards, or journalists who attack public figures. Similarly, the First Amendment's freedom of religion has been invoked most often to protect the right to be different. Even some of the less prominent constitutional rights place a comparable emphasis on separation: we can keep and bear arms, presumably to protect ourselves against tyrannical governments and threatening fellow citizens (Second Amendment); we do not have to quarter soldiers in our homes in time of peace (Third Amendment); and we need not tolerate unreasonable government searches of our persons, homes, or effects (Fourth Amendment).

Freedom from unwanted connection to others, it is argued, is a male concern. According to Gilligan and others, women, because of their socialization, tend to seek and value the very connections against which men seek legal protection (West 1988:13–18). From this perspective, the Bill of Rights is a male document with no female counterpart. Where, for example, is the constitutional counterpoise to the freedom of speech, the legal requirement that we assume responsibility for the offense that we give to others? Why does the law value the pornographer's right to be offensively different over the interests of the women whom his work dehumanizes? Why does there often seem to be such an imbalance between an accused criminal's right to due process and a community's right to security?

Other areas of the law will support a similar argument. For example, Anglo-American law has long exalted the contract as the ideal way to manage a relationship, whether between spouses or between strangers conducting an anonymous business transaction. A written contract is preferred over an oral one; the more specific its provisions, the better. From the law's perspective, the ideal contracting party is a person who fears entanglement with others. Before entering a relationship, such a person thinks through everything that might go wrong. The ultimate objective of the contract is to identify every sort of misconduct that might occur and specify the consequences if it does. Through this logic, the law of contract treats separation as the basic human condition and connection as an aberration requiring careful advance preparation.

The point of these examples is that the ideal of equal rights may be illusory in the sense that the rights being offered are not equally relevant to the different social circumstances of men and women. Although this was originally a feminist argument, many feminists came to reject it (see, for example, West 1988; Fineman 1991). Opponents contend that it "essentializes" women in a misleading and potentially dangerous way. The characterization of rights-based thinking as male, it is said, denies women's capacity for autonomy. These critics argue that when the law is "feminized" — as, for example, when litigation, with its emphasis on confrontation, is replaced by mediation, which stresses reconciliation — the results are often even worse for women.[1] The reason seems to be that male interests dominate the "reformed" procedure just as they have historically dominated every other legal procedure, but now the fact of reform effectively deflects criticism and demands for further change. The critics' solution, much oversimplified, is for women to take control of the apparatus of rights adjudication and radically restructure it to advance women's interests.[2]

Whatever their differences, however, feminists remain united on the point that American law is patriarchal. However differently individual feminists may interpret the paths through which patriarchy works, there is general agreement that the law continues to favor identifiably male interests. Significantly, many feminist scholars speak of the law's patriarchy in terms of discourse. Political scientist Zillah Eisenstein (1988:20; see also Henderson 1991:418) has described the law as "an authorized language of the state," a "discourse" suffused with the power of the state. To the extent that the law embodies male values and advances male interests, it is an authoritative *patriarchal* discourse.

As we have observed in other chapters, not only is discourse a way of talking about something, it is also a way of thinking and acting with respect to that subject. Thus, the patriarchal discourse of law is a way of talking and thinking about women, and acting toward them, in legal and political contexts. As long as the dominant legal discourse is patriarchal, women will be talked about, thought about, and acted on as subordinate to male interests.

We have also seen in the previous chapters that discourse can both reflect and reproduce dominant cultural values. The dual role of discourse, this double duty as simultaneously cause and effect, can best be appreciated by examining the linguistic practices through which it is translated into social action. Ground-level linguistic practices take the forms and have the effects that they do because of the power of the values that they enact. At the same time, the repeated use of such practices reaffirms that power.

The patriarchal discourse of law provides another demonstration of this dynamic. Recall the discussion of rape in chapter 2. We argued there that the discourse of rape remains, at every level, a discourse of subordination. We asked how that could be, in the face of repeated efforts at legal reform. The answer lay in the linguistic analysis of rape trials. Normative law reform (rape shield laws, for example) has been ineffective, we concluded, primarily because it has been inattentive to the linguistic practices that continually ratify the cultural value of subordination.

In the remainder of this chapter, we reexamine some of our own empirical work in an effort to discover additional linguistic practices that simultaneously reflect and reproduce the law's patriarchy. First we review our research on the speech styles of trial witnesses, arguing that the speech practices of the courtroom exhibit a clear preference for a distinctively male style. We then examine the way in which different kinds of witnesses structure accounts of their problems, concluding that here as well there is a strong, if subtle, male bias. The point of both examples is that efforts to modify the law's patriarchy are likely to be futile without an understanding of how it manifests itself at the most concrete linguistic level.

Stylistic Variation in Courtroom Talk

When we began our collaborative research on courtroom language in the 1970s, we were strongly influenced by sociolinguistics' then-current focus on the social conditioning of language variation. Linguists such as William Labov (1972a, 1972b) and Gillian Sankoff (1980) were demonstrating through careful research that people do not simply speak differently, but that variation in language reflects such social dimensions as class, race, ethnicity, and age. In 1975, Robin Lakoff published her influential book *Language and Woman's Place*, in which she added gender to the list of social variables that influence language. All of this work, with its common goal of illuminating the social conditioning of language variation, represented a major break with earlier generations of linguists, who had emphasized the universal aspects of language to the point of ignoring variation or treating it as insignificant.[3]

Importantly, the influence of these groundbreaking sociolinguistic studies reached beyond the disciplinary bounds of linguistics. Anthropologists, sociologists, and others began to appreciate the significance of language variation as a window into the complexity of social organization. We found ourselves in this camp as we began to investigate the dynamics of the courtroom. We were motivated to ask such questions as these: What kinds of variation are there in the ways that witnesses present their testimony? To what degree does this variation reflect social differences among witnesses (i.e., do men and women, blacks and whites, or well-educated and poorly educated people talk differently in court)? And if people do talk differently when they testify, do these differences have practical consequences?

To answer questions such as these, we undertook an empirical study of language in the courtroom.[4] First, we spent several weeks in court observing and listening. Although we could imagine some of the possible dimensions of language variation, we wanted to specify exactly what happens when different kinds of people talk in court. Some of the topics we ultimately studied had not occurred to us in advance but emerged only from the process of repeated observations. We noticed, for example, that lawyers and hostile witnesses interrupted each other regularly and in elaborately patterned ways. We then designed an experimental study of interruption, finding that jurors are attuned to subtle variations in the pattern and that these variations influence their evaluations of both lawyer and witness.[5] In addition to studying issues that emerged during our own observations of courtroom dynamics, we selected other topics that had already been identified in the literature and then developed them empirically. Our study of language and gender in the courtroom falls into this latter category.

As we began our research, Lakoff's *Language and Woman's Place* had heightened our awareness of the possible significance of gender differences in speaking styles. Lakoff argues that women, as a result of their socialization, speak a language of subordination. Through such stylistic features as hedge words (*kind of, sort of*), polite forms (*sir*), tag questions appended to declarative statements (*The meeting's at three, isn't it?*), exaggerated imprecision about quantities (*It was about a mile, but I'm not very good at distances*), and a rising, inquisitive intonation in normally declarative contexts (*Six-thirty?* in response to a question about when dinner will be ready), women project deference and uncertainty. Thus, Lakoff concludes, women's speech both reflects and reinforces their subordinate position in society.

Against this background, we paid particular attention to female witnesses. Not surprisingly, we found many who spoke what Lakoff terms "women's language." But we also found that not every woman spoke this way and that some men did. The women who did not were usually expert witnesses such as physicians or psychologists (there were not very many female experts in the 1970s), while the men who did were typically poor and uneducated. These findings complicated our conception of women's language, but they did not diminish the fact that some witnesses spoke a language of deference, subordination, and nonassertiveness, whereas others spoke in a more rhetorically forceful style. We coined the term *powerless language* to reflect what we had actually observed: that the speech style Lakoff had identified was associated primarily with the speaker's status in society (O'Barr and Atkins 1980). Given the social realities of the 1970s, most powerless speakers were in fact women, but the correlation of powerless language with gender was not exact.

Powerlessness and Patriarchy

Once we had defined powerless language and described its occurrence in the courtroom, we set about to answer another question: Does it make a difference? We conceived of the trial as a situation in which a number of people present conflicting versions of what happened. In the end, the judge charges the jury to decide (or decides him/herself if there is no jury) which of the various versions to believe. When there are competing versions, the jury cannot give equal credence to all of them; some must be believed more than others. We were specifically interested in knowing whether witnesses who presented their testimony in a powerless style were evaluated as less credible than those who spoke in a more assertive manner.

To answer this, we conducted controlled social-psychological experiments. In simulated courtroom situations, we found that language style did indeed influence the credibility of testimony. Experimental jurors were significantly more likely to believe those witnesses who spoke assertively than those who spoke powerless language. Our findings, since confirmed in many subsequent studies of powerless language in and out of court,[6] demonstrated that style is a critical factor in the courtroom and that the relative credibility of witnesses is influenced by the manner in which their testimony is presented.

Although we did not fully appreciate it at the time, this research has important implications for understanding the subtle workings of the law's patriarchy. While we had found that powerless language was not strictly a gender-based phenomenon, the fact remained that most of the witnesses who used powerless language were women and that most men did not use it. This meant that most women, most of the time, were speaking in a style that the legal system devalued; men, by and large, did not suffer this disadvantage.

When we presented this research to audiences of practicing lawyers, as we often did, they invariably jumped to the same pragmatic conclusion: *If you want to win the case, teach women to talk like men!* We initially scoffed at these comments as yet another instance of the philistinism of lawyers. Gradually, however, we began to appreciate what they were telling us about the nature of the law. Through the credibility assessments of jurors, the law was expressing a strong preference for a speech style that was, as a matter of social fact, distinctively male. We mean "distinctively male" in two senses: in the strict empirical sense that men employed it more often than women, and in the sense that, at least in the 1970s, women seemed to have little opportunity to learn it. Justice was thus more accessible to men than to women. The law's patriarchy was both reflected and reproduced in the most fundamental linguistic practices of the courtroom. The jurors' credibility assessments reflected patriarchal values. The lawyers' strategic responses ensured that those values would be reproduced.[7]

There is, of course, no rule of law that requires witnesses to speak in a power-ful style. Jurors are not instructed to believe powerful speakers. On the contrary, if they are instructed on credibility at all, they are simply told to rely on their general experience and common sense.[8] And that is what they do: they apply their everyday standards to the evaluation of witnesses, and those standards include the preference for powerful speech. "The law" as an institution is com-plicit in punishing women for their speech habits to the extent that it remains silent as jurors act on their cultural values.[9]

So is it appropriate to use the powerless speech phenomenon as linguistic evidence of *the law's* patriarchy? Or is it evidence only of the general patriarchy of society, which the law must inevitably reflect? This is a difficult question to answer. The law often looks like a conservative, reactive institution, changing only when necessary to catch up with changes in society. Recall, for example, that legal prohibitions on birth control were being litigated in the Supreme Court as late as 1972.[10] On race relations, however, beginning with *Brown v. Board of Education* in 1954 and continuing through the affirmative action era, the law has tended to be out ahead of general social values. The best one can say is that the law can be an agent of change when it (that is, the judges and legislators who determine the law's content) chooses to be.

By tolerating jurors' preferences for powerful speech, the law offers subtle but significant support for society's patriarchal values. It is subtle in the sense that it is masked by the pervasive rhetoric of equal protection and due process and by the very real protections with which the law backs up that rhetoric in many contexts.[11] It is significant, however, in that for certain witnesses the pref-erence for powerful speech can vitiate those protections. Any judge would im-mediately dismiss a juror who announced before the trial that he was more likely to believe the testimony of men than of women. But how different is this from what jurors do every day when they give greater credence to powerful speech?

The Logic of Legal Accounts

During the 1980s, the focus of sociolinguistic research shifted from speech style to what was termed "discourse." In place of the former emphasis on variation in individual elements of phonology and lexicon, sociolinguists began to ex-amine larger units of speech. There was particular interest in "narratives" in the traditional sense of self-contained stories or accounts.[12] Sociolinguists paid in-creasing attention to such things as how narrators structure their accounts, how they claim authority for their stories, and how they interact with their audiences.

Motivated in part by this new theoretical focus, we began to study the structure of legal accounts. But we were also stimulated by a lingering issue from our prior research on courtroom speech styles. During post-trial interviews with the witnesses we observed in the 1970s, we repeatedly heard about their sense of frustration with the legal process. A constant refrain was "I never got a chance to tell my story. If I'd only known how bad it was going to be in court, I never would have gone." When we pressed for details, it became clear that what they meant was that the structure of courtroom discourse had short-circuited their expectations about testifying—expectations we discovered to be based on everyday storytelling habits. They had been unable to structure and illustrate their accounts as they did in ordinary conversation, and that disturbed them.

This suggested a research question: What would their stories sound like if they *did* get a chance to tell them unconstrained by courtroom rules? This question in turn suggested an obvious research setting: small claims courts, where laypeople can assert legal claims in a relatively informal environment, usually without the advice or assistance of lawyers. In small claims courts, people give accounts of legal problems in whatever ways they deem appropriate. In their accounts, they act out their beliefs about what kinds of problems the law should deal with, what constitutes evidence and proof, and what sorts of remedies they expect the law to provide.

As we studied litigant accounts given in more than one hundred trials in six different cities, a striking pattern emerged: there are two very different ways in which litigants structure their accounts. *Rule-oriented* accounts base claims for legal relief on violations of specific rules, duties, and obligations, such as those inscribed in contracts. They are arranged sequentially, retelling events in a straight line from beginning to end. They deal explicitly with cause and effect, as well as with the identification of the human agents responsible for events. Importantly, these accounts conform to the logic of the law and reflect an accurate understanding of the law's sense of relevance. They emphasize evidence that bears directly on the specific rule violation being asserted and exclude evidence extraneous to the claim, in particular those details that are of a personal or social nature.

Relational accounts, by contrast, base their entitlement to relief on general rules of social conduct. Their thesis is often that decent people who meet their social obligations have an entitlement to fair treatment. Because relational accounts focus on personal status and social position, they tend to be full of details about the life of the speaker, details that the law usually deems irrelevant. Issues of time and of cause and effect are often dealt with in highly idiosyncratic ways.

The Rule-Oriented Account

Text 4.1 is the paradigm of the rule-oriented account. The witness (Hogan) is a sales executive who is appearing in court on behalf of her company, the

defendant in the case. The plaintiff (Webb), a former sales representative for
the company, is suing over the company's refusal to pay him a commission on
the sale of an expensive scientific instrument.

As she presents the company's defense, Hogan deals directly with the issues
the judge must resolve to decide the case. She treats the dispute as a contractual
problem between two parties and does not discuss personalities or social relationships. The description of the dispute's context is limited to what is directly
relevant to the narrow contractual issue on which she believes the judge will
focus. Hogan's account is given in sequential order (note how in lines 28–41
the account progresses from March 1984 to November 1986) and is highly
factual (e.g., "1500 manufacturers," line 18; "60,000 products," line 18; "it
was not 400 but only 200," lines 66–67). Names (note the repeated references
to Mr. Harper, Mr. Webb, and Diller and Macy), dates (lines 62–64 stress the
significance of November 15 and December 15, 1986), and the contents of
conversations (e.g., lines 57–60) and documents (see, for example, her recapitu-
lation of Mr. Harper's letter in lines 51–55) are reported precisely. Unlike many
relational accounts, this one presumes no prior knowledge of people, places,
and events on the part of the listener.

TEXT 4.1 (Conley and O'Barr 1990:63–66)

JUDGE: We'll come back to you in just a moment. Let's turn over to
you ma'am. We do need your name, business address, and connec-
tion with the uh, Instrument Supply Company.
HOGAN: My name is Lynn Hogan. Uh, my address, do you want my
5   business address or —
JUDGE: Business address is fine.
HOGAN: 1200 Cavanaugh Street. I am the scientific sales manager for
Instrument Supply, Denver.
JUDGE: As such of course you've heard everything that's been stated
10   so far. We have several exhibits. I believe in this case you're probably familiar with all of them.
HOGAN: Yes sir, I am.
JUDGE: But if not, you're certainly free to look them all over and your
opportunity to react to what you've heard and to further develop
15   whatever answer or defense you may have.
HOGAN: Okay, thank you. Um, as uh Dan [*the plaintiff*] stated, uh,
Instrument Supply is a scientific distributor. Uh, we represent over
1500 manufacturers and we sell over 60,000 products. Um, we are
continuously being exposed to gimmicks from our manufacturers to
20   boost the sale of their products. Uh, the only control that management has, um, over these prod–, over these promotions, is to pick

and choose the ones that uh, best support our local selling programs, where we want the local emphasis to be. Um, then it is my responsibility, as well as the district manager, to assist the sales reps in
25 focusing on these sanctioned programs. Uh, in order to keep track of what we have sanctioned, we have a calculation sheet that specifically shows the sales representative what we are sanctioning. This is one for the first half. I have highlighted that that particular promotion for spectrometers was on the first half, from March until August of
30 1984, giving the particular payouts, and as you'll see there is a 200 dollar payout there for 1001 Spectrometer. In the, we, uh, usually will change some of the programs on the second half uh, PIP program. Um, we also as sales managers, provide to the representatives, um, some sort of indication that we are bombarded, our plate is full.
35 So I put out to them in September of 1986, a list of the sanctioned promotions. You will see on there that the Diller and Macy double payout is not on there. Uh, I was unaware that this, um, letter had gone out from D and M. Approximately October of 1986 they did send this out to the sales representative. Uh, I received notification
40 that it was out amongst the reps late October, early November, upon returning from vacation. My management told me of his conversation with Mr. Harper and the agreement was made between John Taylor, uh the dis–, the then district manager and Mr. Harper, that there had been a, uh, an advance notification put out on an unsanc-
45 tioned program through Diller and Macy, not sanctioned by Instrument Supply. And uh, that Mr. Harper was more than uh, uh, uh, he was more than open to go ahead and pay his 200 dollars, but that we would not pay the matching 200 dollars.
JUDGE: What is his basis for that? Which seems to be contrary to the
50 flier that he put out.
HOGAN: Um, Mr. Harper in a, in a letter that Mr., I asked for Mr. Harper to write, which I believe you already have a copy but here is another copy. In there it states the events. It does say that he um, prematurely put the promotion out to the sales force without
55 talking to local management. Um, in early, either late October, early November, I asked him, he told me at that point about um, what was going on with Mr. Webb and I asked him at that time, I said, "Would you please call Mr. Webb and tell him that you have prematurely put a promotion out that's not sanctioned and that you will honor your
60 200 dollars and that Instrument Supply will not." He told me that he had. Uh, it is true that I was semi-aware of this 1001 from um, uh, the sale at Lakeview. Mr. Webb did a quotation to Lakeview on November 15th of 1986, uh, stating on there that this particular quote

was good until December 15th, 1986 to the customer. Um, it is my
65   job to encourage the sales representatives to close sales. At that time
I was not aware of the fact that Dan did not know it was not 400 but
only 200 through Diller and Macy. Upon his resignation, um, when
he came into the office the end of December, he did at that time state
the 400 dollars and I did at that time tell him that it was 200 dollars
70   from Diller and Macy and not a matching 200 dollars from Instrument Supply. Um, at that point, um, Dan continued to pursue it and
um, you know we, you see the answers that we have have uh put out.
So we have paid, we did pay 200 dollars out for Diller and Macy.
Diller and Macy is reimbursing us for that 200
75   dollars through the PIP program. And um, excuse me, if I could just
present one other thing.
JUDGE: Go right ahead.
HOGAN: For the second half, and this goes with that one other thing
that I gave you, this is the second half PIP calculation sheet, and you
80   will see on there is no Diller and Macy payout for the second half.
JUDGE: Anything else before we hear again from Mr. Webb?
HOGAN: No sir.

The Relational Account

Text 4.2, by contrast, illustrates the relational account. Rawls, the ultimately un-
successful plaintiff, has sued her neighbor Bennett for removing a hedge on her
side of their shared property line, failing to control the growth of his shrubbery
onto her property, and generally harassing her. In this text, she responds to the
judge's questions about how the hedge was removed. Previously, he has asked
her a series of specific questions about the location of the property line, but she
has been unable to provide any useful information on that issue.

Here, Rawls describes and analyzes her problem in terms of social relationships rather than the kinds of rules that constitute legal doctrine. She rarely
responds directly to the issues raised in the judge's questions (contrast the answer that begins on line 3 with those beginning on lines 5 and 15). Instead, the
questions evoke lengthy digressions about the history of her relationship with
Bennett. These digressions meander through time and place (e.g., lines 5–11,
where she has to "jump back" three years and describe Bennett's comings and
goings), drawing her audience ever deeper into her social world but providing
little information about the specific issues that are of interest to the court. Her
account contains frequent references to personal status (e.g., her references
to "getting crippled up," lines 31–32, and having only one trash can, line 55),
items that are significant to her social agenda but irrelevant to the court's more
limited and rule-centered agenda. Additionally, the account assumes that the

listener shares her knowledge of background events and places. Although the assumption of shared knowledge is common and appropriate in familiar conversation, it creates difficulties in an institutional setting when a stranger is trying to extract a set of facts and apply legal rules to them.

TEXT 4.2 (Conley and O'Barr 1990:61–63)

JUDGE: You're alleging that these trees and, and the shrubs and apparently the hedge included were removed. When did this happen?

RAWLS: Oh, well now that happened this year. At, uh —

JUDGE: And how did it happen?

5   RAWLS: Well I can, well, well I have to jump back because, uh, for three years when Mr. Bennett moved back — because he was there once before and then he moved and then he come back into that house — and all the time before — I have to say this though judge — because all the time before everybody took care of that hedge and

10   they wouldn't let me take care of it. They trimmed it and I even went to Mr. Bennett when he was there before —

JUDGE: Wait a moment. Now the question that I asked you — and I would like to have you answer it — and that is how did the hedge get removed?

15   RAWLS: Well, um, Mr. Bennett said he told me when he moved back in, uh, because I was taking care of my trees coming up through the hedge, I was cutting them off and he told me not to do that. He said, "Don't do it," he said, "I'm going to have, the church is going to pay to take them out of there, because my wife wants to put a fence and

20   plant roses on the other side." He said, "Is that alright with you?" I said, "I don't care what you do with it," you know, and I said, "If you need, uh, money for tools, maybe I can rent a tool and help in that respect because I can't dig," you know. And I said, "If you need uh, a tool to help you remove the hedge," I said, "uh, I will," well it wasn't

25   the hedge then it was all the stumps underneath because he wanted that removed because he, his wife wanted the fence and she wanted roses on it. And so then three years went by and they let these trees grow up like you see the picture there. I think you've got it. And they're so big and then when he told me to stop taking them out

30   because he was gonna take out that hedge, uh, the stumps, why uh, in the meantime I called a man and I had them, because I'm getting crippled up and I can't bend down sir, and here I was still taking out those trees and he wasn't coming to help me like he said he was. So then I had a man come — here Jim give him this — and I paid 45 dol-

35   lars. There's the bill there and he cut it right off down level with the

ground. Well, I knew that wouldn't take it but at least it would keep
me for a little bit trying to get them tree things out of that shrubbery
there. Well, um, Mr. Bennett, when he finally come out he said,
"You know, that isn't going to do it," and that's when he told me,
40   "My wife wants to put a fence," and he said, "You know that isn't
going to do it. Those stumps are going to have to be taken out." And
that's when I told him, and he said he would do it, "I and the church
would take them out," and I, that's when I told him, "If you need, uh,
money for a tool or something to help you. I'll pay for the tool
45   or whatever." And he told, didn't do it, and so then I just had a, the
Milehigh, uh, Tree Service come uh, uh, and um, a, and Mr., I had
his name here — Mr., uh, Cook come and he come in the house and
sat down with me and he looked at that and he said well he surely
should help in the shrubbery in the back because there's shrubbery in
50   the back that was over on my line that I've got to take out and I've
got pictures of that too, sir. And he said he didn't know what the man
or hat the man was because the tree was dead why didn't he take it
out? Well all he wants to do is harass me so he leaves it there so I
have to keep taking the stuff out and bending over and using my
55   trashcan, you know. This is something else. I only got one can. Why
don't he pick up his own trash? And so I went ahead and aid it. He
told me he would come if I need. He says, "I'll cut it when you need
me." Yet I could never get this man. I tried to have him subpoenaed,
yet I could never get him because I think Bennett got to him first.
60   But, anyway I got the Milehigh Tree Service here for 275, and I got
his mess in the backyard — if you look at the pictures here — that's
what I took them for. Did you give him the ones with the trees?

The rules-versus-relationships dichotomy implicates some common gender
stereotypes. The structure of the rule-oriented account reflects some defining
beliefs that many men have about themselves: men think in straight lines, they
get right to the point, they emphasize "facts" rather than emotions, and they
have faith in general rules that apply to everyone regardless of personal circumstances. The relational account, on the other hand, evokes a widely held male
stereotype of female thought and behavior: women are imprecise in dealing
with time, they wander off the point when telling stories, they let their emotions
get in the way of the facts, and they get too engrossed in context to develop and
apply general principles.

Our research indicates that gender does influence the distribution of the two
kinds of accounts, but in an indirect way. Most of the rule-oriented litigants
we observed were men, and most of the relational litigants were women, although this was not a hard-and-fast correlation.[13] Indeed, in Text 4.1, the rule-

oriented litigant is a woman, while another case that we discussed elsewhere in identifying the contrasting orientations involved two men (Conley and O'Barr 1990:68). The ability to produce rule-oriented accounts seems to be an acquired skill. The crucial factor associated with this skill is exposure to the culture of business and law. Lawyers have this skill, of course; so do landlords, merchants, and other businesspeople, big and small. Because it is still the case in our society that these roles are most often occupied by men, the ability to give rule-oriented accounts remains largely a male prerogative.

This imbalance is highly significant because the law has a strong preference for rule-oriented accounts. Although relationally oriented small-claims litigants do prevail on occasion, most legal decision makers find it far easier to deal with the structure and content of rule-oriented accounts. In interviews with us, judges described relational litigants as hard to follow, irrational, and even crazy, while praising the straightforward efficiency of rule-oriented accounts. They reported that in order to respond to a relational account, they first had to restructure it in their own minds around whatever legal rules might apply, selecting and reordering the relevant facts, while discarding the extraneous ones. This was hard work, and they often did not bother. The implication of these comments is, of course, that relational litigants — which often means women — have a harder time gaining access to justice than do their rule-oriented counterparts.

Despite what the judges say, relational accounts are not illogical. It is just that their logic differs from that of the rule-oriented accounts that the law prefers. Relational accounts tend to predicate legal entitlement on personal need and social worth: *I am a person in need. I meet my obligations to other members of the social network and help them when they are in need. Therefore, the law should help me now.* Given this outlook, the details of one's personal life and social relations are highly relevant. If one is not concerned with the deductive application of rules, there is no compelling need to present events in chronological sequence or to be precise about such things as times, dates, and quantities. As we discuss at the end of this chapter, other societies in other places have built legal systems around this kind of logic. This suggests that, at least in theory, we could, too.

We emphasize "in theory." Many would object to such a revolutionary transformation on grounds of practical utility or their own philosophy of justice. Those who would welcome the change would confront a monumental task: undoing our system's historical connection with a rule-oriented system of reasoning. If that reasoning is indeed patriarchal, then the law's preference for it both reflects and reinforces the essential patriarchy of legal discourse.

When the law, as personified by judges, reacts more favorably to rule-oriented accounts, it is granting privileged status to linguistic practices that historically have been more associated with men than women. In Gilligan's terms, the law is preferring the abstract, rule-driven logic typical of men to the more contextual reasoning that characterizes women (Gilligan 1982). In this way, the law's linguistic practice reveals its fundamental patriarchy. The details of the interactions between judges and rule-oriented litigants comprise the mechanics of translating patriarchy into social action.

As in other contexts, though, linguistic practice is both cause and effect. Every time a judge prefers the rule-oriented structure, this act sends a message to those who would interact with the law. The message is that the easiest mode of access is to conform to the logic of the system, however gender-biased that logic may be. Anyone who is in regular attendance in courtrooms and law school classrooms can attest that people respond to this message in a pragmatic way. As more and more women enter the system as lawyers, litigants, and judges, it is they who change, not the system. Opportunities for resistance are ignored as people make the practical judgment that they need to speak the language of the law. Every time the law's linguistic practice is reenacted, the patriarchy of its macrodiscourse — that is, the way things are thought about and acted upon — is reaffirmed.[14]

Conclusion: An Alternative Vision of Justice

In this chapter, we have reviewed two of our own investigations of how legal processes actually work at the microlinguistic level. The findings we have reported are at variance with the law's ideal of equal access to justice. In this regard, our results are no different from those of most other sociolegal projects. Over and over, such studies have shown the gap between the claims of law-in-theory and the realities of law-in-action.

The particular focus of our research has been on the preference of the law for certain linguistic practices. Witnesses come in all varieties — they are old and young, educated and uneducated, and from varied ethnic backgrounds, and, importantly for the argument we develop here, they differ in terms of how they talk. The legal system prefers some of these ways of talking over others, and it expresses its preferences in complex ways.

At the level of speech styles, the system gives greater credence to those who speak in a powerful and assertive style. Conversely, those who speak in a powerless style, which is marked by deference and imprecision, are less likely to be believed. Since men are more likely to have learned a powerful speech style than women, this preference, we believe, is a manifestation of the law's patriarchy at the most elemental linguistic level.

One response to this claim is that it is inaccurate to attribute this gender bias to "the system." After all, it is not legal officials who are evaluating men and women differently, but the lay jurors, who are the law's fact finders. To the extent that the powerless phenomenon reflects a patriarchal bias, it is the bias of our society as a whole. Since a fundamental purpose of having juries is to incorporate societal values into the law, the system will never get very far ahead of society — nor should it.

This argument is largely irrelevant to our principal point. That point is that patriarchal values are inscribed in the linguistic details of the day-to-day workings of the law. Whether the law is leading or following the larger society does not alter this reality. Moreover, the law is more than a passive conduit for the values of society as expressed by jurors. As we noted earlier, it takes active measures to screen out many of the biases that jurors might bring into the courtroom, and this could be true with regard to language variation as well.

The law exhibits a similar preference for a characteristically male epistemology in the way that it responds to different kinds of account structures. In our study of small claims courts, we found that rule-oriented accounts articulate better with the logic of the law than do their relational counterparts. Small claims judges can deal relatively easily with rule-oriented accounts, with their emphasis on rule violations and their exclusion of social context. For a relational litigant to receive a comparable hearing, a judge must be willing to make the effort to listen to the account — rather than dismissing it out of hand, as often happens — and then restructure it in terms of legal rules. Litigants who are able to construct rule-oriented accounts are typically those with exposure to the culture of business and law; it is still the case in our society that men gain such exposure far more readily than women. Once again, legal patriarchy, in the sense of favoring male interests, is realized in the linguistic details of courtroom interactions.

These processes parallel other ways of inscribing patriarchal discourse in the workings of law. How else are we to understand what we saw in chapter 2 regarding rape trials? And what about mediation? Although one might expect that women would fare better in mediation, with its ideology of conciliation, than in adversarial adjudication, the evidence we reviewed suggests the opposite. Here as well, the law remains consistently patriarchal in its linguistic practice. Methodologically, these various examples all point to the critical role of linguistic analysis in understanding the mechanics of domination and privilege. Because it is at the level of language-in-action that abstractions such as patriarchy become reality, linguistic analysis is of more than academic interest. Those who would transform the law's patriarchy are probably wasting their time unless they are prepared to challenge the practices that both reflect and reproduce it.

Finally, it is worth asking what a legal system that does not favor patriarchal interests might look like. Could the law exhibit different preferences than it does at present, or might it treat different ways of saying things more equitably? Could the law have different priorities than it now does?

Take the case of Mrs. Rawls. Her difficulties with the court had to do with the fact that she was unable to structure her problems according to the template of the law. Her logic was not that of the law. She could not seem to separate the hedge, the property line, and the concept of ownership from the complexities of social relations, unneighborly neighbors, and twenty years of bad feelings. The judge described her to us as a crazy old lady whom the law could not help. Imagine for a moment the possibility of a legal system that adjusted to the logic of its constituents, rather than insisting that they make the accommodations. What would such a legal system look like?

One need not look far: the ethnographic record of legal anthropology suggests some answers. Anthropologists have described numerous legal systems that show us different ways to listen to litigants and make decisions. The village courts of the Tiv of Nigeria and the Barotse of Zimbabwe, as described long ago by, respectively, Paul Bohannan (1989) and Max Gluckman (1955, 1965), remain instructive examples. Despite major differences between the two legal systems, both Tiv and Barotse courts allow litigants to say whatever they have to say and allow those who sit in judgment to ask whatever they want to know, call for whatever evidence they deem important, and visit places where events occurred. They are not bound by Western-style constraints on who can talk, what speakers can say, and how talk must be structured. Far from being extraneous, social context is central. In the cases that Bohannan and Gluckman describe, judges often seek out the social context when the litigants fail to provide it. In contrast to their Western counterparts, Tiv and Barotse judges are not strangers operating in an abstract universe without reference to the social world where disputes occur and where the parties will return after the hearing. Their overriding concern seems to be to ensure that decisions reached by the law are ones that will work in society.

In these respects, the Tiv and Barotse legal systems come much closer to the everyday understanding of disputes exhibited by relational litigants like Mrs. Rawls. It is tempting to speculate on how she would fare in such environments. Those courts would be interested in the history of her relationship with her neighbor and her claim that he had violated community norms. Their solutions would look less to past violation of rules than to future compatibility. The judges would probably maintain an interest in her affairs and would be neither surprised nor displeased to see her again if changing social circumstances warranted.

We should not be too quick to romanticize this vision of Mrs. Rawls in Barotseland, however. Despite the appeal of their legal process, Tiv and Barotse societies are at least as patriarchal as our own. Indeed, many of the cases that Bohannan and Gluckman report involve women being shuttled back and forth between kin groups like livestock. And even their enlightened procedures look very much like the mediation strategies that Fineman and others have found wanting as a solution to the patriarchy of American divorce law.

Our point is simply that there *are* alternatives to the microlinguistic structure of our legal system. Radical as some of them may seem, they have worked, more or less, in other places and at other times. Some of the alternatives might subvert the law's patriarchy; others might reinforce it, perhaps in unexpected ways. But whatever form the linguistic practice of the law takes, it will interact with the law's higher-order macrodiscourse in a relationship of mutual influence, with profound implications for the distribution of power among the law's constituents.

Postscript on Current Events

Since we published the second edition, there have been two sets of developments that are especially worthy of comment. First, as we write this third edition in the late fall of 2017, the United States is witnessing an unprecedented challenge to the status quo of male power. Large numbers of women are coming forward to accuse powerful men in politics, the media, entertainment, and business of sexual abuse and harassment. For perhaps the first time in history, these accusations are being taken seriously, and many of the accused are resigning their positions of power, sometimes with admissions of guilt. In fact, as we were writing this paragraph on December 7, 2017, US Senator Al Franken (D.-Minn.) announced his intent to resign in the face of such allegations. Only time will tell if these developments will bring about a fundamental shift in the gender dynamics of power.

Second, recent social changes have added another layer to the analysis presented in this chapter by contesting traditional concepts of sex and gender. The rapid and widespread recognition of gender nonconformity has led to a new critique of the law as not just patriarchal but also heteronormative. The law has begun to respond, albeit haltingly — most notably in the Supreme Court's 2015 decision in *Obergefell v. Hodges*, which recognized a constitutional right to same-sex marriage.

But, as the label "same-sex" suggests, that case begged the question of a fluid definition of gender. Courts and legislatures are just beginning to address that issue, in ways that are both helpful and unhelpful. A newly enacted California law, for example, will allow people to choose "nonbinary" for the gender entry on state government documents like birth certificates and driver's licenses. At the other extreme, North Carolina's now-repealed "bathroom bill" required users of government-provided restrooms to use the one that corresponded with the gender on their birth certificates.

Law and language scholarship is also beginning to address the complexities of gender definition. One of us, for example, did a linguistic analysis of a state court trial in which a transgender person was prosecuted for marrying a person of the same sex (R. Conley 2008). More recently, anthropologist Hadi Deeb (2013) analyzed the oral arguments before the California Supreme Court in a pre-*Obergefell* same-sex marriage case. These two articles probe the ways in which the microdiscourses of the law both reflect and reinforce the law's heteronormative assumptions, while simultaneously providing avenues for challenging those assumptions. This is an area in which law and language scholarship, effectively communicated to general audiences, can be especially influential.

CHAPTER FIVE

A Natural History of Disputing

How do disputes begin? What do they look (or sound) like in their earliest stages? How does an injury or wrong develop into a full-blown dispute or even a legal case? These are perplexing questions for sociolegal scholars. The obvious solution—to follow a dispute from its very beginning through its development and eventual resolution—has enormous intellectual appeal. But is it possible to do so?[1]

In this chapter, we consider the history of disputes. We ask whether different kinds of disputes tend to unfold in regular ways and, if so, what accounts for the regularities. Our starting point is a model of dispute evolution—or *transformation*, as it is usually called—that has shaped sociolegal research on disputing for almost two decades. We then review what is known linguistically about the behaviors that occur at each of the posited stages of a typical dispute. The chapter concludes with a new model of the disputing process that is built inductively from the bits and pieces of available linguistic evidence.

The evidence considered in this chapter is all drawn from US courts. Consequently, the inferences we draw and the models we propose should be evaluated with that limitation in mind. Legal anthropology teaches us that disputing practices are culture-specific, and other models may apply in other cultures.

Naming, Blaming, and Claiming

Some of the best answers to questions about the history of disputes have emerged from the conceptual framework formulated by William Felstiner, Richard Abel, and Austin Sarat in their still-influential 1980 article, "The Emergence and Transformation of Disputes: Naming, Blaming, Claiming. . . ." They propose a logical model of three developmental stages through which disputes pass in their early phases. In practice, the stages are complex, reactive, and unstable, making them difficult to isolate or describe fully. Nonetheless, the conceptualization of naming, blaming, and claiming as the developmental stages of a dispute has lent useful structure to the study of disputing behavior.

Naming refers to the phase in which a particular experience is understood as injurious. Until the injured person says to himself or herself, "I have been hurt or wronged; what has happened has damaged me in some way," the injury remains unperceived *as an injury*. Many of life's untoward events never move into the naming phase. Consider such examples as a health problem arising from daily labor in a hazardous workplace, the aggravation caused by a neighbor who ignores a property line and builds a corner of his garage on someone else's property, or the annoyance or trauma resulting from a coworker's unwanted sexual advances. But until these problems are perceived as injuries and named as such, they remain embryonic disputes.

Blaming marks an important transformation in the development of a dispute. In this phase, a link is made between the perceived wrong and the party believed to have caused it, whether that is another person or a social entity of some sort. An employer is blamed for creating the hazard in the workplace, a neighbor's building contractor is held responsible for encroaching on the property line, or a coworker is said to have sexually harassed another person by making unwanted advances. At the completion of the blaming stage, the injury has been defined and the principals in the dispute identified.

Claiming occurs when the injured party voices the grievance to the party believed to be responsible and asks for a remedy. The employer might be asked to remove the hazard from the workplace, the contractor to rebuild the garage so that it does not cross the property line, or the harasser to act in a different way. If the party believed to be responsible complies, then the problem is solved. But this is not what always happens. The party who is held responsible may resist the claim. This denial of the claim marks a final transformation of the incipient controversy. At this point, when the parties are at loggerheads and no simple resolution is in sight, a full-blown dispute emerges.

Useful as it is, the Felstiner-Abel-Sarat framework is a logical model of disputing rather than a description of what actually happens in particular instances.[2] In reality, the three stages might occur in rapid succession, or one or another of them might be recycled a few times as a person ponders the seriousness of the injury and the possibilities of whom to hold responsible. In some cases, the transformation process might extend over a very long period of time—even a lifetime—as a victim gradually perceives the wrong and begins to move toward blaming someone and seeking resolution. (Think about recent cases in which lifelong smokers have sued tobacco companies and adults have come forward with claims of childhood sexual abuse.) What this logical model of conflict cannot do is to tell us much about what happens in each of the stages or what specific events trigger the developmental transformations.

A more complex model of the emergence of disputes can be derived from microlinguistic analysis of trouble talk in everyday life. Like the Felstiner-Abel-Sarat model, this model is built up logically from what we know about how people talk about trouble in the early phases of perceiving injury and blaming others, well before disputes as such have fully developed. But what a language-based model can add is an understanding of just what it is that people say when they perceive injuries, name them, and blame others. It can thus offer an explanation of how the various transformations actually occur. As we shall see, the interactive component of the various transformations — that is, what other people do and say — is also a critical part of what happens.

In this chapter, we assemble linguistic data from a variety of sources in an effort to expand and elaborate on the naming-blaming-claiming dispute model, and thus to appreciate the microdiscourse of disputing. Our effort is twofold: to develop a fuller understanding of the language people use when they name, blame, and claim, and to consider what happens when disputes go beyond the claiming stage into the realm of ongoing confrontation. At the end of the chapter, we synthesize our linguistic observations into a new model that seeks to account for all the contingencies that may ensue during the life history of a dispute.

A Language-Based Model of Naming and Blaming

Ever since we began our own study of disputes more than forty years ago, we have had the fantasy of being present at the birth of a dispute, of being able to hear the first voicings of the process of naming, blaming, and claiming. Perhaps these would be words spoken to a spouse at breakfast, a friend at work, or a neighbor across a back fence. In such intimate moments, people tell significant others what has happened. They put into words their feelings and perceptions and share them with someone willing to listen. But just what is it that they say? Is there a way to study these first tellings, these embryonic narratives about troubles? Were we able to sit at the breakfast table, eavesdrop on a telephone conversation, or stand at the fence, what would we hear?

It is extremely difficult to position oneself strategically in these intimate spaces and then wait for dispute-related topics to emerge. Nonetheless, conversation analysts have managed to collect and study bits and pieces of naturally occurring conversation about troubles in everyday life. From these fragments, it is possible to build a reasonably complete linguistic model of what people say in the earliest stages of naming their troubles as injuries and blaming others for them.

Some significant insights into the earliest phases of disputing come from Anita Pomerantz's (1978) early study of trouble talk in everyday contexts. She notes that "unhappy incidents" in daily life are often announced without any attribution of responsibility. It is only later, through the interactional work done by the recipients of the talk, that responsible agents are connected with the actions. What people seem to do in everyday contexts is to mention their troubles to spouses, friends, and neighbors in fairly general terms. The recipients of the talk then ask a series of follow-up questions that initiate a collaborative search for a responsible party who can be blamed for the problem.

Pomerantz gives some examples of how this works. In each case, someone announces a problem — something's hurt, something's broken, something's wrong. What follows is a response from the recipient of the talk that begins the effort to complete the equation by identifying the person responsible for the bad outcome.

TEXT **5.1** (Adapted from Pomerantz 1978:116–17)

(1) ANNOUNCEMENT: My face hurts.
     QUESTION: Oh, what did he do to you?
(2) ANNOUNCEMENT: It [the car engine] blew up.
     QUESTION: What did you do to it?
(3) ANNOUNCEMENT: The cat's been eating our dinner.
     QUESTION: Did you leave it out so that he could get to it?

These examples provide a prototype of how people talk about trouble in everyday contexts. As Felstiner, Abel, and Sarat theorized, the original event in the linguistic history of a dispute is indeed the description, the noticing, the naming[3] of the problem. But as Pomerantz shows, this initial announcement of the problem often occurs without any attribution of responsibility. Blaming comes later. Significantly, her data show that the second stage of the transformation occurs collaboratively. One person names the problem; another helps affix responsibility for it.

The recipient of the trouble talk may respond with varying degrees of directness. In examples (1) and (3) in Text 5.1, the recipient moves immediately to the identification of a suspect (a "he" evidently known to both parties; "you") and the specification of the guilty act (an all-but-explicit accusation of physical violence; a charge of leaving the dinner out). In example (2), the recipient names the agent ("you") but merely raises the question of what that agent might have done to cause the problem.[4] Moreover, it is interesting (although not remarked on by Pomerantz) that all three examples reflect an effort not simply to find some responsible agent but also to find a responsible *human* agent. Although exceptions come readily to mind (such things as lightning bolts out of the sky, car crashes resulting from mechanical failure, and illnesses that seem to be merely a part of the human condition), collaborative searches for blame, in this culture at least, seem to exhibit a strong preference for discovering human agents.[5]

A second body of evidence about embryonic disputes comes from the work of Gail Jefferson (1980, 1985, 1988), one of the founders of conversation analysis. In a 1985 article entitled "On the Interactional Unpackaging of a 'Gloss,'" Jefferson's concern is the impact of the interactional environment on the telling of troubles. She finds that we often offer tokens of or hints about stories that we might tell (i.e., that might be unpacked more fully), but the actual form and complexity of the tellings that ensue depend on the behavior of those to whom we drop the hints. We say, for example, that something bad has happened, but a full-blown story does not get told unless the audience does its work by encouraging elaboration. Jefferson provides examples of lengthy conversations in which potential stories are offered or introduced several times, but only when the listeners affirmatively signal their willingness to hear elaborated versions do the stories actually get told in that form.

Other work by Jefferson discloses further details of the process of co-producing stories about trouble. The process is variable and often complex. The requisite audience participation can take a variety of forms. Sometimes, for example, the trouble will be announced by an unexpectedly detailed answer to a "How are you?" kind of question; the recipient may ignore the hint or, as in Text 5.2, invite elaboration of the problem.

TEXT 5.2 (Adapted from Jefferson 1988:422)

QUESTION: How are you feeling now?
ANSWER: Oh, pretty good I guess.
INVITATION: How is your arthritis? You still taking shots?

In other instances, the announcement of the problem comes in the form of a statement. The recipient may then invite elaboration by what Jefferson calls *affiliation responses*. These are words, phrases, or other utterances that express the recipient's sympathy and interest in hearing more about the problem. Text 5.3 illustrates the process.

TEXT 5.3 (Adapted from Jefferson 1988:428)

ANNOUNCEMENT: I been taking antibiotics ever since Sunday.
AFFILIATION: Ohh.
ELABORATION: And uh I, when I lie down or when I get up it feels like the flesh is pulling off my bones.
5   FURTHER AFFILIATION: How awful.
FURTHER ELABORATION: Oh I have, listen I was in such excruciating pain yesterday . . .

Yet another possibility is that the recipient will help the telling along by offering a *second story*. The recipient will signal a willingness to hear more by responding to some detail of the unfolding story with a statement such as "Yeah, that sounds like when I tore that thing in my shoulder a couple of years ago — I thought I was gonna go crazy it hurt so much." Second stories seem to have the effect of motivating the original speaker to produce even more elaborate versions of the original problem.

Whatever their specifics, most of the features of co-produced trouble narratives discovered by Pomerantz and Jefferson share two related characteristics. First, in the instance when troubles get fully told, the recipient plays an active and helpful role. Second, the linguistic relationship between teller and recipient moves in the direction of ever-greater intimacy as the teller offers more and more personal detail and the recipient signals a willingness to receive it. Significantly, such features require a friendly audience and an informal conversational environment. Thus, there is likely to be a stark disjunction when the aggrieved party moves beyond naming and blaming to the claiming stage and beyond. The story must now be retold to the potentially hostile responsible party. If that proves unavailing, the claimant may have to move into the professional world of lawyers and judges. In either of those environments, helpfulness and intimacy are unlikely, and a new set of linguistic issues will come into play.[6] We turn next to what is known about the linguistic details of the latter phases of the disputing process.

The Claiming Process

Claiming, as specified in the Felstiner-Abel-Sarat model, occurs when the injured person articulates the wrong to the blamed party and requests a remedy.[7] It is easy to imagine a variety of possible responses: (1) the blamed party agrees with the claim; (2) the blamed party denies the claim; or (3) some complex intermediate state emerges, and the two parties become entangled in an argument. In case (1), the controversy presumably ends; in case (2) or (3), a full-blown dispute can emerge. Let us examine these possibilities in more detail.

Recall our discussion in chapter 3 about conversational interaction. A major characteristic of verbal exchanges is that many sequences occur as *adjacency pairs* (Atkinson and Drew 1979:57–61). Questions-answers and requests-replies are common adjacency pairs. In some adjacency pairs, the first part invites only one possible response (or second part). Thus, a greeting calls for a return greeting; any other response is out of order conversationally. Other first parts may evoke alternative second parts: invitations may occasion acceptances, rejections, or counteroffers, while requests may be granted or denied. In most instances where the first part allows multiple second parts, only one is usual and anticipated — or, as conversation analysts put it, *preferred*.[8] An acceptance is the preferred response to an invitation, as compliance is to a request. Other responses — rejecting an invitation and denying a request — are said to be *dis-*

preferred. Linguistically, dispreferred second parts tend to be more elaborate than preferred second parts, often involving explanations or excuses. For example, an invitation may be accepted with a simple "Yes, I'll be there," whereas a rejection will typically take the form of "I'd love to come, but I have to. . . ."

Claiming—that is, the actual confrontation of the accused by the accuser with a claim about responsibility—is the first part of an adjacency pair. From the perspective of the wronged party, the preferred second part would be an acceptance of the blame. But is this usually what happens?

Some evidence comes from Atkinson and Drew's (1979:112–17) discussion of accusations. They consider the possible second parts to accusations—denials, excuses, counteraccusations, admissions, apologies, and so forth—and conclude that the anticipated second part in everyday situations is one that somehow avoids self-blame.[9] Denials, excuses, and counteraccusations all function to avoid self-blame. Admissions and apologies, which involve some degree of acknowledgment of responsibility, are very infrequent. The logical conclusion of Atkinson and Drew's argument is that claiming is a structurally self-defeating process, one that is usually doomed from the outset. If we accuse someone, the likelihood is that he or she will deflect the accusation, rather than accepting blame.

Consider the following story, told to one of us in the aftermath of Hurricane Fran, which struck North Carolina in 1996. The teller reported that she had been driving her car down a familiar street known by her audience to have been blocked after the storm by a fallen tree. She made the detour through the neighborhood that had come to be everyone's way around the fallen tree in the immediate aftermath of the storm. On this occasion, she encountered linemen who were repairing downed power lines. One of them was directing traffic in the area where the crew was working. The narrator obeyed his directions, but to her dismay, as she drove through the work area, a limb fell on her car, damaging it badly. When she got out of the car to discuss the situation with the lineman, she was astonished when he immediately accepted responsibility on behalf of the power company and offered to pay for the damage to her car.

In her telling of the story, the narrator emphasized three striking ironies. First, her car had survived the hurricane itself but then got wrecked when things had ostensibly returned to an unthreatening normalcy. Second, the damage had occurred as a result of obeying *safety* instructions given by the work crew. Third, and most remarkable, the crew had immediately accepted responsibility for the damage to her car. It was the convergence of these unusual occurrences that made the story worth telling.

From a linguistic point of view, the third irony is an exception that proves Atkinson and Drew's rule about the avoidance of blame. The lineman's immediate acceptance of responsibility was so contrary to everyone's expectations that it became the punch line of an elaborate story. While people might wish for such reactions from those against whom they make claims, they seem to understand that in most cases claiming merely sets the stage for further evolution of the dispute.

At any point in the process of naming, blaming, and claiming, the wronged party may decide to "lump it." *Lumping*, a term widely used in the sociolegal literature (see Miller and Sarat 1980–81:525–26), refers to the possibility that the injured party may decide unilaterally to give up on the dispute and just live with the wrong. The disputing process may seem daunting from the outset, or the aggrieved party may be beaten down by the respondent's attempts to avoid blame. Whatever the cause, lumping remains an option throughout the life of the dispute. When lumping occurs, overt disputing behavior ceases. Lumping may have lingering psychological effects, but the interactional aspects of the dispute come to an end.

But if the wronged party pursues the claim beyond an initial denial or deflection of blame by the accused, what happens next? Another piece of evidence helps illuminate this part of the process. The story in Text 5.4 was told by a plaintiff in a small claims court case. It relates the history of the plaintiff's efforts to assert a claim against a dry cleaner for ruining his suit. He confronted the cleaner with the problem twice. Both times the cleaner denied responsibility, ultimately seeking the support of a third party — a fabric analyst — in denying the man's claim.

Text 5.4 (Adapted from Conley and O'Barr 1990:37–38)

> I bought a suit around the last of May. I wore the suit once and sent it to the cleaners. When the suit came back, there was a spot on it. The man at the cleaners told me that there was a defect in the material. I took the suit home and told my wife what the cleaner had said. We agreed that I should take it back again to the cleaners the next day. He agreed to reclean the suit. When it came back a second time no different from the first, the cleaner offered to send it away to have the fabric analyzed. He promised to refund my money if the analysis proved that he was at fault. He got my suit back two weeks later with a report saying that he wasn't at fault but I don't agree.

This story provides some insight into the complexities of claiming in day-to-day contexts. The man hoped for acceptance of his claim. (Why else would he have bothered to assert it twice?) But the cleaner played his role according to the usual interactional script by denying responsibility on each occasion. Linguistically, sequences such as this one are common: claims elicit denials that elicit restated claims that elicit further denials that elicit restated claims — and so on. Through such sequences, claiming can evolve into argument, and the dispute can become hopelessly stalemated.

Some of the best evidence about the nature of argumentation is found in the work of Angela Garcia, which we discussed in chapter 3. Although her work has focused on how mediation alters argumentation, she nonetheless provides insights into the nature of the problem that mediation fixes. Arguments have the potential to continue endlessly because they consist of sequences of accusation-response adjacency pairs. Although an accuser hopes for an acceptance of blame, the usual second part is the opposite: some sort of deflection or denial of blame, often followed by a counteraccusation. When this begins, the back-and-forth of you-did/no-I-didn't/yes-you-did can continue ad infinitum, or at least until one of the parties gives up and decides to lump it. Thus, in the transformation of disputes, the linguistic evidence suggests that argumentation is a likely outcome as an accuser presses a claim. But in the end, argumentation does not solve the problem; each side just continues to restate its position. Beyond putting forth further arguments (or lumping it), one option still remains: turning to the legal system.[10]

What Happens When Disputes Reach the Legal System?

As we have seen, a dispute is likely to pass through several developmental phases before it reaches the legal system. At the very least, the wronged party has to perceive and articulate the problem. Then an equation must be formulated that links the wrong to a responsible party. The claim may be stated to the responsible party directly or through an intermediary, orally or in writing. If the accused does the usual thing and denies responsibility, the accuser must then decide whether to see a lawyer or seek a remedy in an informal, do-it-yourself legal forum such as a small claims court or community mediation center. In either case, turning to the legal system will involve further retellings of the problem to new audiences: lawyers, clerks, mediators, judges, and possibly even jurors. We look next at how the legal system itself interacts with and transforms disputes. The evidence we consider is drawn from detailed studies of the language of disputing in two very different legal environments: the small claims court and the lawyer's office, each of which represents an initial point of contact with the law.

Transformation in the Small Claims Court[11]

Some dissatisfied claimants may turn to a small claims court as their point of entry into the legal system. Although the details of what cases small claims courts can handle vary from state to state, they generally hear simple legal claims involving less than $2,000–3,000. The theory of small claims courts is that people can come to court without lawyers, state their claims in everyday language, and get relief. Consistent with the theory, small claims litigants rarely consult lawyers before coming to court. Some states do not permit lawyers to appear in court; in other states, lawyers are allowed but rarely appear. Small claims judges (who need not even be lawyers in some states) are supposed to conduct hearings in an informal atmosphere; in particular, testimony need not follow the rules of evidence that apply in higher courts.

When a person brings a dispute to a small claims court, he or she is always asked to fill out a complaint form. Although it is represented to be nothing more than a source of background information for the judge, this form, however simple it may be, results in a formalization of the dispute. In many or even most instances, this may be the first time the wronged party has written down what the dispute is about. Such a form requires that the parties be named and that a monetary claim be stated along with some sort of justification for the claim. For example, in one state, the form reads,

PLAINTIFF'S NAME AND ADDRESS

_____
_____
_____

DEFENDANT'S NAME AND ADDRESS

_____
_____
_____

PLAINTIFF'S CLAIM
The Defendant owes me $ _____ for the following reasons:

_____
_____
_____

This form imposes a framing of the dispute that may or may not have occurred to the claiming party. The claiming and resisting parties are renamed as, respectively, plaintiff and defendant. The dispute must be reduced to a stated amount of money that the plaintiff claims from the defendant. And the "reasons" underlying the claim must be set out in a few lines.

Claimants respond to this demand for framing in interesting ways. In some instances, the written statement of the claim seems to capture the entirety of the dispute and is consistent with the account later given in court. For example, a North Carolina man sued a dry cleaner for $198.99: "Defendant ruined my wife's new silk dress with his cleaning procedures and he claims no responsibility in this matter." Subsequent retellings stressed the same three elements: the dress was new, it was ruined when the cleaner returned it, and the cleaner refused to accept any responsibility for the damage.

In other cases, the written statement of the claim is cryptic, barely hinting at what might be told in other environments. For example, a woman in Pennsylvania sued a local merchants' service organization for $550: "For the Juneteenth Crowning Ball, and a sponsor's fee." In later tellings in and out of court, the plaintiff explained that her daughter had won a beauty pageant sponsored by the organization and had expected to receive a scholarship as a result. The mother was suing because the organization had refused to pay the amount her daughter had expected to receive. In another case, a Colorado man demanded $750 from a real estate management company for "Rent deposit. Refused for unreasonable excuses." What emerged in court was a very complex story about responsibility — both legal and moral — for defects in an apartment and credit for repairs allegedly made by the tenant. In a third case, a long and complicated dispute between roommates in Pennsylvania was reduced on the form to a $500 claim for "payment of phone bill."

What is most significant about the complaint form is not so much what the claimant actually says, but the fact that the legal system requires him or her to say something and to do so in a specific format. Through the form, the law interacts with the claimant to co-produce an account of the dispute. The law demands a particular kind of claiming, one that reduces the dispute to dollars and cents and that briefly but explicitly states a justification for the claim. By transforming the claimant's account of the dispute in this way, the law — in this very first encounter with the claimant — has already begun to transform the dispute itself. When the case gets to court, the judge will look to the complaint form for an initial understanding of the dispute. Many litigants report that, when judges restate their understandings back to them, they no longer recognize their disputes.

In one city that we studied, the initial encounter with the legal system occurs as an interaction between the claimant and an intake clerk. In this jurisdiction, each person who comes to the courthouse to file a case has a private interview of several minutes' duration with a well-trained clerk. The clerk listens to the claimant's oral account of the dispute and then types a statement of claim in the form that he or she thinks will be most helpful to the judge. The clerk also collects and appends all relevant documents. The claimant then reads and signs the form. The result of this process is illustrated in the following account of a long and sometimes bitterly personal dispute between a homeowner and a roofing contractor.

TEXT 5.5 (From the authors' files of small claims complaints)

> On 12/19/85, the pltff. contracted the defendant to put white aluminum cornice 3rd flr. frt. roof. Re-roof kitchen 10x10 ply 2nd flr. guaranteed 5 yrs. & 5 more yrs. brush coat. New eves box, barge board and down spout on 2nd flr roof rear coat $1,080.00 Plaintiff paid deft. $500.00.

The deft sub-contracted job, who's [sic] men came to plaintiff's property put down less than $75.00 worth of materials, removed barge board, put up aluminum which fell off in a few days. Pltff. received a check from deft. for $250.00 which he did not cash. Pltff. has paid another contractor $1,410.00 to do the job correctly. Pltff. desires deft. to pay him $505.11 with interest, for mailings, $2.11, xeroxing cost, $3.00, court costs because of defendant's breach of contract, water damages, faulty workmanship, etc. See attached exhibits.

This kind of transformation, though more elaborate, is comparable to that effected by the simple complaint form. In both processes, the law exerts its power to demand a particular framing of the dispute. The blaming must be explicit, and the claiming must be monetary. The clerk-interview process ensures in addition that the reason for the blame is something that the law deems significant—in the above example, a breach of contract—and that the elements of the quantified claim are specifically enumerated and documented. The most significant difference between the two processes is that in the interview with the clerk, the interaction and ensuing transformation are more overt and apparent to the claimants. But the unassisted filling out of the form constitutes just as much of an interactive telling, and the transformation of the dispute that results is every bit as real. In both instances, the law as audience plays a critical role in determining what gets said.

The transformative work of the law continues when a small claims case goes to trial. Each litigant is called on to present an account of the dispute to the judge. Trials typically begin with the judge asking the plaintiff a question such as "Why are you bringing this case?" or "Why are you here?" In turn, the judge asks the defendant a question such as "What do you say?" or "What's your side of this?" Such invitations often leave litigants at a loss for words, perhaps because these questions are so different from the subtle techniques that listeners use to facilitate trouble-tellings in everyday contexts. As the trial moves along, however, judges may interact in more conversational ways—for example, by responding to litigants' statements, asking questions, and raising topics. The product—or, more accurately, the co-product—is an account produced jointly by the litigant and the law.

"The law," of course, is not in itself an anthropomorphic being that listens and responds. Rather, the entity we call the law manifests itself in the behavior of legal officials, such as intake clerks and small claims judges. Because these are real people, their orientations and reactions are not uniform but vary in interesting and important ways. In our study of small claims judges, we found much variation in the ways that they interact with litigants and their accounts.[12] The most significant difference is between those judges who see their authority as closely circumscribed by legal rules that they must apply rigorously and those who believe that they have a broader mandate to disregard the letter of the law in pursuit of "just" outcomes.

Judges who see themselves as rule-bound often work to frame litigants' accounts within categories to which rules will apply. Such judges typically respond with interest and affirmation when litigants talk about contracts, property lines, or documents, but they react passively or negatively when litigants seek to introduce lengthy personal histories into their accounts. Rule-bound judges frequently told us that litigants who sought to mix the personal and the legal were unfocused, unintelligent, or even crazy.

Among those judges who have a broader conception of their role, some pursue personal moral agendas, whereas others see consensus-for-consensus's-sake as the highest value. Those pursuing personal agendas react to litigant accounts in unpredictable ways. For example, a single mother who was a defendant in a debt collection action began to tell of the ways in which the legal and welfare systems had failed her. The judge, who regularly decided cases on the basis of his personal moral values, deflected her account by asking why she kept having babies.[13]

Judges who seek consensus are most attentive to those aspects of litigant accounts that hold some promise of compromise regardless of whether the issues are relevant to some potential rule of decision. When a litigant expresses some ambivalence about one of his or her demands, for example, the judge may try to develop the point through expressions of support and elaborating questions. A similar reaction may be evoked when a defendant expresses agreement with a prior statement by the plaintiff. Consensus-oriented judges frequently offer to suspend the hearing so that the parties can talk privately. They may also "preview" the possible legal outcome of the case and urge the parties to settle on similar terms.

The general point is that all types of judges interact with litigants to transform the disputes before them regardless of whether the judge stresses legal rules, personal values, or the process of conciliation. Although the account of the dispute that emerges in the small claims courtroom is likely to be very different from versions told earlier in the disputing process, it will be yet another co-produced account. In this critical linguistic respect, the role of the judge is no different from that of the neighbor across the back fence or the spouse at the dinner table who might have participated in previous transformations.

Transformation in the Lawyer's Office

Another point of entry into the legal system — and therefore a potential locus of transformation — is the lawyer's office. In their book *Divorce Lawyers and Their Clients* (1995), Sarat and Felstiner show that the interaction between client and lawyer is above all a contest between competing discourses. By approaching a lawyer in the first place, a layperson acknowledges that he or she wants a legal remedy for a problem. The lawyer listens and responds to what the client says through a template built of legal understandings and framing mechanisms. Whether or not the client's problem ultimately ends up in court, the encounter with a lawyer produces linguistic transformations similar to those observed in small claims courts.

For many people, this encounter with law-in-practice is a jarring experience. As they attempt to tell about the trouble that brings them to the lawyer's office, they do not always find sympathetic, affirming listeners such as those described by Jefferson. Rather, they often find themselves telling their stories to professionals who value distance over affiliation and control over support.

In a study of more than forty divorce cases, Sarat and Felstiner found two overarching ways in which lawyers transform their clients' disputes. First, whereas clients typically frame disputes in terms of moral blame and legal rights, lawyers use a variety of linguistic strategies to recast them as battles over such tangible issues as houses, support payments, and visitation schedules. Second, while clients' initial accounts usually envision cases as going to trial and being decided by judges or juries, lawyers are constantly at work in subtle ways to move clients around to the view that settlement is preferable to adjudication. Significantly, lawyers almost never tell clients that they are wrong or that they must repudiate their view of the case. Instead, they induce clients to volunteer successive new accounts of their cases until the tellings that emerge are compatible with the discourse of lawyers. By imposing changes on their clients' microdiscourse, lawyers effect a shift in the macrodiscourse of the disputes.

One linguistic strategy that the lawyer employs to change the focus of the dispute from moral to tangible issues is to offer unsupportive responses to a client's rhetoric about blame. In Text 5.6, a woman provides a poignant moral account of why her marriage failed. Her lawyer responds neutrally to this information and then changes the subject.

TEXT 5.6 (Sarat and Felstiner 1995:32)

CLIENT: There was a harassment and verbal degradation. No interest at all in my furthering my education. None whatsoever. Sexual harassment. If there was ever any time when I did not want or need sex, I was subject to these long verbal whip lashings. Then the Bible
5   would be put out on the counter with passages underlined as to what a poor wife I was. Just constant harassment from him.
LAWYER: Mmn-uh.
CLIENT: Then he undertook to lecturing me, and I'd say, "I don't want to hear this. I don't have time right now." I could lock myself in the
10   bathroom and he would break in. And I was just to listen, whether I

wanted to or not. And he would lecture me for hours. Literally hours.
There was no escaping him, short of getting in a car and driving
away. But then he would stand outside in the driveway and yell,
anyhow. The man was not well.
15 LAWYER: Okay. Now how about any courses you took?

By contrast, in Text 5.7, when the client's talk focuses on the disposition of
common property, the lawyer's neutrality is replaced by supportive and encouraging responses.

TEXT 5.7 (Sarat and Felstiner 1995:38)

LAWYER: Have you discussed any more getting rid of the van and
getting yourself another vehicle?
CLIENT: Yes. I talked it over with him, and asked if he would be
willing to release the van if I were to find a car.
5 LAWYER: Yeah.
CLIENT: And he said, "If he thought it was a fair deal, or a decent
deal," or something. And I said, "Well, if I'm going to be making the
car payments, what does it have to do with you? All I want from you
is to release the van." He still wants that control.
10 LAWYER: He's looking at everything as dollar signs. Pretty typical
reaction. He's going to be defensive on all those things. Have you
been looking for vehicles?

Lawyers may also deflect client rhetoric about morality and blame by bringing the talk back around to the legal process. In Text 5.8, a husband refers to
his wife's character defects in an effort to explain her refusal to negotiate a
property settlement. The lawyer ignores this theme. Without commenting on the
client's assessment of the wife, the lawyer instead responds with a procedural
suggestion about how to move more quickly toward settlement.

TEXT 5.8 (Sarat and Felstiner 1995:39)

LAWYER: What would happen if the two of you sat down and started
talking?
CLIENT: Well, anytime we've ever had discussions, they always
turn into arguments. There are a number of other things besides the
5 getting a job issue that I feel are inequitable in our relationship. On
the rare occasions that she actually listens, she's not a good listener.
When she actually listens and senses that she'd better change her
ways, that may last for a week before it's back to the same old thing.
And she's tied up with her hobbies. We were really broke this winter,

10   and I tried to discuss it with her. She said I should go see a financial
     counselor. She one evening said, "Well, when I get my inheritance I
     should share that with you." And I said, "Well, that would help." But
     then she'd just start ranting and raving, as if I had the nerve to con-
     sider that any of her inheritance would be mine. So she doesn't mean
15   it when she does ever make a concession. And it's very temporary
     and fleeting.
     LAWYER: Maybe she'd make a stronger commitment to a counselor
     that can listen to your two points of view.

Throughout their dealings with clients, lawyers enhance their authority by stressing their knowledge, skill, and expertise. Perhaps surprisingly, they rarely base their authority on their knowledge of legal rules. Rather, they freely admit that "official" rules almost never determine outcomes. They emphasize instead their familiarity with the pragmatic details of how the system "really" works. This doubles the client's dependency: he or she must rely on the lawyer not only to deal with the law's official rules but also to negotiate the subtle but informal practices that actually determine outcomes.

This relationship of client to lawyer is illustrated in Text 5.9, in which the lawyer counsels a wife whose husband has just obtained a restraining order keeping her away from the marital home. The wife, who is confused and out-raged, asks two apparently straightforward legal questions. The lawyer's responses show off his mastery of the court's basic procedures, as well as his special access to insider knowledge.

TEXT 5.9 (Sarat and Felstiner 1995:89)

     CLIENT: How often does a case like this come along—a restraining
     order of this nature?
     LAWYER: Very common.
     CLIENT: It's a very common thing. So how many other people are
5   getting the same kind of treatment I am? With what, I presume, is
     very sloppily handled orders that are passed out.
     LAWYER: I did talk to someone in the know—I won't go any further
     than that—who said that this one could have been signed purely
     by accident. I mean, that the judge could have—if he looked at it
10   now—said, "I would not sign that," and it could have been signed
     by accident. I said, "Well, then how does that happen?" And he said,
     "You've got all this stuff going; you come back to your office, and
     there's a stack of documents that need signatures. . . . There's some-
     one else that needs your attention, so you go through them, and
15   one of the main things you look for is the law firm or lawyer who is
     proposing them. And you tend to rely on them."

By increasing the client's dependency, such assertions of authority support the lawyer's efforts to move the client's focus from moral to tangible issues. If the law as practiced is indeed an all-but-impenetrable enigma, then what basis can the client have for resisting the lawyer's reframing of the dispute? The same strategy can also help the lawyer achieve a second major objective: positioning the client to forgo an adversarial confrontation and accept settlement.

This evidence from Sarat and Felstiner's study of talk in divorce lawyers' offices provides another window on the interactional details of how disputes are transformed through encounters with the law. Lawyers' ways of responding condition and shape clients' accounts and attitudes. Subtly, the lawyers advance a particular view of rights and wrongs and of the solutions that should be effected. Clients' stories about blame and moral responsibility for marital troubles get cool receptions. Instead, lawyers encourage talk about property and settlement strategies. They also emphasize aspects of law and the legal process that make them indispensable to the solution of their clients' problems. Their discourse embodies a view of law as flexible and indeterminate and of legal processes as liable to be influenced by the personalities and prejudices of particular judges.[14] Although a sampling of interactions between divorce lawyers and their clients is hardly a basis for strong universal claims, the evidence that Sarat and Felstiner adduce is surely indicative of the kinds of transformations that occur when lay clients bring other kinds of problems to legal professionals.

Reflections on Transformations

In this chapter, we have explored the evolution of a dispute from its early phases of naming, blaming, and claiming through the further transformations that the legal system effects. It has become evident, we hope, that a dispute does not exist in isolation from the contexts in which it is expressed. Rather, the account of a dispute that is given at any point in time is the dispute. All the contexts in which a dispute is expressed are interactional, and each such context shapes the dispute in unique ways.

Additional evidence about how the legal system transforms disputes comes from what litigants have to say after their cases have moved through the legal process. In these moments, litigants reflect on what has happened to them and on their efforts to achieve justice. As a part of our study of small claims courts in the late 1980s (Conley and O'Barr 1990), we interviewed litigants after their cases were decided. We sought to understand how their actual experiences with the law differed from the expectations they had going into the legal process. What the litigants told us in these interviews[15] adds a final note to the study of dispute transformation.

First, litigants expressed surprise that the accounts given by opposing parties had managed to transform the dispute. Before going to court, they had understood their disputes only from their own points of view; indeed, many litigants had failed to imagine that there might be alternative perspectives, let alone what accounts given from those perspectives might sound like. So confident were they in the inherent truth of their own stories that they had not contemplated the possibility of counternarratives that might have their own plausibility. Only after the fact did they realize that these counternarratives had so altered the courtroom discourse as to create new disputes whose form and content were unforeseen and often unnerving. We heard the same lament again and again: "The case that came out in court wasn't the one that I filed; maybe I should've known that this would happen, but I didn't."

Second, we learned that people had not foreseen that the law itself would have a similar transforming effect, reworking their stories into disputes that were sometimes unrecognizable. When these litigants filed their cases, things had seemed straightforward: they had been wronged; the opposing parties were at fault, had failed to rectify the problems, and needed to be punished in some way. They had been unprepared for how the law would strip their stories of their emotional and evaluative dimensions. They had been equally unprepared for the way in which the courts would shift the focus of their cases from such global issues as moral probity and social responsibility to specific questions about contractual language and monetary remedies. Once again, there was a recurrent theme: "The judge didn't want to hear what I had planned to say; he kept asking about things that had nothing to do with the problem."

Third, litigants — both winners and losers — often expressed dismay about the way that judges had responded to their stories. They had imagined that the inherent veracity of their own narratives would carry the day. They had expected, it seemed, that judges would have no recourse but to affirm and agree with their stories. They had failed to appreciate that judges might sit impassively as they talked or respond neutrally to what they had to say. When it happened, as it often did, that judges sided with the opposing parties — by seeming to assist them in getting out their counternarratives or by finding in their favor at the moment of decision — they were dumbfounded. The complaint was usually along these lines: "I can't believe that the judge paid any attention to what those people were saying; it was so obviously a bunch of lies."

The litigants we interviewed thus recognized, at least after the fact, that the legal process had changed the nature of their disputes. They identified three sets of agents who had collaborated in this transformation: the opposing parties, the normative requirements of the law, and the judges. In revealing these discoveries to us, the litigants reaffirmed the fundamental principle that disputes have no life separate from their particular tellings in specific contexts.

But how do litigants explain this transformation process to themselves? In particular, how do they account for what has happened to them and deal with their failure to foresee it? One obvious response would be to blame the system, to say that the law is an oppressive institution with no concern for justice. This was not what the litigants told us, however. What they did instead was to blame themselves or the particular judges who had heard their cases. The litigants held themselves responsible for their failure to prepare for the transformations their stories had undergone. Many also criticized the judges for failing to help them, usually adding that other, "better" judges would have done more.

Whatever its therapeutic value for litigants, this personalizing reaction to adverse experiences clearly works to the benefit of the system. This focus on the microdiscourse of the dispute deflects attention away from analysis of the macrodiscourse of the legal process itself. It precludes a consciousness of law that understands such experiences as inherent in the nature of law and legal practice. Such an understanding might promote resistance to the power of the law. Instead, the litigants' personalization of the difficulties they experienced leaves the law's hegemony unchallenged.

Although the litigants' analyses may have the unintended consequence of promoting the status quo, they are in another respect unusually perceptive. By individualizing their experiences, they call attention to the fact that the law's power is realized through concrete linguistic events. And when they reconcile themselves to the system by blaming their problems on themselves, they demonstrate that those linguistic events not only reflect but also reaffirm the law's power.

Conclusion: Toward a Natural History of Disputing

We began this chapter by reviewing the *naming-blaming-claiming* model that has shaped the analysis of dispute transformation for almost forty years. We then considered what is known linguistically about the processes of naming, blaming, and claiming, as well as about subsequent phases of disputing not covered by the original Felstiner-Abel-Sarat model. We are now in a position to propose a model of our own. Our model, which is summarized in the figure below, is based on linguistic and ethnographic evidence. Its purpose is to elab-

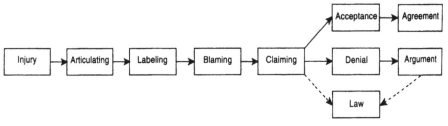

Notes: Lumping can occur at any point.
Articulating and labeling are both included in Felstiner, Abel, and Sarat's (1980–81) "naming" stage.

orate on and extend the original: elaborate on by offering additional empirical depth, and extend by tracking a dispute past the point of claiming and through its final disposition. To emphasize its empirical derivation, we call the model a *natural history of disputing.*[16]

The naming-blaming-claiming continuum forms the core of the new model. We have added the antecedent phase *perceiving the injury* and have separated *articulating* and *labeling* from each other. We then follow the dispute beyond the claiming stage to delineate two possible outcomes: acceptance, leading to agreement, and denial, leading to argument. Recourse to law and lumping are options at various phases.

Like all models, this one has its limitations. The real world is so complex and the variations on what can and does happen are so numerous that it is impossible to account for all the possibilities. We make no claim to have covered every contingency in the life of a dispute or to have brought every relevant piece of empirical evidence into our formulation. Our more limited objective is the same one we have pursued throughout this book: to challenge existing ways of thinking about legal processes by paying closer attention to their linguistic details.

CHAPTER SIX

The Discourses of Law in
Cross-Cultural Perspective

hus far, we have considered the multiple discourses of law solely from
an Anglo-American perspective. We have relied entirely on English-
language evidence from American and English legal proceedings to develop the argument that the linguistic practice of the law reflects, reproduces,
and sometimes challenges its dominant ideals. In this chapter, we explore the
cross-cultural applicability of this approach. Specifically, we ask whether it is
possible to dissect the linguistic enactment of legal power in the non-Western
societies that have been the traditional concern of legal anthropology and, if
so, how legal anthropology's received knowledge would hold up in the face of
such analysis.

A useful starting point may be to ask, What do we think we know about
legal discourse from a cross-cultural point of view? The answer is that we—
that is, the sociolegal community, particularly legal anthropologists—think we
know quite a bit about both the theory and the practice of non-Western law.[1]
To illustrate the point, consider the contributions of five of the most important
figures in the history of legal anthropology: Karl Llewellyn, E. A. Hoebel, Max
Gluckman, Paul Bohannan, and Laura Nader.

In *The Cheyenne Way* (1961, orig. 1941), Llewellyn and Hoebel try to reconstruct the "law-ways" of a Cheyenne culture that had disappeared more
than fifty years before they did their research. Their principal resource is the
memories of elderly Cheyennes who had observed or, more often, heard about
"cases of hitch or trouble" (Llewellyn and Hoebel 1961:26). These memories
became the basis of a detailed theory of legal principles and dispute resolution. Several years later Gluckman published *The Judicial Process among the
Barotse of Northern Rhodesia (Zambia)* (1955). On the basis of his own observation of contemporary cases, Gluckman claimed to have discovered the

Anglo-American concept of "the reasonable man" in the jurisprudence of a Zimbabwean society. Gluckman was subsequently taken to task by Bohannan (1969) for imposing Western legal categories on the Barotse materials, and a famous debate ensued. Drawing on his work with the Tiv of Nigeria, Bohannan (1989, orig. 1957) argued that each society's legal categories are unique and therefore not even translatable; Gluckman (1969) continued to insist that his cross-cultural comparison was both appropriate and correct. Significantly, neither questioned the other's ability to lay claim to an understanding of the logic of a non-Western legal system. The final example, Nader's *Harmony Ideology: Justice and Control in a Zapotec Mountain Village* (1990), explores the complex legal ideology of Mexico's Zapotec people. Her thesis is that as a legacy of colonialism the Zapotec idealize harmony as the ultimate end of law and that this ideology defuses challenges to the status quo.

Our point in mentioning these canonical works is an epistemological one: the intellectual claims of legal anthropology are exceedingly robust. As these few examples illustrate, for more than seventy-five years legal anthropology has claimed insight into the principles, procedures, decision-making logic, and ideology of non-Western law. All of these topics are contentious ones in our own society, of course, the subject of never-ending debate among legal scholars. If wisdom is so elusive when we are looking at our legal system, which operates in our own language, it seems only reasonable to look critically at the basis for legal anthropology's claims. In other words, *how* does legal anthropology know what it purports to know?

The short answer is "ethnography." At least since Bronislaw Malinoswki's *Crime and Custom in Savage Society* (1985, orig. 1926), legal anthropology has relied on patient fieldwork by participant observers. Its claim to authenticity relies on the ethnographer's opportunity to see and hear disputes evolve and to watch, transcribe, and (at least in recent decades) record legal proceedings. But how deep has this ethnography been? Inferences about issues such as decision-making logic and ideology are statements about the discourse of law in a particular society. Has the ethnography penetrated far enough toward the level of linguistic practice to justify such inferences? Is the ethnography linguistically rich enough to show us how the dominant discourses of law are reproduced, reaffirmed, challenged, and transformed in other societies?

To be fair, legal anthropology has always been sensitive to these questions. Back in 1926, Malinowski railed against relying on informants who "retail the Ideal of the law" (1985:120); he argued that the ethnographer must take care to test the informant's report against the evidence of actual disputes. In the 1950s and 1960s, the Gluckman-Bohannan debate took the methodological self-consciousness of legal anthropology to a more sophisticated level. Whereas Malinowski seemed to be drawing a contrast between subjective and objective knowledge of another society's law, Gluckman and Bohannan argued over the very possibility of knowledge. Gluckman, analyzing his Barotse cases, claimed to see Anglo-American tort law's "reasonable man" standard operating there as well. Bohannan, arguing from his Tiv materials, suggested that such comparisons are inevitably infected by the epistemological biases of the analyst, and therefore are suspect. In other words, once we open up the possibility of comparing other societies' legal reasoning to our own, we tend to see what we want to see. According to Bohannan, it is better to leave native legal concepts untranslated, to be appreciated on their own terms.

The Gluckman-Bohannan debate has continued in updated versions (see, for example, Comaroff and Roberts 1981:6–11). Subsequent legal ethnographies such as Nader's *Harmony Ideology* begin to exhibit sensitivity to the full range of contemporary concerns about the contingent nature of knowledge. But even as legal anthropology has become more thoughtful in questioning the bases of what it claims to know, a gap has remained. Sociolinguist Brenda Danet puts her finger on the problem in an influential review essay published in 1980. Commenting on the anthropological analysis of the role of questioning in dispute processes, she observes, "Most of the anthropological literature is insufficiently detailed to permit precise statements about the nature of the procedures" (Danet 1980a:516). In reviewing the work of a number of ethnographers, Danet (1980a:516–18) makes statements such as these:

> We know little about the exact conditions under which claim construction is transformed from direct argument to some combination of direct argument and indirect claims made in response to questions.

> In Kpelle trials . . . Gibbs [1962, 1967] provides no information on the exact structure of questioning or the rules that govern turn-taking.

> Despite a wealth of materials on Lozi court cases, however, [Gluckman (1955, 1965, 1973)] does not describe the exact sequence of events in court. . . .

> Yakan litigation also combines narrative presentation of claims with questioning, though Frake (1969) gives no details on the latter.

Danet's point seems to be that as of 1980 legal anthropologists had rarely given us the kind of linguistic data necessary to evaluate their claims. An examination of a more recent legal ethnography such as Nader's suggests that not much has changed.[2] We are given rich descriptions of "cases" that state the underlying "facts" of the dispute; report the court proceedings, often with generous quotations from the principals; present the result and rationale given by the decision maker; and sometimes provide an epilogue about the subsequent relations of the disputants. However rich the description, though, there is a vast gap between the linguistic practice that constituted the actual dispute and what is made available to the reader. Most of that practice is summarized or paraphrased; the speech that is reported directly is translated into idiomatic English. The reader must put a great deal of trust in the ethnographer.

There are many reasons why the presentational style of legal anthropology has developed as it has. The case-reporting strategy described above is exactly what is found in the published decisions of Anglo-American courts. The law professor Llewellyn brought the case method to the Cheyenne materials; the legally trained Gluckman took it to Zimbabwe. It would be unfair to suggest that these and other legal anthropologists have been thoughtlessly imposing a familiar method on data from other societies. On the contrary, it has always seemed to fit. In the preface to the 1989 edition of *Justice and Judgment among the Tiv*, Bohannan captured the prevailing sentiment with characteristic eloquence:

> I used the case method first because I admired the method as it had been used by Llewellyn and Hoebel in *The Cheyenne Way*, and I had been taught it by Max Gluckman. Moreover, the Tiv drove me to the case method. My self-assigned task was to discover as much as I could about what they were interested in. They put a lot of their time and effort into cases. (1989:vii)

An additional reason for adopting the law's case-reporting conventions has to do with sample-size concerns. Conventional social science wisdom holds that the more instances that can be cited in support of an interpretive argument, the more persuasive it becomes. However, publishers, teachers, and students all prefer short books. Thus, if you are going to rely on numerous cases to make your point, you must condense them. Extended transcripts are casualties in the quest for a broader base of support.

Technological limits have been another factor working in favor of the summary approach. For much of the history of legal anthropology, recording equipment was unavailable or impractical. Even when it has been available, the desirability of using it has been questioned. We turn once again to Bohannan, this time in his preface to the original edition of *Justice and Judgment among the Tiv*:

> By other techniques, such as sound recording, it would have been possible to get fuller transcriptions of the cases. I am not sure that it would be desirable, for I have found, in trying to use it, that gadgetry so absorbs the attention of the field worker that it is very easy for him to forget that he must gear his life to the people he is studying, not to his gadgets. . . . The only sensible gadget for doing anthropological research is the human understanding and a notebook. Anthropology

provides an artistic impression of the original, not a photographic one.
I am not a camera. (1989:xxiii, orig. 1957)

Others have made the related argument that raw transcription produces more
data than the anthropologist can intelligently interpret (e.g., Epstein 1967:222).
    Some scholars have refused to accept these principled defenses of legal an-
thropology's reliance on summary and paraphrase. In a strongly worded critique
in 1975, David Turton wondered whether ethnographers of law and politics
were not simply covering up the fact that they were not fluent in their subjects'
languages. Considering the question of why anthropologists have given little
attention to public political discussions, Turton wrote,

> I should offer some explanation as to why this whole subject has been
> overlooked, even by those anthropologists who have presumably had
> to sit through many hours of political oratory during the course of
> their fieldwork. It could be, of course, that after due study and con-
> sideration they came to the conclusion that this public discussion was
> mere window dressing, masking the underlying principles of social
> organisation. They may have been helped to this conclusion by ob-
> serving that there is very little element of surprise in the decisions
> reached by public meetings—that the decisions are, more often than
> not, foregone conclusions. From personal experience, however, I think
> it is just as likely that the anthropologists concerned simply did not,
> and indeed could not, understand well enough what was going on in
> public discussions until it was too late. (1975:164)

Turton's concern cannot be lightly dismissed. Think about the difficulty that
even educated laypeople who are native speakers of English have following
the proceedings in American courts. Now add to this inherent difficulty the
problems faced by an anthropologist who may have had only a few months'
experience with the radically unfamiliar language in which the court is being
conducted. Bohannan wrote in 1957, "My wife and I used no interpreters
among the Tiv until we had been with them for almost a year. By that time we
spoke Tiv quite fluently and understood it well" (1989:xxi). How many legal
anthropologists could say this? How many could claim the kind of fluency that
Turton argued for? We must at least consider the possibility that some of our
canonical knowledge is suspect because the researchers did not fully understand
what was being said.
    Whether because of conscious methodological choice or communication
difficulties, the present record of legal anthropology is not one that permits
much analysis of the details of the discourse of legal proceedings. The potential
consequences of this state of affairs are obvious. First, our ability to evaluate

the discipline's claims about law and legal procedure is impaired. Suppose, for example, that we want to ask whether there really was a "reasonable man" in Barotse jurisprudence. For all the breadth and depth of Gluckman's cases, we still cannot pursue the question with the same intensity that Gregory Matoesian brings to the issue of the revictimization of American rape victims. Even Bohannan, with his very real concern for the authentic Tiv perspective, does not afford us this luxury. As we contemplate instance after instance, we are left wondering whether the whole field of comparative law might not look different if the data permitted us to test claims about law and legal discourse on the microlinguistic level.

The state of the ethnographic record may also have compromised legal anthropology's concept of culture. Most classic ethnographies of law suggest a cultural model wherein rules direct action. The contentions of litigants and the decisions of Tiv *jirs*, Barotse courts, and Cheyenne councils are explained in terms of the substantive principles and forms of argument that constitute part of every member's cultural literacy. There are moments of resistance and opportunities for change, but it is clear that rules direct action and not vice versa.

The current idea of culture is considerably messier. In a study of police culture, criminologists Clifford Shearing and Richard Ericson (1991) provide a fascinating example of the application of contemporary notions of culture in a law-related context. They look closely at the stories that police officers tell about how they do their jobs. Sets of rules prove to be too simple to account for the cultural knowledge that these stories reflect. Instead, "[s]omehow competent officers know what to do" (Shearing and Ericson 1991:487). In their effort to understand what the officers know and how they know it, Shearing and Ericson ask, "What if we took police stories seriously as *stories?*" (1991:488). Some stories, they find, are merely short-lived descriptions of the world as police officers experience it. Others are told and retold until they reach mythic status as "carefully crafted poetic pieces that capture the insights and wisdom of countless officers who have, through their telling of it, embellished and polished the story" (Shearing and Ericson 1991:491). Stories are thus revealed to be both reflections of the police officers' world and resources for reproducing and sometimes transforming it.

Reflecting on what police stories suggest about the nature of culture, Shearing and Ericson reject the image of officers learning rules that are then followed or violated. Rather, the officers "are active participants in the construction of action" (Shearing and Ericson 1991:500). The stories provide open-ended information to other members of the police culture — "gambits and strategies" that they can use in constructing culturally appropriate action in new and often unforeseen circumstances. Culture itself is less a set of rules than a flexible set of resources, "a poetic system that enables action through a trope and precedent based logic" (Shearing and Ericson 1991:500). Importantly, it is the stories — the linguistic practice — that enable the interpretation of culture, and not the other way around. We are left to wonder whether legal anthropology's understanding of culture may have been impoverished by the unavailability of equivalent stories.

Questioning Huli Women

Laurence Goldman was an early and strident advocate of the view that the record of legal anthropology is linguistically inadequate. Remarking caustically on Bohannan's claim a generation ago that the "literature in legal anthropology [was] small and almost all good" (1964:199), Goldman writes that "this same and now large corpus of works is, in certain critical and fundamental respects, inadequate and almost all bad" (1986:350). That inadequacy derives from "problems of legitimation and ethnographic reliability" (Goldman 1986:350) — in particular the absence of authentic discourse from case reports.

In his initial effort to prove the point, Goldman (1986) examined gender dynamics in the dispute processes of the Huli, a people of highland Papua New Guinea. His investigation begins in the informal, ad hoc public moots, where many disputes are heard and mediated. Goldman notes that the traditional ethnographic view has held that the moots are a striking instance of gender equity in a society that "in most domains is typified by a rigid role differentiation along sexual lines" (1986:355). A preliminary analysis tends to support this view. For example, although only men can serve as mediators, women may speak as disputants, witnesses, or supporters, and the stated norms for receiving their testimony are strongly egalitarian. Moreover, the moot procedure seems unchoreographed. Litigants present their claims in many ways, and there are no preset rules for deciding who talks when. Consistent with the open-ended nature of the process, "women are not subject to any constraint on the length, locale or format of their speaking turns" (Goldman 1986:355).

In 1973, the national government created a multilevel official legal system to function alongside the moots. Village courts form the lowest level of the government system. Although their stated purpose is to mediate informally in the manner of the moots, the village courts have evolved into adjudicatory rather than conciliatory bodies. Significantly, village court procedure quickly moved away from the unrestricted conversation of the moots and toward the controlled question-and-answer style (Goldman calls it "ping-pong") characteristic of Western courts.

Among the questions Goldman poses are, first, whether the reputedly egalitarian norms of the moots have been carried over to the village courts and, second, whether the moots actually practice the gender equity that is conventionally attributed to them. After a study of question forms in cases involving illicit premarital sex that is strikingly similar to Matoesian's work on rape trials, Goldman answers both questions in the negative.

With respect to the first question, Goldman's data on the distributional patterns of question forms are especially compelling. He reports initially that questions in general are four times more common in village courts than in moots. This confirms the accepted view that the village courts have gravitated toward foreign procedures.[3] Goldman also finds that in the village courts almost four times as many questions are addressed to women as to men. Because so many of the questions asked of women involve "the extraction of a high degree of detail about the sexual acts committed," he concludes that they reflect an "attempt to shame women" (Goldman 1986:375). Finally, examining the use of WH questions (who, what, where, when, why, how) in village courts, Goldman (1986:377) notes that "why" questions are commonly put to women but *never* to men. The reason for this disparity, he believes, is that women are made to feel that they must explain their actions, while men are comfortable leaving their motives ambiguous: "they leave it up to their 'male' audience to construct possible reasons for their actions" (Goldman 1986:377).

Addressing the second issue — whether even the moots really are egalitarian — Goldman finds that comparable, if subtler, gender inequities are present in the linguistic practice of the moots. For example, questions that take the form of declarative statements with interrogative intonation are put to women much more often than to men. Goldman believes such questions to be coercive because "they tell more than they ask" (1986:375). He also examines relative frequencies of "affirmative/negative" questions, which call for yes/no answers, versus types of questions that permit more discursive answers and even invite the display of rhetorical skills. The former, which are inherently more controlling and coercive, are directed at women substantially more often than at men. Goldman further notes that when affirmative/negative questions are put to men, they are often softened or "rendered non-confrontative"; thus, the coercive form is revealed to be "the dispreferred form for soliciting responses from male addressees" (1986:375).

Having reviewed these and numerous other details of question structure, Goldman concludes that there is a "remarkable degree of fit or internal consistency . . . in terms of the hypothesis that, on the evidence of interrogative form, both moots and courts are more coercive of women" than of men (1986:377). As between moots and village courts, he finds that the deferential, nonconfrontational style of the former has been carried over to the latter only in instances of interaction with men. Thus, the ideology of gender equality is an illusion in both venues, and even the egalitarian formalities have disappeared in the village courts. But the illusion can be appreciated only through the microanalysis of the actual language of disputing.

Goldman sees a relationship between these microlinguistic practices and the dominant discourse of gender relations among the Huli: "One could go on to argue that this [linguistic coercion of women] is related to male power or discriminatory ideologies typical of Highlands [New Guinea] societies. The interrogative process becomes a means of playing out inter-sex dramas, the process *is* the punitive repercussion of male power" (1986:377). In other words, the interrogative process not only exemplifies the patriarchy of Huli society but also helps to ratify and reproduce it.

As in the Anglo-American cases we have examined, linguistic practice is both effect and cause of the dominant discourse about Huli gender relations. And as in those cases, new insights into that discourse have been made possible only by detailed linguistic analysis. This is a level of analysis, Goldman argues convincingly, that has been absent from legal ethnography, perhaps by conscious choice or perhaps because of a lack of understanding of what people are saying.

Goldman on Accident

In subsequent work on Huli law, Goldman continues to press the point that a meaningful understanding of law needs to be based on a genuine appreciation of the discourse that constitutes it—whether that discourse takes place in English or some other language. In his book *The Culture of Coincidence* (1993), Goldman uses Huli linguistic data to attack a widely accepted precept of comparative jurisprudence: the idea that non-Western people do not recognize the possibility of accident.

According to this traditional view, as Goldman describes it, the non-Western legal mind cannot accept that an injury has occurred for no reason at all and instead insists on finding a responsible agent. Sometimes the agent is a human being who both intends and causes (in a Newtonian sense) the injury, as in the case of a person who deliberately strikes another with a rock. This kind of responsibility is compatible with Western notions of fault. In other cases, however, there is no evidence of an agent of this conventional sort. In such cases, the traditional analysis holds, non-Western legal reasoning assumes that someone must have used supernatural means to cause the harm and seeks out likely suspects. When a plausible candidate is found, that person is held responsible, regardless of whether he or she actually caused the harm through intent or negligence. The idea of accident—that is, the occurrence of misfortune without a human agent behind it—is claimed to be missing in most non-Western societies. (This is not to say that Westerners do not prefer to assign blame, merely that they recognize cases in which accident must be the accepted explanation.)

For example, in a case reported from the Brazilian Kuikuru (Dole 1966:76), when two houses in a village burned down, there was no thought that it was just an accident. Instead, a shaman conducted a divining ceremony during which he conversed with interested members of the community and then fell into a trance. He named as the culprit a man who had left the village several years ago and never returned. Because changing residence was regarded as an admission of being a troublemaker, the shaman's explanation met with general acceptance; Sherlock Holmes–style questions about whether the suspect could really have "done it" were never raised. The traditional view thus ascribes to non-Western legal systems a theory of strict liability. Liability is strict in two senses: someone must be liable for every harm, and a suspect cannot avoid liability by saying that he or she did not intend the injury or was not physically responsible for it.

To set the stage for his examination of Huli legal discourse, Goldman revisits some of the great classics of anthropology and their arguments about the role of accident in non-Western law. The idea that the non-Western mind cannot accept accident dates back at least to Lucien Lévy-Bruhl's *La mentalité primitive* (1923). In a passage Goldman (1993:45) quotes at length, Lévy-Bruhl writes, "[T]he very idea of accident is inconceivable to the primitive mind. . . . In fact, there is no such thing as chance. The idea of accident does not even occur to a native's mind, while on the contrary the idea of witchcraft is always present."

The most famous ethnographic explication of Lévy-Bruhl's theory is E. E. Evans-Pritchard's *Witchcraft, Oracles, and Magic among the Azande* (1937). His prototype of Azande reasoning about misfortune is the case of the falling granary. A man was sitting in the shade beside an elevated grain-storage vessel. As the man leaned on the granary, one of its wooden supports broke. The heavy granary toppled over, killing the man. In such instances, how do the Azande explain what has happened? They do not, Evans-Pritchard asserts, call them accidents, as we almost certainly would. Rather, the Azande see these occurrences as manifestations of the supernatural powers of witches. Such happenings occasion searches for the human agents whose evil intentions were played out through witchcraft. In the end, every death and serious illness is someone's responsibility. Things do not just happen; people make them happen through the machinations of witchcraft.

But just how did Evans-Pritchard come to these conclusions about Azande thought? What sort of data did he collect, and how? How did he analyze the data? Asking such questions leads into the now-familiar territory of reflexive anthropology, where it is fashionable to dismiss nearly all that has come before as hopelessly biased and irretrievably useless. If we reexamine Evans-Pritchard according to those standards, we learn that much of his work was conducted on the veranda of his house or in front of his tent, through interpreters, and that he did not know much about the Azande language. It now seems clear that he did not know enough to avoid subtle misunderstandings of how the Azande talk and reason about misfortune. Perhaps the "Azande" theory of misfortune, which has become a paradigm case in the anthropological literature, would be unfamiliar to the Azande themselves.

Goldman (1993:66–67) documents the export of Evans-Pritchard's Azande model — with all its faults — to other African societies and later to the Melanesian ethnographic literature. Even the hill tribes of Papua New Guinea, the neighbors of the Huli, are said to conform to the Azande paradigm. In case after case, ethnographers report the rejection of accident in favor of strict liability. For example,

[N]o distinction appeared to be drawn between intentional and unintentional killing, as among the Kikuyu, Kamba and certain Nigerian tribes. . . .

[A]mong the Arusha "no jural distinction" is made between premeditated and accidental homicide. . . .

Among the Ashanti, all accidents are understood as ultimately the result of offences against supernatural agencies. . . .

"[T]he Melanesian view about compensation for injury caused to person or property is far more like one of absolute liability than liability based on fault" . . . .

[T]he Jale [of New Guinea] . . . do not "distinguish between intent, negligence, inadvertence, and accident as aggravating or extenuating circumstances". . . .

Cases such as these lead to an impression of fundamental differences between *us* and *them*. They become the basis for arguing that *our* legal system is rational and fair, whereas *theirs* is magical and arbitrary. Our worldview, our legal culture, our system of thought—all are different in their core from those of more "primitive" people. In short, we are not like them; we and they inhabit different worlds of thought about causality, responsibility, and blame. But, argues Goldman, the linguistic support for this conclusion is suspect. By sitting on the veranda (figuratively, if not literally) and by failing to know the local language well enough to have a real understanding of what was being said, non-discourse-oriented anthropologists may have been imposing our linguistic, legal, and cultural templates on other societies.

To test the reliability of legal anthropology's conventional wisdom about accident, Goldman adduces further linguistic evidence from his long-term study of the Huli. This evidence suggests that the Huli do indeed distinguish between accident and intentionality, but—and this is the critical point—they do so in ways that differ fundamentally from how we do so in English. As a result, unless we understand their language in considerable depth, we run the risk of drawing an erroneous conclusion about the differences between our legal reasoning and theirs.

"In English," Goldman observes, "our notions of accident frequently discriminate between actions that are under the control of agents and happenings that are essentially non-agentive in nature" (1993:1). A primary way we indicate this difference in English is through the use of adverbs such as *intentionally, willfully,* and *deliberately,* versus *accidentally, inadvertently,* and *unintentionally.* These adverbs qualify statements such as "X hit Y." With one of the former adverbs, we blame; with one of the latter, we exonerate. Similarly, terms such as *arson* and *murder* convey intentionality, whereas *setting on fire* is ambiguous with respect to intention. But these are English-language concepts and modes of expression. It would be a great mistake to assume that their simple presence or absence in another language indicates that we do or do not share that society's approach to legal responsibility. Rather, we need to be prepared for the possibility that another society might linguistically encode similar legal concepts in other ways — ways that are so fundamentally different from our own that we may miss them altogether if we cannot hear what is being said with an almost-native ear.

The Culture of Coincidence examines a number of Huli discussions about a death that had occurred. The facts are simple; the interpretation is not. A woman named Gegai was visiting another woman. The second woman's home burned down, and Gegai died in the fire. Was this occurrence an accident, or was it someone's fault? These are the questions with which the Huli struggled. The occurrence was discussed in various ways over a period of time in Huli public life. The sum total of all that got said by all the parties involved constitutes the Huli equivalent of an inquest or a trial. It is this public talk that Goldman examines in an effort to understand how the Huli manage accident and blame.

Goldman's conclusion is that the Huli do indeed think of some occurrences as accidents, much as we do, and make no effort to assign responsibility for their occurrence to a human agent. His evidence is complex. The discussion transcripts themselves require ninety-two published pages and his analysis of them more than two hundred additional pages. We review only a small segment of that evidence here. But the following examples serve to illustrate Goldman's method and more generally to demonstrate the essential role of microlinguistic analysis in revealing Huli legal theory.

Verb Forms and Accidents

In the first example, Text 6.1, two members of the community discuss the fire and then begin to draw analogies to other events that our legal system might characterize as accidental. (In this and the following texts, each italicized Huli line is followed by Goldman's translation into idiomatic English. In most of the Huli lines in Text 6.1, one word is in Roman type. This is a *habitual* verb form, which is discussed in the paragraph following Text 6.1. The translation for the habitual verb form is in italics in the English line that follows.)

TEXT **6.1** (Goldman 1993:90–91)

SPEAKER *1*

(1) *Anda dalu* daga
(2) When houses burnt, then people *used to get burnt.*
(3) *Wiya dagua dedagoni*
(4) What was there got burnt like this.

SPEAKER 2

(5)   *Iba* piaga[4]
(6)   People *used to drown.*

SPEAKER 1

(7)   *Iba* piaga
(8)   People *used to drown.*

SPEAKER 2

(9)   *Iba longai* piaga
(10) Misadventures *occur* involving trees.

SPEAKER 1

(11) *Iba longai* piaga
(12) Misadventures *occur* involving trees.

SPEAKER 2

(13) *Uli* piaga
(14) People *used to fall* into holes.

SPEAKER 1

(15) *Uli* piaga
(16) People *used to fall* into holes.
(17) *Nde kira kirali kirahowa mendego* pilaga *wiyagoni*
(18) Whilst two people were together *one used to fall* down.
(19) *O biago ale bidagoni*
(20) Like the event[s] referred to it [this one] has happened.

None of the Huli words in Text 6.1 can be translated directly as some variant of "accident." Yet it is perfectly clear that the two speakers intend to put
the present burning incident in the context of similar misfortunes that have no
human cause. They accomplish this, Goldman argues, through the repeated
use of the habitual verb form (the nonitalicized Huli words, translated in italics). This form indicates that the described action occurs customarily, typically,
usually. The habitual form is gnomic, meaning that it is used to state timeless,
proverbial truths. It is a way of showing *grammatically* the normal, unremarkable quality of what is being talked about. In English, by contrast, we usually
convey the same idea *adverbially*, by our choice of words. Rather than simply
changing the form of the verb, we add such words as *usually* or *customarily*.[5]

In Text 6.1, the habitual form of the verbs indicates the ordinariness of
what happened in the case under consideration. Sentence (1), translated as (2)

"When houses burnt, then people used to get burnt," is a statement about how things usually work in Huli. The logic is this: people live in grass houses; grass houses catch fire easily; when houses burn, people can get burned, too. Sentence (1) — like the others describing analogous misfortunes — neither identifies a human agent nor compels a search for one. When properly understood, it is clear evidence that accident as we know it is also a logical possibility in Huli. Without the detailed understanding of the habitual form that Goldman provides, however, we would probably miss the point entirely. Looking only at a literal translation into English, we might well conclude that the text has nothing to do with recognizing the possibility of accident.

This single piece of evidence might suffice to make Goldman's point, but there is much more. For example, in the following two English sentences, note that identical verb forms are used to convey very different meanings:

(1)   The man hurt.
(2)   The man hurt the woman.

In sentence (1), the verb *hurt* describes the state the man was in at some point in the past. It lacks an object of any sort. It simply describes how things were. By contrast, sentence (2) employs *hurt* to express the idea that the man did something to the woman that resulted in her being in a particular state. Outside its context, we cannot tell which meaning of *hurt* is intended; the verb form alone does not resolve the ambiguity. It is easy to imagine a person who lacks facility in English becoming confused about the logic of the two sentences.

But this is English. The Huli language does not allow for this sort of confusion. Sentences (1) and (2) could not be confused in Huli because different forms of the verb would be used to express the different ideas of state of being (1) and cause and effect (2). For example, the verb *burn* in Huli would be *da* if describing a state of being and *dela* if implying cause and effect. Thus, sentences (3) and (4) below, which employ identical verb forms in English, would employ the distinct forms *da* (3) and *dela* (4) in Huli (Goldman 1993: 95–96).

(3)   The house burned.
(4)   X burned the house.

The point of this example is once again that Huli grammar not only permits but indeed *requires* the speaker to distinguish between an accidental burning and one caused by an agent. In talking about the case in question, Goldman emphasizes, Huli speakers and listeners were constantly attuned to this distinction — a distinction that makes sense only to people who recognize the possibility of accident. As in the example in Text 6.1, the distinction could be readily lost in the process of translating Huli into a language (such as English) that lacks separate forms for transitive and intransitive verbs. We are left to wonder, as Goldman wants us to, whether Evans-Pritchard and others might have missed such subtle encoding mechanisms in reaching the conclusion that the non-Western legal mind does not recognize accident.

Ergativity

A final illustration involves the property of *ergativity*. In languages that have this property, nouns and pronouns that are the subjects of transitive verbs — that is, they are the *agents* responsible for the action of the verbs — are grammatically marked so as to distinguish them from nouns and pronouns that are intransitive subjects (Dixon 1979). English obviously is not an ergative language in this sense.[6] When the first-person-singular pronoun is the subject of an English sentence, it is always *I*, regardless of whether the sentence is *I jumped* or *I hit the ball*. If English were ergative, the *I*'s in the two examples would be different in some way. Typically, the transitive subject carries a marker, as in *I (AGENT) hit the ball*. But since English is not ergative, the form of the word *I* does not reveal its status as an agent; we must listen for the information to be provided by additional words.

Huli, by contrast, is ergative. The two Huli sentences that follow are among Goldman's many examples of how ergativity functions to mark agency and responsibility. In each case, Goldman's English translation follows the Huli sentence (Goldman 1993:121).

(5)   *Ibu andame dene . . .*
(6)   She got burnt by means of the house.
(7)   *Kenobi one biagome inaga ainya delara*
(8)   Kenobi's wife burnt my mother.

In each of these examples, the key element is *-me*, the suffix that marks an agent or instrument. In sentence (5), *-me* is affixed to *anda-* (house) and connotes that the house is the responsible agent. *Ibu* (She), the subject of the sentence, is unmarked, meaning that *She* is not an agent. The ergative features of the sentence thus imply that the burning was an accident, in the sense that an inanimate object — the house — rather than a person is identified as the responsible agent. A more idiomatic English version of the same idea might be *She accidentally got killed when the house burned down*. In sentence (7), the agentive suffix is attached to part of the phrase identifying Kenobi's wife (the word for *wife* is *one*; *biago-* is an intensifying particle, which emphasizes the identification). The word for *mother* (*ainya*), the object of the verb, is unmarked. The agentive suffix identifies Kenobi's wife as the responsible agent. To achieve the same effect in English, we might use the adverb *intentionally*, or perhaps we would say *Kenobi's wife was responsible for burning my mother*.

The ergativity problem is a further reminder that the absence of a vocabulary of accident in a particular language does not mean that its speakers do not recognize the concept. What we do in English by using an adverb such as *accidentally* or *intentionally*, the Huli do with grammatical forms. But to know this, we have to understand the details of how Huli grammar works and how such notions are encoded within their language. If we work in another culture with a limited understanding of the local language or through an interpreter, as many anthropologists do, we run the substantial risk of missing the point of what is being said. Under such circumstances, we are likely to hear through our own linguistic template or that of an interpreter who strives to say things in ways that will make sense to the English-speaking anthropologist. If we do not hear the equivalents of such words as *accidentally* and *intentionally*, we may conclude that the other culture does not recognize the concepts that these words encode in English. The substance of what is being conveyed through the *structure* of the other language may get misunderstood or lost altogether. It is this problem, Goldman suspects, that lies at the heart of anthropology's longstanding but erroneous presumption that *they* differ from *us* in their inability to comprehend the possibility of chance occurrence. Goldman's linguistic analysis suggests an alternative presumption: that all cultures have notions of accident but use different linguistic strategies to express them.

Repairing Relationships in Weyewa

Much other work in linguistic anthropology confirms Goldman's methodological point about the importance of detailed analysis of actual legal discourse, even as — ironically — it challenges his thesis about the prevalence of the concept of accident. In *Power in Performance: The Creation of Textual Authority in Weyewa Ritual Speech* (1990), Joel Kuipers reports on his extended study of ritual speech performance by the Weyewa people of eastern Indonesia.[7] Although its substantive goals are somewhat different, Kuipers's book is strikingly similar to Goldman's in the depth of its linguistic analysis and the richness of the transcript evidence that is adduced to support each argument.

Kuipers's subject is a form of ritual speech, generally constructed in poetic couplets, that is employed in all Weyewa ceremonial events. This speech is conceived of as "words of the ancestors." Such words "transmit the ancestral 'voice' in formal, poetic, but intelligible monologues that narrate the history of promises, obligations, and commitments to ongoing relationships of ceremonial exchange" (Kuipers 1990:ix). Their ritual purpose is to remind people of and thus restore a set of essential relationships. For the Weyewa, "complete saturation in the words of the ancestors is an important goal guiding the stages of a prolonged ritual process of atonement and exchange between the ancestors and their descendants, between wife-givers and wife-takers, and ultimately between life and death" (Kuipers 1990:1–2). Kuipers focuses on the details of the "sociolinguistic trajectory," whereby talk about some problem progresses "from a squabbling debate to an utterly unified and monologic *performance* of the words of the ancestors" (Kuipers 1990:2). He calls this process *entextualization*, a linguistic concept that has roots in the early twentieth-century work of the Russian semiotician Mikhail Bakhtin (1981, orig. 1935) and is the subject of a vast contemporary literature (e.g., Bauman and Briggs 1990; Silverstein and Urban 1996; Heffer, Rock, and Conley 2013).

One of Kuipers's specific topics is the question of how people talk about misfortune or calamity in ritual contexts. Misfortune is typically characterized as "personal, isolating, disorienting, violating, sudden, extraordinary and 'hot'" (Kuipers 1990:38). Its personal quality is reflected in the Weyewa word for misfortune itself (*podda*), which refers simultaneously to the disastrous event and the experiences of the victim. Misfortunes are reported in phrases that vividly depict the event as being aimed at the victim (for example, "*wolota mawennal*/the blowgun strikes exactly" and "*reketa manindo*/the dart hits its mark"). Such characterizations are consistent with the testimony of victims about their sense of being singled out and personally attacked by the event. For example, a man whose father died suddenly cried out, "*rudduka pandoku-ngga*/I was set down wrongly"; "*bondala pa-ndenga-ngga*/I was just placed aside" (Kuipers 1990:39).

But who or what aims misfortune at the victim? The answer often lies in "ruptured *relationships* among specific actors who participated in the event," and in particular in neglect of the bonds between the human and the spirit worlds (Kuipers 1990:42). As Kuipers's italics suggest, the word *relationships* is critical. Weyewa do not usually blame misfortune on the malevolence of an individual human or spirit agent. Instead, they ask whether the relationships among all those — human and spirit — with an interest in the event have been conscientiously maintained. Kuipers illustrates the point with the case of a man who broke his arm when his horse threw him after seeing a snake. A diviner seeking the cause of the misfortune ultimately focused on the man's late father's failure to fulfill a bargain he had made with the earth spirit and on the man's subsequent failure to assume responsibility for the bargain after his father's death. No one was deemed solely responsible for the calamity; rather, there was a collective lack of attention to the essential lines of communication between father and son and between the human and the spirit worlds. As the diviner put it, "*nda'iki li'i pana'u*/there were no words of instruction"; "*nda'iki li'i pananggo*/there was no voice of command" (Kuipers 1990:42).[8]

What emerges from this subtle analysis is a picture of a society whose outlook on misfortune is difficult to pigeonhole. On the one hand, it would be an oversimplification to class the Weyewa among Lévy-Bruhl's "primitives," to whom "the very idea of accident is inconceivable" (Goldman 1993:45). On the contrary, Kuipers reports that many Weyewa are familiar with Western scientific explanations of calamity and see them as useful in certain limited circumstances. But it would be grossly inaccurate to describe Western notions of chance and causation as dominant or even widely accepted among the Weyewa. As Kuipers concludes, "For Weyewa, misfortune (*podda*) results when persons exercise their judgment as individuals and thus fail to recognize the authority of, or otherwise abide by, collective agreements and conventions" (1990:53–54). Such failures lead to imbalance in relationships among people and between people and spirits; that imbalance, if uncorrected, can lead to calamity.[9]

Conclusion: Has Legal Anthropology Missed the Point?

So is Goldman wrong? Does Kuipers's analysis, drawing on linguistic resources as rich as Goldman's, undercut the latter's claim that legal anthropology has missed the point about accident? In a narrow sense, perhaps; but in a broader sense, the answer to these questions is clearly no. In fact, the Weyewa case helps to make Goldman's ultimate point even more convincingly. The Weyewa case, while it may not support the universality of accident on the Western model, does underscore the significance of a language-based anthropology of law.

In earlier editions, we ended this chapter as follows:

> This realization leads us back to the most fundamental question: Whether the whole discipline of legal anthropology stands on suspect terrain because of its early practitioners' lack of linguistic skills. Only time and more work like that of Goldman and Kuipers will tell. But regardless of what it eventually proves about the soundness of legal anthropology's received wisdom, such work does demonstrate incontrovertibly that in any culture a full appreciation of the law and its power depends on a thorough understanding of everyday linguistic practice.

From the perspective of 2018—after time and more work have told, as it were—it is clear that legal anthropology has come to terms with the suspect terrain of its origins. The discipline has survived and prospered. This relative prosperity owes much to contemporary legal anthropology's commitment to "a thorough understanding of everyday linguistic practice." We conclude this third edition of this chapter with a brief recent example that illustrates this point.

Anthropologist Larry Nesper (2007) has studied legal discourse in the tribal court of the Lac du Flambeau Ojibwe tribe in Wisconsin. He describes the development of tribal courts as part of a process over the past fifty-plus years that "has transformed American Indian tribes from largely powerless and impoverished kinship-based communities into neocolonial statelike structures" (Nesper 2007:675). Tribal court proceedings have become sites where tensions between a kinship-based tradition and a state-like present are worked out. These courts, like all courts, are "local theatrical sites" (Nesper 2007:676). As such, Ojibwe courts have become "sites of display, contest, and reproduction both for a traditional model of community relations and for relations organized under the political ideology of sovereignty as a Tribe" (Nesper 2007:677; compare Richland 2008).

Nesper focuses on the *pragmatics*—the study of the contribution of context to meaning—of several cases involving alleged violations of recently codified tribal law regulating on- and off-reservation hunting and fishing. In one revelatory case, the defendants were cited by a state game warden when hunting deer at night with a spotlight ("shining") from a road along the reservation boundary. Apparently, the road itself was inside or right on the boundary, but the deer were outside the boundary. The critical legal issue was whether the defendants were engaged in shining outside the reservation, which violates state law, or doing it within the reservation, where the warden had no jurisdiction.

Nesper draws on the microdiscourse of the trial to illuminate the opposition—at the macrodiscourse level—between the state-like tribal code and the customary community relations. For example, when the prosecutor asked the warden what he was *thinking* and *believing* when he issued the citations, the defendants' "lay advocate," a prominent tribal politician, initially objected but then withdrew the objection, almost ostentatiously. By doing so, Nesper infers, the advocate was laying the groundwork for an epistemological challenge to how knowledge about the boundary of the reservation should be evaluated. In one view, the boundary is an objective product of surveying and cartographic representation; in another, it is a more fluid product of traditional knowledge and experience—less a product than a cultural production.

In presenting the defendants' case, the lay advocate first cross-examined the game warden about his lack of knowledge of treaty issues, using *deixis* (linguistic pointing, discussed at length in chapter 10) to emphasize "the great gulf between 'our people'—the defendants and, implicitly, defense counsel and the judge—and 'this man,' the warden" (Nesper 2007:684). (Nesper notes that tribal court participants speak a mix of Ojibwe-English and American Standard English dialects. Among other things, Ojibwe-English speakers generally avoid asking direct questions, which complicates cross-examination.) The defendants' advocate then cross-examined another prosecution witness, a state land-surveying official, to raise doubt about the ostensible certainty of surveying and mapping the reservation's boundary. The advocate then offered three expert witnesses—representatives of "our people" and their ways of *thinking* and *believing* about the boundary and the legality of hunting along it. According to these witnesses, on the basis of their lifelong experience and knowledge of community custom, "as long as your feet were on the reservation or, for that matter, as long as one of the wheels of your car was on the reservation — you could shine a light and then shoot at what your light could reach" (Nesper 2007:684).

In the end, the judge showed respect for both the tribe as state and the tribe as a customary community. In a nod to the former, he accepted the rational boundary model, which he justified as a necessary safety regulation, and found each defendant guilty of one charge. But, out of respect for custom, he dropped two other charges against each and suspended their sentences on condition of good behavior for the rest of the hunting season. The case thus becomes, in Nesper's view, "a lesson in the cost of domestic dependent sovereignty, which is that the Tribe will come to look rather like all of the other sovereigns" (2007:689). Yet it also establishes the tribal court as "a site for negotiating the significance of the cultural distinctiveness of the community" (Nesper 2007:689). Nesper's particular contribution is to show the power of microdiscourse to reveal these larger issues, and in so doing reaffirm the continuing vitality of a linguistically sensitive legal anthropology.

CHAPTER SEVEN

Language Ideology and the Law

Much of the contemporary work on the relationship between language and power has been done under the heading of *language ideology*. (*Ideology of language* and *linguistic ideology* are used more or less synonymously.) In everyday usage, the word *ideology* suggests a body of ideas, a philosophy, or an outlook. It often has political connotations, as in "Marxist ideology" or "conservative ideology." The word also frequently has a pejorative undertone, an implication that one who holds to an ideology is an inflexible and uncritical true believer—I have a well-reasoned political philosophy, but you are a "mere ideologue."[1] Applying everyday thinking to the term *language ideology* yields a definition along the lines of "a body of ideas about language," with a particular focus on political contexts. Although the scholarly definitions of both ideology and language ideology are endlessly debated, the most common social-science usages do not differ materially from their everyday counterparts.

The linguistic anthropologist Michael Silverstein (1985) provides a vivid historical example of language ideology at work. It involves the history of the second-person pronoun *you*, which modern English uses in both the singular and the plural. In Old English, before the Norman Conquest in 1066, the singular variants of this pronoun were *thou* (nominative, or subject) and *thee* (accusative, or object)—*thou* love me, and I love *thee*.[2] The plural forms were precursors of *ye* and *you*—*ye* love me, and I love *you*. The post-Conquest dominance of Norman French speakers added a new element to this pattern of usage: the French practice of always using the plural form in formal speech or in addressing someone of higher social status. Thus, in French, a teacher would address a student in the singular *tu*, but the student would reply in the plural *vous*. By the thirteenth century, this practice had become established in English as well, to the point where "to *thou*" had become a verb meaning "to speak down to." A French language ideology had been imported into English, leading to a change in the meaning and usage of English pronouns.

By 1700, however, *thou* and *thee* had disappeared from ordinary English usage, and Silverstein asks why. Remarkably, it seems to have been the Quakers' fault. The seventeenth century was a time of great upheaval in England, with the beheading of Charles I, Cromwell's commonwealth, the restoration of Charles II, and finally the Glorious Revolution that brought William of Orange to the English throne. Silverstein (1985:247) identifies two significant ideological themes in this century of tumult: "constant struggles between the authority of institutions — Crown, Church, et cetera — and the authority of what we might term the 'empirical evidence of individuals,'" and the "emergence of consciousness of English as a 'language.'" On the question of authority, the Quakers took an extreme pro-individual and egalitarian position. This had a linguistic manifestation: the deliberate and pointed use of *thou* in addressing any individual, regardless of status. Taking advantage of the growing awareness of English as a language, prominent Quakers advanced linguistic purity as a justification for the practice. Historically, they argued, *thou* and *thee* were always and only singular forms, and *you* was just the opposite. In linguistic parlance, these pronouns "indexed," or pointed to, number and number only. To refer to an individual as *you* was thus without linguistic warrant and simply wrong.

The Quaker practice posed a dilemma for those on the authoritarian side, however. I might be *thou*ing you because I think you are of lower status, but how could listeners be sure that I was not using the subversive, leveling Quaker *thou*? In order to avoid association with a disfavored fringe group, those in the mainstream eschewed *any* use of *thou* and *thee*, and the forms all but disappeared from the language in favor of the universal *you*.

Silverstein's point in telling the story is to illustrate the interaction between ideas about the meaning of language — language ideology — and the very structure of language, in this case the norms for using personal pronouns. Over the course of about four hundred years, speakers of English reversed these norms twice in reaction to political and social forces. In the second instance, the precipitating cause was the subversive effort of a dissenting sect, the Quakers. They played on the evolving idea that there was such a thing as a "language" in the sense of a rule-bound system whose traditions and precedents deserved to be taken seriously. Language ideology thus found itself at the intersection of language and society, and in particular at the center of an ongoing struggle for power. At various points people's ideas about language responded to power, abetted its assertion, and spearheaded an effort to subvert it.

In this chapter we will expand our consideration of law, language, and power by analyzing some more recent examples of language ideology at work in legal contexts. We begin by examining in some detail the efforts of anthropologists, linguists, and others to define ideology generally and language ideology in particular. We will then review two contemporary case studies. The first involves an American criminal trial that was strongly influenced by ideas about the nature of language and the hierarchical relation among languages. The second explores the interaction of language ideologies and cultural ideas about gender in an Islamic court in coastal Kenya. Despite the radically different settings, the two studies make a similar point about how language, interacting with ideology, can simultaneously reflect and constitute power.

Defining Terms

Anthropologist Sally Merry (1990:6) has defined *ideology* broadly and inclusively as "a set of symbols which are subject to various kinds of interpretation and manipulation." Writing at the same time, we defined "the core element of ideology as a system of beliefs by which people interpret and impart meaning to events" (Conley and O'Barr 1990:210n10). Following Merry (1986), we distinguished anthropology's emphasis on ideology as a constitutive system of meaning from the Marxist focus on ideology's role in the maintenance of power relations.

A more recent analysis of the meaning of ideology by another anthropologist, Kathryn Woolard (1998), suggests that these same themes continue to dominate the discussion of this elusive concept. Woolard characterizes the very word "ideology" as "itself a text, woven of a tissue of conceptual strands," four of which she discusses in detail. The first strand treats ideology simply as the realm of mental phenomena, having to do with "consciousness, subjective representations, beliefs, ideas," and forming "the more intellectual constituent of culture" (Woolard 1998:5). Some writers in this tradition have insisted that ideology must have an intentional, deliberate, thought-out element, whereas others see it as "behavioral, practical, prereflective, or structural." In the latter sense, ideology is a matter of "the lived relations by which people are connected" in society (Woolard 1998:6), and overlaps with such concepts as hegemony, Pierre Bourdieu's notions of *doxa* and *habitus*, and Foucault's idea of discourse (or *macrodiscourse*, as we have defined it in chapter 1).

Woolard's second strand builds on the first, adding an element of sociocultural relativity to the basic concept of shared ideas and practices. In this view, which Woolard (1998:6) characterizes as "the most widely agreed-upon," the components of ideology are inevitably "derived from, rooted in, reflective of, or responsive to the experience or interests of a particular social position." That is, even though ideologies are often presented as self-evidently true and beyond the need for explanation, they can always be deconstructed and shown to be the product of someone's wants and needs. Ideology, in other words, is "dependent on the material and practical aspects of human life" (Woolard 1998:6).

The third strand is essentially the second with an important new wrinkle: "a direct link to inhabitable positions of power—social, political, economic." Specifically, "ideology is seen as ideas, discourse, or signifying practices in the service of the struggle to acquire or maintain power" (Woolard 1998:7). In law, for example, we have demonstrated that the "official" ideology retailed by legal professionals reflects their experiences and advances their interests. By contrast, the varied legal ideologies held by lay litigants reflect their very different experiences and support their efforts to challenge professional dominance (Conley and O'Barr 1990:150).

The fourth and final strand adds the element of "distortion, illusion, error, mystification, or rationalization." Often, this can be associated with "the defense of interest and power," as with Engels's notion of "false consciousness" (Woolard 1998:7). To return to the example of law, lawyers have long been accused of using language and symbols to mystify inherently simple concepts in order to maintain their monopoly. Richard Abel (1989:18–19) has described this process as "the task of constructing the professional commodity" and insuring that consumers "purchase it rather than simply produce it themselves."

Woolard (1998:7) sees a "great divide" between the second and third strands, between those who view ideology as "neutral" and those who imbue it with "negative values." In the specific case of language ideology, the prevailing definitions seem to be neutral, but much of the research focuses on power relations. It is as if those who study language ideology begin with a neutral stance but are drawn inevitably to questions of power. That has certainly been our personal experience.

In what may be at once the most elemental and most widely cited definition of language ideologies, Alan Rumsey (1990:346) characterizes them as "shared bodies of commonsense notions about the nature of language in the world"—in other words, ideas about language held by groups of people. Judith Irvine and Susan Gal (2000:35) extend this minimalist definition to encompass the relationship between language and society: "the ideas with which participants and observers frame their understandings of linguistic varieties and map those understandings onto people, events, and activities that are significant to them." The linguistic anthropologist John Haviland (2003:764) glosses these two formulations, elegantly and helpfully, as "what ideas the people we work with (and, indeed, we ourselves) have regarding what language is or what language is good for." He further observes that "insofar as ideas about language rub off onto ideas about people, groups, events, and activities, we may find that linguistic ideologies pervade the very stuff of anthropology: social life and its comparative organization" (Haviland 2003:764).

Tracking the differences in approach to the general concept of ideology, many have focused more explicitly on power. Irvine (1989:255; emphasis added), for example, has defined language ideology as "the cultural system of ideas about social and linguistic relationships, *together with their loading of moral and political interests.*" Haviland's (2003:764) version is "ideas about language and its place in social arrangements or its use and usability for social and political ends." Paul Kroskrity (2016:95) has recently offered "beliefs, feelings, and conceptions about language structure and use, which often index the political economic interests of individual speakers, ethnic and other interest groups, and nation-states." And in a definition that presumes awareness and intent — and is splendidly illustrated by his account of *thou* versus *you* — Silverstein (1979:193) proposes "sets of beliefs about language articulated by users as a rationalization or justification of perceived language structure and use."

The Importance of Studying Language Ideology

Regardless of the details of one's preferred definition, most scholars agree that the current attention to ideology has had two significant effects on linguistics itself. The first is renewed respect for "the linguistic 'awareness' of speakers," or "native consciousness" (Kroskrity 2000:5, 8) — in other words, what people think about their own language. These "local models," in Kroskrity's words, are "by definition 'real' to members of the groups in question" and "can provide resources for members to deliberately change their linguistic and discourse forms." Students of language ideology see the linguistic models of speakers not as "competing with expert or scientific systems," as many early linguists did, but rather as complementary forms of sociocultural data (Kroskrity 2000:7).

With a few exceptions, until recently linguistics had chosen to discount or ignore speakers' linguistic theories in favor of the "scientific" perspective of the analyst (see Kroskrity 2000:6–7).[3] This was true even of disciplines that emphasized the detailed analysis of language usage. Thus, conversation analysis has generally avoided consideration of speakers' ideas, even as it combs transcripts for the rules that those same speakers appear to attend to. Similarly, William Labov (1979:329), who pioneered the correlation of language variation with social factors, dismisses the possibility that ideology could "alter the socially determined pattern of linguistic variation."

Nonetheless, Labov's work, sometimes described as *correlational sociolinguistics*, also provides a vivid illustration of the salience of native consciousness. As we described in chapter 1, Labov demonstrates strong correlations between patterns of linguistic variation and social class. One can read his research as relating not only to speakers' experience of class but also to their class aspirations. In what may be his most famous study, Labov (1966) shows that employees of an upscale New York department store pronounced *r* after vowels (for example, saying "New York" rather than "New Yawk") — thought to be an upper-class tendency — more frequently than their counterparts in a discount store. In addition, the post-vocalic *r* was more common when the speakers were asked to repeat themselves and, presumably, were paying more conscious attention to their speech.

Although Labov (1979:329) expressly denies the power of language ideology, at least in the sense of "native consciousness," to alter the pattern of linguistic variation, the current view would be that he has demonstrated precisely the effect that he denies. Recall that he characterizes the pattern of variation as "socially determined." But how does social determination work? What, specifically, is the social agent of determination? The answer must be *language ideology*. In Irvine and Gal's (2000:35) phrasing, Labov's *r*-pronouncers had some ideas with which they framed their understandings of linguistic varieties, and they mapped those understandings onto events that were significant to them. Labov discovered *how* language can vary according to social context. Language ideology helps to explain *why*.

The influence of language ideology can also be seen in conversation analysis. In the original 1998 edition of this book (pp. 19–20), we wrote, accurately, that "most conversation analysts have limited themselves to the study of *how* people manage conversations, prescinding from such questions as *why* they do what they do. The focus has been on the mechanics of conversation rather than on the social and political objectives the parties may be pursuing." This has changed. Responding to the concerns that have animated the study of language ideology, conversation analysts have increasingly sought to tie speakers' explicit language practices to their implicit purposes. Some scholars doing work that is methodologically indistinguishable from conversation analysis have self-consciously called their research "discourse analysis" in order to distance themselves from conversation analysts' longstanding aversion to questions of power. Some of the more recent work has been done under the rubric of "critical discourse analysis," with "critical" meaning "focused on power relations." Several collections have used conversation analysis to examine ideologies of language and gender (see Hellinger and Bußmann 2002; Litosseliti and Sunderland 2002; McIllvenny 2002). Conversation and discourse analysts have begun to debate "what counts as context for analyzing talk, what it means to say something is relevant to participants, the relative status of analysts' and participants' understandings of participant actions, and, most broadly, the role of objectivity and politics in intellectual inquiry" (McElhinny 2003:849).

The second effect of paying attention to language ideology has been to highlight "the non-referential functions of language" (Kroskrity 2000:7). The most basic definition of *referential* is suggested by its root, *refer*, "meaning simply to point out something for the purpose of describing or saying something about it" (Mertz 1985:8). As the linguist John Lyons (1968:404) put it a generation ago, "the relationship which holds between words and things (their referents) is the relationship of *reference*: words *refer to* (rather than 'signify,' or 'name') things." Thus, the referential function of language involves using it to denote, or refer to, things that are being talked about. This is the function of language that people are most attuned to when they are beginning to study a foreign language, studying lists of words and phrases, listening to tapes, and generally trying to learn "how to say things."

The nonreferential functions comprise everything else that language can do, including constructing, reflecting, and resisting social structure. As Kroskrity (2000:7) points out, "much of the meaning and hence communicative value that linguistic forms have for their speakers lies in the 'indexical' connections between the linguistic signs and the contextual factors of their use — their connection to speakers, settings, topics, institutions, and other aspects of their sociocultural worlds." In other words, much of the work of language is done in the nonreferential realm.

We believe that Kroskrity's claim that attention to ideology has opened up the previously neglected nonreferential aspects of language is somewhat over-stated. To cite one example, our own work in the 1980s and early 1990s on rule-oriented versus relational accounts of legal problems (Conley and O'Barr 1990) seems to be precisely about the connection between linguistic signs and settings, topics, and institutions, even though we failed to characterize it in terms of language ideology. And in his study of *r*-pronouncers, William Labov, even as he disavows the efficacy of language ideology, seems to be proving its importance. We think it might be more accurate to say that the current focus on language ideology has sharpened linguists' appreciation for the nonreferential by making explicit that which was formerly implicit.

Kroskrity also identifies four substantive features of language ideologies that have proven to carry particular analytical power. First, "language ideologies represent the perception of language and discourse that is constructed in the interest of a specific social or cultural group" (Kroskrity 2000:8). This is the self-interested aspect of ideology in the general sense that we discussed earlier. Kroskrity gives the example of national language movements: although their stated purpose is usually to promote efficiency in communication, they can almost always be shown to benefit some groups at the expense of others. In fact, the same argument can be made about linguistic scholarship itself: its ostensibly disinterested (and, in theory, purely referential) texts can "be read subversively as powerful means of controlling the process of producing and receiving dis-course" (Bauman and Briggs 2000:139).

Kroskrity's (2000:12) second point is that language ideologies are "grounded in social experience which is never uniform." That is, language ideologies should be presumed to be multiple, since every sociocultural group can be sub-divided along such axes as gender, class, generation, and elite status. In simplest terms, when you find *a* language ideology, look for more. Third, "members may display varying degrees of awareness of language ideologies" (Kroskrity 2000:18). Awareness is likely to correlate with the way in which an ideology is put into practice. Those who are more aware tend to be more active in contesting existing, dominant ideologies, whereas "merely practical consciousness" typifies "relatively unchallenged, highly naturalized, and definitively dominant ideologies" (Kroskrity 2000:19). The Quakers who advocated for the status-neutral *thou* were certainly aware of the ideological contest in which they were engaged, as were, more recently, the feminists of the 1970s who began the movement to displace the generic *he* (Silverstein 1985). By contrast, before these respective subversive actions, English speakers who made the *thou/you* status distinction or referred to a generic human being as *he* probably thought rarely if ever about what they were doing.

Kroskrity's (2000:21) final point is the subtlest and in some ways the most powerful: "members' language ideologies mediate between social structures and forms of talk." Language ideologies, in other words, are not mere abstractions. They are, rather, bridges between the sociocultural experiences of speakers and the ways in which they actually speak. The Quaker case is again pertinent: one can trace an unbroken link from social and political experience through language ideology to the very structure of the English pronoun system.

An example that illustrates all four of Kroskrity's points is the question of whether *United States* is singular or plural. In the eighteenth and early nineteenth centuries, the United States *were* plural, as in Article III of the Constitution: "Treason Against the United States shall consist only in levying War against them, or in adhering to their Enemies, giving them Aid and Comfort." This usage began to change during and immediately after the Civil War; for example, by its 1888 edition, *Encyclopedia Britannica* had switched to the singular. Now, speaking of the United States in the plural sounds like a conscious archaism or rhetorical flourish, as when someone says "in these United States."

First, both usages reflect ideas about language — specifically, about the significance of the category "number" — that serve the interests of particular social groups. In the Constitution, the plural may be indicative of deference to the sensibilities of those who were reluctant to sacrifice the autonomy of the uniting states. As the states' rights leader John C. Calhoun said in 1849, "the United States are not a nation" (Schwartz 1993:239). Alternatively, it may simply reflect the traditional British practice of rendering governments and other corporate bodies in the plural. Even if the latter interpretation is correct, it is interesting that there was no attempt in the Constitution to make a point by using the singular. In either case, the standard historical view (e.g., Bishop 2003) is that the post–Civil War singular serves a newly ascendant nationalist ideology.

Second, the ideologies in question were not uniform. One can find published examples of the singular usage before the Civil War, as well as the persistence of the plural in the decades thereafter. Surprisingly, the Thirteenth Amendment, which was pushed by the strongly Unionist Radical Republicans immediately after the Civil War, abolished slavery "within the United States, or any place subject to *their* jurisdiction."[4] Third, the historical record suggests varying degrees of awareness of the ideological change. It is widely believed that Lincoln was the pivotal figure in the switch to the self-consciously nationalist singular, but there is evidence of him using both forms — on the same day![5] Now, of course, the once-controversial singular has been fully "naturalized" for as long as most living people can remember.

As to Kroskrity's fourth point, it is hard to imagine a clearer example of ideas about language mediating between changing sociocultural experiences and the forms of everyday talk. The Civil War and the events that precipitated and followed it were the pivotal sociocultural experiences, of course. Mark Twain captured Kroskrity's point about mediation perfectly (and anticipated linguistic anthropology by more than a hundred years) when he observed that the Civil War was fought over whether "United States" was singular or plural (see Venners 1997).

The Power of Language Ideology in Legal Contexts

We turn next to two specific examples of the study of language ideology in legal contexts. In each instance, attention to language ideology helps to clarify the ways in which language functions (nonreferentially) to both reinforce existing power relations and facilitate their subversion. The first example is a report by linguist John Haviland (2003) of an Oregon murder trial in which he served as an expert witness. Several witnesses, including the defendant and the critical prosecution witness, were speakers of Mixtec, an indigenous Mexican language, but the court presumed them to be Spanish speakers because of their nationality. Haviland uncovers the complex ways in which the case was influenced, if not determined, by a set of ideas about language itself and the relationships among languages that are embedded in the American legal system. The second example is the work of anthropologist Susan Hirsch (1998) in Islamic divorce courts in coastal Kenya. Through attention to the linguistic details of trials and of mediation sessions, Hirsch illuminates the interaction between linguistic and cultural ideologies about gender. She reveals the dilemma faced by divorcing wives who must play to one ideology in order to justify themselves as wives and women while simultaneously invoking its opposite in an effort to assert their rights under Islamic law.

Language Ideologies in American Courts

Haviland served as an expert witness for the defense in a homicide case against a defendant he identifies as Santiago V., a Mixtec-speaking Indian from the Mexican state of Oaxaca. The victim, Ramiro, was stabbed to death in a migrant labor camp near Portland, Oregon. According to the prosecution's version of the case, Margarito, a friend of Ramiro, had provoked a fight at a party. Afterwards, the two had driven off into the strawberry fields, pursued by another car full of young men. After Ramiro and Margarito abandoned their car and ran off, the second group—which included Santiago—found it and burned it. They then captured Ramiro and, according to eyewitness testimony, Santiago stabbed him while he was held at gunpoint. The defense contended that there were several cars in the fields, that the lack of bloodstains proved that Santiago could not have done the stabbing, and that the eyewitness testimony had been coerced from men who were under threat of prosecution for the car burning. Santiago V. was convicted and sentenced to life imprisonment. The critical linguistic feature of the trial was that none of the witnesses to the events in question spoke English. Almost all were native speakers of Mixtec, and few had meaningful competence in Spanish. Nonetheless, the only translator provided by the court was a native speaker of Cuban Spanish (which is quite different from Mexican Spanish) who knew no Mixtec.

Haviland's account focuses on some beliefs about language that were critical to the outcome of the trial. The first is the notion of "referential transparency" (Haviland 2003:767). He characterizes this as "the 'Verbatim' theory, or the assumption that expressions in one language can be unproblematically rendered into propositions and translated 'verbatim' into another" (2003:767). This belief underlies the way in which the court structured the relationship between witnesses, jurors, and interpreters. The judge instructed the interpreter to function as a translation machine (Haviland 2003:768): "[T]ranslate the responses of the witness verbatim, word for word. In other words, I don't want you to say, 'Well, the witness says,' forget that part. Just translate it verbatim, word for word." This is impossible, of course, since no one language can be mapped directly onto another in "verbatim" fashion. As Haviland puts it, the judge's instruction rested on the fallacy that "the truth-functional core of what someone says can be decoupled from the actual saying itself" (2003:768).

The same can be said of the judge's instructions to the jury about the translation process. Following a long-established principle of American law, the judge told the jurors that they must ignore any competency that they might have in Spanish.

TEXT 7.1 (Haviland 2003:768)

> The translation of the Spanish language that you must rely on in the course of this case is that translation that is made by the court interpreter that will be translating the language as it's spoken from the witness stand. . . . I don't know whether any of you, as I say, understand
> 5   Spanish, but we don't want to get into a situation where we have some

juror in the jury room saying, "Well, that's not what the witness really said, you know."

Thus, the interpreter's "verbatim" translation of a witness's answers — presumably bereft of any commentary, paraphrases, or, ironically, "interpretation" — was to be the sole source of evidence for the jurors. They were to ignore everything they heard between the lawyer's question and the interpreter's English rendering of the answer, regardless of whether they understood it. This legal rule is apparently informed by a fear of jurors arriving at competing translations that are not verbatim. The rule has an internal logic only if, as Haviland argues, one accepts the verbatim fallacy.

So the *Santiago V.* case, like most US cases that involve non-English-speaking witnesses, began with the promulgation of a flawed language ideology. As the trial progressed, other language ideologies came into play to complicate the situation even further. As we noted earlier, some of the key witnesses were speakers of a third language that neither the English-speaking judge and lawyers nor the English-Spanish interpreter understood at all. In Text 7.2, the testimony of the Mixtec-speaker who claimed to have seen the defendant stab the victim degenerated into dark comedy. Note that the district attorney was speaking in English and the witness in Spanish. The interpreter was going back and forth between the two languages, but the transcript — which forms the sole basis of a defendant's rights on appeal — reproduced only her English renderings.

TEXT 7.2 (Haviland 2003:769)

> DISTRICT ATTORNEY (DA): Do you understand Spanish well?
> WITNESS: No.
> DA: What is the word you know in Spanish for stabbing?
> INTERPRETER: May I ask how I can ask him without giving the word?
> 5 DA: Okay. Let me rephrase the question. What word do you use to
> say how the knife went into the man's body?
> WITNESS: I call it knife.
> DA: How do you describe a knife being stabbed into someone hard?
> INTERPRETER: I don't know if you want it in Spanish or English?
> 10 DA: In Spanish.
> WITNESS: I don't know.
> DA: You don't know the word to describe that in Spanish?
> WITNESS: I don't understand much.
> DA: What language do you usually speak?
> 15 WITNESS: In my village, only Mestica [*sic*].
> DA: Is it different very much from Spanish?
> WITNESS: Yes.

Note the multiple absurdities. First, the district attorney established that the witness had limited facility in Spanish. Then he asked the interpreter to ask the witness, *in Spanish*, for the Spanish word for "stabbing." When the interpreter pointed out the circularity of the request, the lawyer asked the witness to provide a word for sticking a knife into someone. The witness responded with "knife." When the witness demurred to the lawyers' follow-up questions, it finally occurred to the district attorney to ask whether "Mestica" is very different from Spanish.

But even this was not enough to discourage the prosecutor from seeking the testimony he needed. Several pages later in the transcript, he tried to cure the problem by asking the witness to write out an appropriate "Mestica" word and then "spell it in Spanish"! The witness responded that in addition to being unable to speak Spanish, he could not write, at least in Mixtec.

What was happening here? One possible interpretation is that the district attorney was an idiot. How complicated is it to understand that there are people in Mexico who speak indigenous languages? That such languages are radically different from *all* European languages? That an interpreter who speaks Spanish does not necessarily speak every language found in every Spanish-speaking country? The clinching evidence for the DA's idiocy might be his lack of preparation for all of these problems. District attorneys are elected. Murder trials are rare, so there is plenty of time to prepare. Such trials usually command intense media attention. Smart district attorneys try to avoid looking like fools in front of the voters. How hard would it have been to locate an English-Spanish-Mixtec interpreter for this trial?

In considering alternative explanations, it should be pointed out initially that the district attorney won: Santiago V. was convicted and sentenced to life imprisonment. It appears that the "tragicomic" (Haviland 2003:769) discourse did not strike the jurors as sufficiently absurd to upset their faith in the prosecution. So perhaps the district attorney was dumb like a fox.

Haviland's linguistic explanation invokes two additional language ideologies that the district attorney may have shared with the jurors. The first is what Haviland (2003:769) calls the "standard language" notion. That is, the conduct of the trial seems to have assumed not only that verbatim translation is possible but that translation *into English* is especially easy. In linguistic terms, English is treated as "a maximally unmarked and neutral vehicle of propositional communication" — in other words, a "standard language" into which all others should be readily translatable (Haviland 2003:769). The negative implication of this belief is that all other languages must be nonstandard, and thus less suitable than English for unambiguous expression of meaning and generally inferior to it.

The second relevant ideology is what Haviland (2003:769) calls the "handicap" notion. Oregon law treats non-English speakers (along with those whose hearing or speech is impaired) as "disabled persons." The accommodation for this particular disability is the appointment of an interpreter. To Haviland, this approach to language rights reflects a belief that English is not only a standard language but "is also somehow in the repertoire of skills of a 'standard person,' one who is socially and, perhaps, morally whole or 'normal'" (2003:769). Once again, there is a powerful negative implication: those who do not speak English are not only "disabled," but "substandard."

Taken together with the verbatim fallacy, these two additional notions explain a great deal about both the judge's instructions and the district attorney's conduct. The instructions seem built on the premises that (a) verbatim translation is possible and (b) something about English makes it a particularly appropriate endpoint for the process. Point (b), the standard-language ideology, both prompts and is reinforced by (c), the handicap ideology. It works both ways: you are defined as disabled because you cannot speak the standard language, and you cannot speak it because of your disability. With these three ideologies in place, the district attorney can be seen not as manipulative but as simply struggling to deal with an abnormal, substandard person. And this person is doubly abnormal: not only is he unable to speak *the* standard language, English, but he is little better at the next best thing, Spanish. Perhaps the jury sympathized with the prosecutor in his desperate efforts to deal with such a thoroughly dysfunctional person.

Haviland might have added a fourth point to his list of ideologies: the notion of national languages.[6] Taken as a whole, the trial embodies the idea that nations have languages that are standard, normal, and natural. In the United States, that language is English, of course. However, the ostensibly ludicrous employment of an English-Spanish interpreter to aid the Mixtec-speaking witnesses implies the belief that Mexico, too, has a natural language: Spanish. Stupidity or sheer malice could explain the court's failure to have a Mixtec interpreter present, as well as the district attorney's befuddlement at his witness's stubborn refusal to be able to speak Spanish. But it is also possible that this tragic farce was set in motion by the operating assumption that "normal" Mexicans would be able to speak their country's "normal" language. Once again, the jurors, sharing this ideology, might have sympathized with the prosecution's dilemma.

Haviland concludes on a discouraging note. He admits that his readers will inevitably expect "a triumphal cry for linguistic anthropology as an antidote to bad theories of language" (2003:773). But he concedes that he has no practical solutions, and we cannot do much better. There are barriers to reform at every level, some legitimate and some spurious.

First, the legal system has a compelling reason for reducing every trial to an English-language transcript: facilitation of appeals. Appellate review of judicial decisions has long been viewed as a fundamental component of due process. Unless appeals are to involve a live retrial of every case—a logistical impossibility—then trials must be reduced to written transcripts in a language that every appellate judge can be presumed to understand.[7] In this country at this time, the reality is that there is only one such language, English. Even under the simplest circumstances, transcribing is an act of interpretation (Ochs 1979). The problems become infinitely more complex when multiple languages are involved. Courts can do a better job of addressing these problems, certainly better than the Oregon court in Haviland's case, but no amount of ideological adjustment will make them go away.

A related practical issue is how much linguistic competence and sophistication courts can be expected to have. The competence aspect of this issue is whether every defendant has a right to interpretation in every language spoken by every witness. In a murder or other major felony case, we think, the answer is clearly yes; it violates any reasonable standard of fairness to send someone away for life on the basis of a colloquy between a lawyer and a witness who barely understood each other. It seems equally obvious that a traffic case should not grind to a halt while an interpreter in a rare (in that venue) language is found, trained, and qualified. Where to draw the line is an excruciatingly difficult question that is beyond the scope of this discussion.

The sophistication prong of the issue brings us back to Haviland's lament about the "bad theories of language" that are so much in evidence in the *Santiago V.* case. That is, is there any hope that judges and lawyers will become knowledgeable consumers of the theory of language ideology? On the evidence of the transcript excerpts that Haviland quotes, the answer would be a resounding no. Haviland's reported experience suggests that legal practitioners are just too dim to get it.

But can this be true? Every day, lawyers everywhere make use of extremely complicated scientific theory and data, from genetics to toxicology to economics. As the following chapter demonstrates, forensic linguists are becoming increasingly prominent as experts. Why, then, is language ideology such an impenetrable mystery? One answer might be that Haviland participated in a truly unrepresentative case, with the lawyers and the judge exhibiting extraordinary levels of incompetence. We have no reason to think so, but, as is almost always the case with qualitative research (including our own), it is impossible to determine how well a particular set of data represents any larger population.

Another factor might be the way that linguists and anthropologists write about language ideology. That is, maybe lawyers and judges would be interested in language ideology and capable of dealing with it were the writing on the subject not so unnecessarily dense. Haviland's own article is the exception that proves the rule, straightforwardly written and probably comprehensible to most educated nonspecialists (lawyers, for example). Regrettably, this is not the case with much of the work in the field. The development of specialized terminology is inevitable as a discipline matures. But obscure diction and convoluted syntax are not. Language ideology both deserves and is capable of straightforward exposition. Instead, we find the very mystification for which social scientists rightly criticize the law. In fact, too much of the writing about language ideology embodies its own language ideology: the apparent belief that obscurity is a mark of theoretical sophistication.

A final question about the relationship between linguistics and American law is also prompted by Haviland's complaint about "bad theories of language." What about linguists' theories of law? Are linguists' ideologies of law as flawed as lawyers' ideologies of language? Two points that Haviland makes are especially provocative.

First, Haviland describes his expert efforts on behalf of Santiago V. as "trying to get an innocent man (and he was innocent) out of prison" (2003:770). In a footnote appended to the parenthetical, he explains that "post-conviction research by defense investigators, as well as by the author and Lourdes de Leon aided by others from the accused man's village in Oaxaca, soon revealed the identity of [*sic*] actual knife-wielder." Few things are as problematic to critical theorists as the law's historical claim to determine "truth," what "really happened." A trial is seen as a competition of narratives (Bennett and Feldman 1981), with the outcome contingent as much on power dynamics as the "facts." Yet here a critical theorist states a conclusion about "what really happened" without any reflection on the problematic nature of truth, or any apparent awareness of the extraordinary irony of his absolute claim. Even allowing for the limitations of space, it is striking that words such as "innocent" and "actual" are unexamined. Linguistics claims a position of privilege that it would not (and should not) grant to the law.

Haviland concludes his discussion of the *Santiago V.* case with an ambivalent "postscript" on the final outcome. The conviction was ultimately reversed and the innocent defendant freed after five years in prison. However, to Haviland's evident regret, the release "was based not in the least on the theory-laden analysis and critical deconstruction of the linguistic flaws in the investigation and trial." Instead, "it was based on a *technicality*. His lawyers persuaded the court of appeals that he had been incompetently defended, since his lawyer had refused to allow him to testify in his own defense" (Haviland 2003:773; emphasis added). The word *technicality* carries heavy ideological baggage. To nonspecialist observers of the legal system it has such implications as "insubstantial," "unrelated to the merits of the case," and, often, "inconsistent with the interests of justice," as in "the high-priced lawyer got the crook off on a technicality." Yet here it is applied to a right — the assistance of counsel — that is explicitly enumerated in the Constitution (the Sixth Amendment) and that most lawyers would regard as a cornerstone of justice. By what warrant, and for what purpose, does Haviland treat it so dismissively? Is it not an exercise in ideology to value the assistance of counsel below "theory-laden analysis and critical deconstruction"?

Haviland's remark about Santiago V.'s lawyers having "persuaded the court of appeals" is also interesting. Recall that Haviland's own judgment about guilt and innocence was pronounced with unproblematic authority: the man *was innocent*. No such certainty attends the appellate court's judgment about the competence of the defendant's trial lawyer. We are told not that the lawyer *was incompetent* but rather that a higher court was *persuaded* that he or she was. Once again, why is it that the law's construction of reality needs "critical deconstruction" by linguistics, while the linguist's version of the same process is to be taken for granted?

None of this is intended to detract from the excellence of Haviland's analysis. He demonstrates, persuasively, how language ideology came into play in the trial of Santiago V. and how its manipulation led to a denial of justice. His work is a model for a new level of linguistic analysis of the production and maintenance of legal power. Our point, rather, is one made frequently by students of language ideology, including Haviland himself: linguistics, like any other institutionalized activity, has its own language ideologies.[8] It is anomalous that Haviland, otherwise so acutely attuned to ideological relativism, chooses to ignore this point in dissecting his own interaction with the law. Perhaps this anomaly can help to explain why the law proved so unreceptive to his approach: physician heal thyself and all that.

Language Ideologies in Kenyan Divorce Courts

Anthropologist Susan Hirsch (1998) studied language ideology in the Kadhi's Courts of coastal Kenya. A *kadhi* is an Islamic judge who is empowered by the state to apply Islamic law in certain cases (including divorce) that involve Muslim parties. Hirsch's particular focus is on ideas about language and gender that are implicated in what she calls "the discursive construction of gender" (Hirsch 1998:17). The title of her book, *Pronouncing & Persevering*, captures an ideological dichotomy that has long been powerful in Kenyan Swahili[9] society, the contrast between "a Muslim husband pronouncing divorce and his persevering wife silently accepting the decree" (Hirsch 1998:2). In this stereotype, the husband's authority to pronounce both reflects and reaffirms his autonomy and agency, whereas women, "devoid of agency" (Hirsch 1998:1) in language and in fact, "are expected to endure marital hardships without complaint and to accept divorce in the same spirit" (Hirsch 1998:3). Hirsch sets for herself the task of questioning this beguilingly simple paradigm through the analysis of the language of divorce cases.

Lacking the power to pronounce, wives who find themselves in intolerable marriages must go before the kadhi and make a case. By Hirsch's account, women confront a seemingly irreconcilable dilemma. Swahili women should personify the cultural ideal of *heshima*, which involves respect, honor, and modesty. An important part of *heshima* is shielding private matters from public scrutiny; instead of making public complaints about marital troubles, one perseveres quietly. A parallel cultural ideal is that of *haki*, which includes the concepts of justice and rights. It is especially powerful because *haki* is guaranteed by Islam and Islamic law. The obvious quandary is that in order to seek *haki* in the marital context, a woman inevitably jeopardizes *heshima*. To achieve her rights as a wife, a woman puts at risk the very qualities that make her deserving of such rights. But women regularly bring and win divorce cases (they lost fewer than 2 percent of the cases Hirsch studied), meaning that they somehow walk this exceedingly fine line.

The solution seems to lie in the ability to negotiate a minefield of culturally significant and often conflicting language ideologies. Specifically, women invoke ideologies that index, or point to, themselves as proper wives, while at the same time stepping outside the traditional bounds of propriety to assert their rights. As Hirsch (1998:219) puts it, "Swahili women who complain in court embody a contradiction. Through their participation in cases and mediations, they generally stand in gross violation of appropriate speech, and yet, in so many dialogues, they are also routinely depicted as compliant wives."

One important language ideology involves the belief that "words expose"; that is, "exposing household problems is damaging to family members" (Hirsch 1998:229). As one divorcing husband described the principle, "It's shameful like that. People stay, they — they conceal together about anything they have, they don't have. Indeed, this is how people get along" (Hirsch 1998:230). For a wife to bring a divorce case, or even to protest her treatment, is inevitably to violate this belief, leading many husbands to complain about their wives' complaining. As one of them testified, "She took the opportunity to — to bring my brother-in-law to the house and to mention these matters . . . I don't want her speaking to him about anything at all" (Hirsch 1998:230–31). For the wife, however, there is no alternative. To win her case, she must persuade the kadhi that she has persevered in the face of her husband's unjust behavior, so that behavior must be exposed. In other words, in order to justify her breach of the linguistic norm, the wife must breach it even more.

A related belief is that "words harm": "bad words 'cause' bad events" (Hirsch 1998:232). Talk about conflict produces more conflict, bringing down evil on speakers and hearers. As a kadhi said in urging a husband and a wife to stop arguing and reconcile, "But don't — don't you, don't be ready all the time to cause trouble, meaning, it's bad to argue" (Hirsch 1998:233). In a similar vein, a husband reported that after an argument with his wife, "I went out to avoid this evil" (Hirsch 1998:232). Here again, a wife seeking a divorce must necessarily go against a belief that Hirsch describes as "widespread in Swahili culture" (1998:232). To compound the problem, the violation is at two levels. The first occurs simply by virtue of talking about trouble in the marriage. In addition, to show that she has been a persevering wife, the woman must describe the trouble in graphic detail, repeating many of the argumentative and abusive "bad words" that her husband has directed at her. The repetition of profanity is especially problematic. So strong is the cultural antipathy to bad words that kadhis will often interrupt wives' narratives with such admonitions as "leave aside these careless words" or "don't say those things here" (Hirsch 1998:234).

All of this takes place against a more general ideological background pertaining to language and gender. Specifically, women are expected to be storytellers: "Swahili women perform experiences of conflict as animated stories, using many conventions of narrative common to storytelling outside court" (Hirsch 1998:140). By contrast, "[m]en tell stories less frequently, and their stories include fewer features of storytelling performances" (1998:140). Consequently, women must tell stories to "index" themselves as women, and those stories must contain the private details of their perseverance. In order to conform to one ideological norm and to create an entitlement to relief, wives must violate other strongly held beliefs. Their husbands are quick to criticize these transgressions, both in and out of court. Yet wives persist and succeed.

Hirsch's analysis suggests no simple explanation of how they do it. One hypothesis might be that women are effectively subverting the dominant ideologies through their resistance, but Hirsch finds no evidence that this is happening. Instead, it seems that women accommodate themselves to the existing belief system. Hirsch reports that the cases that come to court involve truly compelling stories of patient and long-suffering perseverance. She believes that the barriers posed by language and gender ideologies exert a screening effect on the filing of cases. Given the adverse reactions that their unavoidable violations of these norms will provoke, women wait until they have an unimpeachable record of their own compliance with the obligations of *heshima* and their husbands' contempt for the ideals of *haki*. Thus, women almost always win when they seek a divorce, but their winning percentage is illusory, since they only try in the direst of circumstances. If the denominator were bad marriages rather than divorce cases filed, women would appear far less powerful.

Another sign of the power of prevailing ideologies is a decline in the prestige of the Kadhi's Courts during the time when Hirsch was studying them. She reports that men constantly criticized the kadhis for giving relief to women who breached the norms of *heshima*: "Accordingly, kadhis face the hostility of men who lose in court and of other men who criticize their lack of solidarity" (Hirsch 1998:129). Men condemned the Kadhi's Courts as "women's courts," unfaithful to the true tenets of Islamic law. One such man expressed his dissatisfaction with a decision by stabbing the kadhi. Although this judge heroically returned to the bench, and others soldiered on in less dramatic fashion, there was, when Hirsch wrote, a real danger that these courts would not survive.[10]

Hirsch, like the Kenyan women whose cases she studied, finds ironies and contradictions at every turn. Initially, wives who are badly treated seem trapped by a set of interlocking ideologies of language and gender. But, as Hirsch discovered, some of them prevail in court by the tactic of openly and notoriously violating those same ideologies. The necessity of using that tactic, however, dooms all but those with the most egregious cases to persevere in silence. Finally, we learn that the men who lose when women win may defeat the insurgency by simply pronouncing the dangerous system out of business.

Conclusion

Contemporary studies of language ideology represent, in our view, not an entirely new theoretical perspective but a useful reframing and refocusing of work that has been going on for a generation or more. In the first edition of this book we criticized conversation analysis and other methods of linguistic microanalysis for deliberate inattention to connections between language and social, cultural, and political contexts. We particularly emphasized the need to consider the role of language in creating and reflecting power relations. The current focus on language ideology has been a strong corrective to this inattention. By making context a starting point rather than an afterthought, language ideology scholars remind us that we cannot usefully study how people practice language without paying attention to how they think about it.

For people like us who have done comparable research framed in terms of discourse, the concept of language ideology may provide greater analytical precision. We have written extensively, for example, on the rule- and relational "orientations" that laypeople have toward the law (Conley and O'Barr 1990). We would have done better to characterize these orientations as language ideologies, for that is exactly what they are: shared ideas about language. Specifically, they are ideas about the linguistic practices that are appropriate in legal contexts. Because different social groups have differential access to these divergent ideologies, and because only one is compatible with the dominant ideology of the law, the power implications are clear.

The two research projects we have reviewed in detail in this chapter — Haviland's analysis of a multilingual American trial and Hirsch's study of Kenyan divorce courts[11] — demonstrate further the power and potential of the concept of language ideology. Haviland uncovers a subtle but strong, even determinative connection between shared ideas about language (and individual languages) and the workings of the American criminal justice system. For those of us who are as much interested in the law as in its language, the next step is to figure out what to do with his revelation. Hirsch, working in a very different setting, reminds us that the power relations embedded in language ideology are neither simple nor linear. Her sometimes contradictory findings are compelling evidence of the power of attending to power in studying language.

CHAPTER EIGHT

Forensic Linguistics

In their book *Speaking of Crime* (2005), the lawyer-linguists Lawrence Solan and Peter Tiersma tell a remarkable story of the role of a self-proclaimed "author attribution expert" named Donald Foster in the still-unsolved Jon-Benet Ramsey murder case. JonBenet, a six-year-old beauty queen, was killed in her Boulder, Colorado, home on Christmas night in 1996. At the center of the case is an unsigned ransom note that was found at the scene. In June 1997, Foster wrote a dramatic and apparently unsolicited letter[1] to JonBenet's mother Patricia, a prime suspect, saying, "I know that you are innocent — *know* it, absolutely and unequivocally" (quoted in Solan and Tiersma 2005:158). He concluded that the ransom note had been written by a young adult with an addiction to crime literature and Hollywood thrillers and pointed the finger at John Andrew Ramsey, JonBenet's half brother. Foster believed that this young man was communicating over the internet using the name "Jameson." When it turned out that "Jameson" was really a woman, Foster changed his theory to allege that John Andrew Ramsey and the woman had worked together. Finally, when the Boulder police consulted with Foster, he changed his story once again, claiming that the child's mother was actually the author of the ransom note. Foster's key piece of evidence, it seems, was the way that Patricia and the unknown author wrote the letter *a*.

Knowing only this much, most people might conclude that Foster was a crackpot. But who is he in fact, and why did many people, including the police, pay attention to what he had to say? Donald Foster is indeed a serious person, a well-known Shakespearean scholar who is an English professor at Vassar College. In 1989, he had published his PhD dissertation as a book called *Elegy by W. S.: A Study in Attribution*, in which he claimed, on the basis of stylistic similarities, that Shakespeare was the author of a poem entitled "A Funeral

Elegy" (Foster 1989). His claim did not go unchallenged, however. Another Shakespearean scholar found fault with Foster's analysis on several grounds (including the facts that Shakespeare's style had changed by the date the text was published, that Shakespeare did not have a known connection to the subject of the poem, and that Shakespeare's name was appropriated by many others in this period before the advent of copyright). After this and other challenges, Foster withdrew his claim about Shakespeare, and the literary community now considers the real author to be someone else.

Foster had also achieved some popular acclaim shortly before interjecting himself into the JonBenet case. A 1996 best seller called *Primary Colors* depicted a presidential campaign conducted by a thinly disguised Bill and Hillary Clinton and a raft of characters who closely resembled prominent Clinton insiders. The author was listed only as "Anonymous," a gimmick that greatly enhanced the book's cachet. It was endlessly discussed in the media as the Washington elite alternated between looking for themselves in the text and trying to guess who wrote it.

On the basis of his notoriety in the Shakespeare controversy, *New York* magazine hired Foster to analyze the text of *Primary Colors* and attempt to determine its author from a list of thirty-five "suspects." Applying his best techniques (e.g., looking for unusual words, spellings, syntax, and so on), Foster concluded that Joe Klein, a *Newsweek* columnist, was the author (see Foster 2000). After the *Washington Post* acquired a copy of the manuscript annotated in Klein's handwriting, Klein capitulated. Foster had been right this time.

What does this unusual series of episodes say about the role of language scholars in the courtroom? If the Ramsey case ever goes to trial, Foster is unlikely to have any part in it. After Foster's multiple flip-flops, a police source quoted by Solan and Tiersma concluded that "the defense would eat him alive" (Solan and Tiersma 2005:159). In the end, the sober Shakespearean scholar had devolved into the writer of the overwrought letter to JonBenet's mother and a caricature of the self-promoting "expert." It was not a good time to be arguing that students of language have important contributions to make to the litigation process.

In this chapter we review some of the areas in which linguists and other language experts have been routinely welcomed as expert witnesses, as well as some areas in which the role of linguistics has remained controversial. We compare the legitimate contributions of language experts with the more dubious efforts that are exemplified by the Foster fiasco. We argue that, although such experts have made important contributions to litigation, their work has not been without at least three sets of troubling consequences.

The first issue concerns who gets the benefit of linguistic expertise. In some cases, it seems to be a simple question of who can pay. In other situations, language scholars have donated their services in pursuit of fairness and equity.

Even in those cases, however, there is evidence of another form of rationing, this time along political lines. A second and related question deals with subsequent access to the work that experts do. In an adversary system, the work of experts is usually viewed as proprietary, effectively owned by the party for whom it is done. Is it appropriate for language researchers to devote significant time to work that may never see the light of day? Third, there is reason to be concerned about the effect of allowing the needs of the legal system to determine which issues get addressed. While all kinds of research are, of course, influenced by practical considerations (see, for example, the ongoing debate about whether medical research funding is directed disproportionately to "men's" or "women's" diseases), we argue that the problem is particularly acute here, as a vast amount of research time and energy is devoted to pursuing an agenda set by the law. As we have done in other chapters, we explore the implications of these issues for the power relations that are embodied in the legal system. We turn first, however, to a brief digression on the law that applies to expert testimony.

The Law of Expert Witnesses

In court, most witnesses are limited to testifying on the basis of firsthand knowledge — things that they actually saw, experienced, or (rarely) heard. "Experts" are people with special qualifications who are allowed to express opinions about topics that ordinary jurors cannot be expected to understand. A doctor, for example, would be allowed to testify that a person suffered a concussion as a result of an automobile accident. A psychiatrist might be allowed to express an opinion that a criminal defendant was incompetent to stand trial, or an engineer might be allowed to opine (the legal verb for "give an opinion") about the cause of a building collapse. Had the police and prosecutor in Boulder tried to use Donald Foster in a case against any of the suspects he identified, the questions for the court would have been (1) whether he was qualified, based on his specialized linguistic knowledge, to offer an opinion about the authorship of the ransom notes; and (2) whether that opinion would be sufficiently reliable.

In answering these questions, all federal courts must follow Federal Rule of Evidence 702 (as must most state judges, as a practical matter, because most states now have evidence rules based on the federal model). According to Rule 702, "a witness qualified as an expert by knowledge, skill, experience, training, or education may testify in the form of an opinion or otherwise," as long as "(a) the expert's scientific, technical, or other specialized knowledge [will be helpful to the judge or jury]; (b) the testimony is based on sufficient facts or data; (c) the testimony is the product of reliable principles and methods; and (d) the expert has reliably applied the principles and methods to the facts of the case."

Rule 702 raises several distinct questions. We consider them specifically with reference to Donald Foster and the JonBenet case. First, is the witness qualified? Note that the rule is very flexible about forms of qualification: an MD degree with specialized board certification might be necessary in one case, whereas years of experience as an auto mechanic would suffice in another. Foster, with his PhD, his Shakespeare book (a serious endeavor, even if he was ultimately proved wrong), his years of teaching and research experience, and his successful unraveling of the *Primary Colors* mystery, would be found to be a qualified practitioner of author-identity scholarship by any judge in the country.

That finding would lead us to a second, more difficult question: Would such expertise be helpful to the jury? Initially, most judges would conclude that author identification is a highly technical field in which few jurors would have any competence; this would weigh in favor of admitting Foster's testimony. But even so, would knowing about this field and Foster's findings really help the jurors to decide the case, or would it simply mislead them? This gets us to the issue that pervades the second half of the rule and that proves decisive in most determinations of the admissibility of expert testimony: Will the expert's opinion be *reliable*?

The rule instructs the judge to apply a three-part test of reliability. First, is the opinion based on "sufficient" facts or data? In other words, did the expert look at all the available evidence, and was there enough there to support a conclusion? This would be hard to determine in Foster's case. How could a court tell whether Foster had looked at all the available evidence, short of commissioning another author-identity expert to study the entire case? And are there any standards in the field for determining how much evidence is enough?

The second part of the test would be even more difficult: Was Foster applying "reliable principles and methods"? In a 1993 case called *Daubert v. Merrell Dow Pharmaceuticals, Inc.* (which is still good law), the United States Supreme Court held that "scientific" experts should base their opinions on the scientific method.[2] The Court instructed judges to examine experts' methods for indicators of reliability usually associated with positivist or "hard" science (experimental physics, for example), including testability of theories, calculation of error rates, peer-reviewed publications, and general acceptance in the scientific community. Then, in a 1999 case called *Kumho Tire Co. v. Carmichael*, the Court held that in dealing with experts who did not fit the scientific model (in that case, a "tire wear expert"), the trial judge should still insist on a showing of reliability but could be more flexible in deciding what factors to consider.[3]

How would Foster fare under these standards? For starters, is his work "scientific"? If so, his general methods of investigation had surely been peer-reviewed (if nothing else, his dissertation must have satisfied a faculty committee), and the long and serious debate over his Shakespeare conclusion suggests that his methods were viewed as generally accepted. But are those methods testable? It would seem possible to devise a test for authorship analysts, but has anyone done so? Have rates of error ever been calculated? And if Foster is not a scientist, what alternative measures of reliability might a judge employ?

Finally, Rule 702 requires that the reliable principles and methods be reliably applied to the facts of the case. That is, an expert with a track record of reliability cannot depart from his or her established methods and say whatever comes to mind. If we assume that Foster had developed and employed reliable methods in his earlier work on Shakespeare and Klein, were his inferences about the JonBenet case based on the same methods conscientiously applied? Or was he using his credentials as a license to speculate?

We have both worked as expert witnesses, and one of us teaches scientific evidence and has examined many experts in court. We doubt that many trial judges would admit the sort of opinions that have been attributed to Foster in the Ramsey case. The point we seek to make is more general, however. It is that those who seek to appear in court as linguistic experts must satisfy not their fellow linguists but judges seeking assurances of "reliability." We remind our readers to keep this standard in mind as they consider the examples that follow.

Defining Forensic Linguistics

The word *forensic*, derived from the Latin *forum*, means (according to the Oxford English Dictionary) "of, used in, or pertaining to a court of law." Thus, in its most straightforward sense, *forensic linguistics* means "linguistic expertise applied to legal cases." It should be noted, however, that many people now use the term as synonymous with "law and language." For example, in his preface to John Gibbons's *Forensic Linguistics: An Introduction to Language in the Justice System* (2003), the distinguished linguist Peter Trudgill locates it within the context of applied linguistics (itself defined as the application of the findings of linguistic research to the solution of real-world problems). For Trudgill (2003:vi), forensic linguistics is "the application of linguistic research — in socio-linguistic areas such as discourse analysis, dialectology, linguistic variation and stylistics, and other core linguistic areas — to different societal issues connected with the law."

Gibbons (2003:12) himself distinguishes between a narrow and a broad definition of forensic linguistics. In the narrow sense, the term refers to linguistic evidence used in and by the law. In the broad sense, it refers to the entire range of law and language issues, including (1) the language of the law, both the written language used in legal documents and the language spoken in legal fora; (2) legal translation and interpretation; (3) efforts to alleviate linguistic disadvantages resulting from the language of the law; (4) linguistic evidence provided by experts in court; and (5) linguistic expertise applied to problems of legal drafting and interpretation.[4]

In this chapter we will focus on the fourth element of Gibbons's definition, largely because the preceding chapters are devoted to the other components. And as we have done elsewhere in this book, we emphasize the relationship between forensic linguistics and power.

Tracking the Footprints of Linguistics in the Law

In the United States and other common law countries where lawyers must make their cases in an adversarial process, they seek expert testimony on an enormous range of topics. Thus, it is not surprising that in some situations they would turn to linguists and other scholars of language for assistance. Two scholars, Elizabeth Loftus and Roger Shuy, began their work in the 1970s when such expert testimony was novel and rare. As a result, their articles and books became foundational texts in the emergent field we now call forensic linguistics. Although Loftus holds a PhD in cognitive psychology rather than linguistics, her work deals directly with language. Shuy was educated as a linguist and taught linguistics for many years at Georgetown University. Examining their work is instructive because it illuminates both the contributions that language experts have made to the law and the problems that their work has raised.

Elizabeth Loftus and Eyewitness Testimony: Access to Expertise

The psychologist Elizabeth Loftus began studying eyewitness testimony in the 1970s. Although her focus as a psychologist is on cognition and memory, the fact that what is remembered is typically reported *through language* makes her work of interest to law and language scholars. In her early and perhaps best-known research, Loftus (1979:77–78) studied eyewitness testimony by asking questions of experimental subjects who had watched a videotape she had produced showing a car crash. In a particularly provocative set of questions, Loftus asked subjects how fast two cars were going when they collided with each other. She varied the words used to describe the action of the cars in the videotape: *How fast were the cars going when they hit/smashed into each other?* Subjects reported variations in speed from twenty-five miles per hour to more than fifty-five, depending on the verb used to describe the action. Not surprisingly, the subjects who were asked the "smashed" version of the question reported much higher rates of speed.

In a follow-up study a week later, Loftus asked the same subjects, *Did you see any broken glass?* There had been no broken glass in the videotaped accident. Nonetheless, those subjects who had been given the "smashed" question the week before reported seeing broken glass almost three times as frequently as those who had been asked the "hit" question — presumably, Loftus (1979:78) infers, "because broken glass usually results from accidents occurring at high speed." Loftus interprets these results as evidence of the power of new information to influence an eyewitness's memory of a complex event. (Linguists would also be reminded of the extraordinary power of language to shape understanding.)

Findings such as these convinced Loftus that the formation of memory is an ongoing process subject to external influences, not a discrete event that creates an immutable record. The obvious significance of her findings for law led to opportunities for her to work as an expert witness, assisting lawyers in and out of court in assessing the validity of eyewitness testimony.[5] As she became more involved in legal issues, she came to question the law's historical practice of elevating eyewitness testimony above other forms of evidence, and to worry about the harm that it might cause. As Loftus acknowledges in the very first sentence of her now classic *Eyewitness Testimony*, "A major reason for writing this book has been a longstanding concern with cases in which an innocent person has been falsely identified, convicted, and even jailed" (1979:xi).

Loftus has appeared as an expert witness in numerous reported cases, almost always to testify on behalf of criminal defendants about the unreliability of eyewitnesses. Judges have varied in their willingness to admit such evidence. According to one recent decision by a federal appellate court (*United States v. Smithers*), "[c]ourts' treatment of expert testimony regarding eyewitness identification has experienced a dramatic transformation in the past twenty years and is still in a state of flux."[6] When such evidence began to be offered in the 1970s—largely in the person of Elizabeth Loftus—courts were skeptical, finding, among other things, that the scientific theory was not generally accepted, or that jurors, aided by cross-examination, could figure the question out for themselves. During the 1980s, courts increasingly found such testimony admissible, influenced by the mounting body of research that suggested, in the words of the *Smithers* decision, a "dichotomy between eyewitness errors and jurors' reliance on eyewitness testimony" (2000:311). Indeed, the *Smithers* court cited Loftus for the proposition that "half of all wrongful convictions result from false identifications" (2000:311n1). Currently, under the evidence rules reviewed at the start of this chapter, trial judges are required to give close scrutiny to the reliability of eyewitness expert testimony and its capacity to help or mislead the jury. The 1980s trend toward admissibility seems to be continuing, although not without exceptions.[7] Psychology and linguistics have appeared too "unscientific" to some judges.[8]

Loftus's work raises squarely the question of access to language expertise. When experts charge a fee, then help is available only for defendants who have the money, or whose states provide subsidies for experts. And even if all the available experts were to work pro bono all the time, only a tiny fraction of the criminal defendants around the country who were facing eyewitness accusers could possibly expect to get help. It is logical to assume that experts appearing without charge would limit themselves to cases in which they thought the defendant was deserving of their help.

A remarkable example of the latter point — and the difficulties that political screening of cases can create — is provided by Loftus's involvement in the case of John Demjanjuk, a Cleveland autoworker alleged to have been "Ivan the Terrible," a notoriously cruel guard at the Treblinka death camp during the Holocaust. He was convicted of crimes against humanity by an Israeli court in 1988. According to an account Loftus gave in a 1987 *Newsweek* op-ed piece (Loftus 1987), she was called by one of Demjanjuk's lawyers before the trial. He said that he believed in his client's innocence and asked for her help in challenging the eyewitness testimony of the elderly Treblinka survivors on whose identification of Demjanjuk the prosecution's case rested.

Loftus wrote that her initial reaction was sympathetic. Her entire research career had led her to question criminal convictions based solely on eyewitness identifications — particularly those based on observations made long before the trial. This was just such a case. Loftus then referred to her desire to promote the legal ideal of insuring a fair trial for all defendants, even unpopular ones. Loftus also cited her obligations to what she called "my science," implying that a scientist has a duty to pursue significant research opportunities regardless of personal and political consequences.

In the end, however, she rejected the engagement because of personal and social conflicts. Her own Jewish heritage played a part in the decision. Most troubling to her, however, was the hurt expressed by some close friends, also Jewish, when she raised the possibility of helping Demjanjuk. They persuaded Loftus that giving the expert testimony sought would heap a final and terrible indignity on those Holocaust survivors who claimed to recognize Demjanjuk more than forty years later.

This was obviously an excruciating personal judgment that we are glad we did not have to make. Nonetheless, the analytical and emotional process that Loftus chose to detail in the press raises some important questions about forensic science. Few research scientists would share her sense of obligation to contribute to the legal system, and we suspect that just about all would have rejected the case out of hand on political grounds. So Loftus came closer than most would have to offering her expertise even to the most unsympathetic of defendants. But in the end she could not do so, underlining the problem of selective access.

Loftus's work also helps to frame the issue of the proper relationship between basic and applied research. Her career in the laboratory and the courtroom would appear to represent an ideal progression from theory to practice, from basic research to real-world application. She has made significant and fundamental contributions to the science of memory. She is absolutely correct when she writes, "My work has helped to create a new paradigm of memory, shifting our view from the video-recorder model . . . to a reconstructionist model" (Loftus and Ketcham 1994:5). Lawyers discovered her work and asked her to apply it. She has done so, guided by an admirable ethic of concern for the unjustly accused.

But as her work has developed, one might wonder about the relationship between science and law. In 1994, she reported having "testified in hundreds of court cases where a person's fate depended on whether the jury believed the eyewitness's sworn testimony" (Loftus and Ketcham 1994:3). Even spread out over fifteen or twenty years, "hundreds" of court appearances represent a phenomenal commitment of time. As she described it, again in 1994, "my world has been turned upside down. As grant applications pile up in the corners of my hopelessly cluttered office, I spend my days talking on the phone to strangers accused of the most loathsome crimes imaginable" (Loftus and Ketcham 1994:5). Her published output also came to focus heavily on the legal application of her research. In 1991, for example, she wrote *Witness for the Defense: The Accused, the Eyewitness, and the Expert Who Puts Memory on Trial* (Loftus and Ketcham 1991), while her 1994 book, *The Myth of Repressed Memory* (Loftus and Ketcham 1994), deals entirely with her experiences in sexual abuse cases. (Both books were coauthored by Katherine Ketcham, a writer of popular self-help and recovery books.)

We admire Loftus's commitment to the rights of the accused. What concerns us is the prospect of a major field of research — in this case, the study of memory and its interaction with language — having its development driven primarily by the needs of a class of litigants, needs that happen to coincide with the political beliefs of the field's principal figure. We do not mean to suggest in any way that Loftus's *answers* are driven by the interests of her clients; her integrity and competence are unimpeachable. We do mean to wonder about a field in which the *questions* seem to be dictated by those interests.

Recall Loftus's reference to her obligation to "my science" in her *Newsweek* piece about the Demjanjuk case. She agonized over whether, *as a scientist*, she was duty-bound to try to answer a question posed *by the law*. Helping the legal system might be part of one's duty as a citizen, but is it one's duty as a scientist (or a basic researcher in any field) to pursue an agenda set by a legal advocate? Is that in fact "science"? Does a researcher's responsibility not include the framing of the questions to be studied?

Roger Shuy's Linguistic Battles: Questions of Ownership and Agenda-Setting

Roger Shuy's distinguished career is similarly revealing of the strengths and weaknesses of the field of forensic linguistics. Shuy is a widely published and highly regarded linguist who has worked often as an expert in legal contexts (according to his website, he has consulted on over six hundred cases and testified in fifty-four). As he wrote in 1993, "I have worked on behalf of a number of nationally known public figures, entertainers, politicians, industrial giants. I have also worked on behalf of the little guys" (Shuy 1993:xvii). Two of his books (Shuy 1993, 2002) can be characterized as chronicles of his courtroom experiences in, respectively, criminal (*Language Crimes: The Use and Abuse of Language Evidence in the Courtroom*) and civil (*Linguistic Battles in Trademark Disputes*) cases.

Language Crimes is a compelling book that details some of the ways in which linguistic evidence can promote criminal justice. In separate chapters dealing with bribing, agreeing, threatening, admitting, truth-telling, and promising, Shuy (1993:8) outlines basic linguistic understandings of how these speech acts work and shows some of the ways the law can misinterpret them. He begins his analysis by discussing some common misconceptions about language: meaning is found primarily in individual words; a single listening to a tape is enough to determine its content; reading a transcript is as good as hearing a tape recording; all parties to a conversation understand the same things by their words; people say what they mean and intend. For a linguist, these assumptions are problematic. They become the basis for Shuy's demonstration of what applied linguistics can deliver to the law.

For example, in discussing the problem of bribery, Shuy (1993:43–65) points out that there are a variety of ways that offers can be made, ranging from the overt (or performative) offer to the indirect and embedded varieties. The most direct sort of offer would be something like *I hereby offer you a bribe for such and such*. One could make the same offer indirectly, as in *If you will do me a little favor, I'll make it up to you real good*. Least direct of all is the embedded offer, which "lacks both the explicitness of the performative offer and the inferred comprehension of the indirect offer" (Shuy 1993:55). It might consist of nothing more than the mention of two activities occurring simultaneously, such as an otherwise legal campaign contribution to a politician and some action to be taken by the politician. How overt and direct does an offer of a bribe have to be in order to count legally? How should the above examples be interpreted? Should the law consider them bribes or not? The answers to these questions are, of course, legally consequential: they could mean the difference between a jail term and going free.

In another chapter, Shuy (1993:118–35) asks how direct an admission must be in order to be legally binding. Or alternatively, how indirect may it be and still be considered by the law to be an admission? These examples illustrate the quandary: *I admit that I overslept / I slept till 7AM / I missed my bus / I was here as soon as anyone else / My alarm clock didn't go off*. These statements vary from the direct, performative admission (*I admit that . . .*) to the indirect admission (*I slept till 7 AM; I missed my bus*) to the excuse that contains an implied admission (the last two).

Linguistic distinctions like these proved consequential in a case in which

Shuy testified in 1986, *State of Alaska v. Larry Gentry*. Gentry was charged in a homicide, and a critical question was whether he had admitted that he knew in advance that his car was to be used in a murder. In an earlier hearing concerning a search warrant, Gentry's statements had included the following: "I *wasn't too sure* on it even being a shooting . . . I *wasn't sure*, but I *kind of knew* and I *kind of didn't know*" / "I was *pretty sure* of it, yes" / "*I'd done figured it out*" / "No, *I did not know* he was going to use that car" / "I was still *trying to ignore it*" (Shuy 1993:124–25; italics in original). Analyzing these and other inconsistencies, Shuy argued that Gentry had never made anything that the law should characterize as an admission. Finding that the issues were beyond common understanding, that Shuy had used established linguistic techniques, and that his testimony would help the jury, the judge allowed him to testify. Nonetheless, "the jury deliberated briefly and found Gentry guilty as charged" (Shuy 1993:135).

Despite the adverse outcome, it is hard to dispute that Shuy's presence assured Gentry of a fairer trial than he otherwise would have gotten. Indeed, in all of his criminal cases Shuy is undoubtedly using his expertise to advance the interests of justice when he appears in court to demand that language issues be addressed in a linguistically sophisticated way. Nonetheless, the issue of access remains. Who gets the kind of help Shuy can provide? Is politics a determinant, as in Loftus's case? Economics? Shuy (1993:xxi) writes that he is politically neutral: although he has testified only on behalf of defendants, he has consulted with prosecutors and stands willing to help them. But in the course of speculating about why prosecutors almost never call on him, he mentions that "[t]here may be budget constraints" (Shuy 1993:xxi), suggesting that money plays a role in the allocation of his expertise.

Linguistic Battles in Trademark Disputes (Shuy 2002) recounts the civil side of Shuy's career as an expert witness. The role of linguistic experts in trademark cases is longstanding and well established. A trademark is a distinctive word (*Coca-Cola*), phrase (Nike's *Just do it!*), symbol (the Nike swoosh), and so forth that identifies a company's product or service. The decisive issue in most cases is whether the defendant's mark is so similar to the plaintiff's that it is likely to confuse consumers about the source of the relevant products (suppose, for example, that a competitor of Nike adopted the slogan *Go ahead and do it!*). In some cases, the defendant claims that the plaintiff's mark is invalid because it has become the generic name for a class of products; cellophane, aspirin, trampoline, and escalator are all former trademarks that fell victim to "genericide."

Linguists regularly contribute to the resolution of these issues. One of the cases Shuy (2002:125–43) writes about, *AutoNation, Inc. v. Acme Commercial Corp. d/b/a CarMax*, is illustrative of the types of analyses they do. The legal issues were (1) whether "AutoNation USA" was confusingly similar to CarMax's "AutoMation" trademark (the name of its computerized inventory system); and (2) whether AutoNation's slogan, "The Better Way to Buy a Car," was confusingly similar to CarMax's "The New Way to Buy Used Cars." The jury ultimately found in favor of AutoNation.

Shuy was initially contacted by AutoNation's lawyer, with whom he had worked in the past. Because the case was far from his home, Shuy suggested that the lawyer contact his friend and colleague (and ours), Duke University linguist Ron Butters. A few weeks later, Shuy got a call from CarMax's lawyer. He had used Butters in the past and had intended to hire him here. But when he learned that Butters was already working for the other side, he offered the engagement to Shuy, who accepted. Beyond being mildly amusing, this story speaks volumes about the role of linguists in trademark cases. Everyone understands that, in every significant case, there will be a "battle of experts"; there are a limited number of "regulars"; everyone knows everyone else; and experts compete without hard feelings. Indeed, the professional behavior of the experts seems indistinguishable from that of the lawyers (including being well-compensated). Implicit in this is the understanding that a good linguist, just like a good lawyer, should be able to construct a plausible argument for either side.

Shuy and Butters prepared reports for their respective clients and testified in depositions (sworn testimony given before a trial, usually in a lawyer's office, to permit the opponent to learn what the witness will say). The technical linguistic issues they debated included the following:

1. *Phonetic similarities and differences*: The two experts agreed on the number of sound units, or *phonemes*, in the AutoNation USA and AutoMation marks. Butters emphasized, however, that the "o" in AutoNation was long, whereas in a CarMax television commercial the "o" in AutoMation was pronounced "uh" (what phonologists call the "schwa" sound). He argued that this difference helped to prevent confusion. Shuy emphasized the similarity of the "n" and "m" sounds in the respective marks and pointed out that they are easily misperceived or confused by listeners. He also stressed the visual similarity of the two marks.

2. *Morpheme differences*: Butters contended that the "Auto-" morphemes (a morpheme is a unit of sound that conveys meaning) in the two marks were different: in AutoMation, auto means "self," whereas in AutoNation it means "automobile." Shuy pointed out that both were derived from the Greek *automata*, meaning "self-directed" or "propelled," and hence were a source of potential confusion.

3. *Pragmatic meaning differences*: Butters testified that AutoNation and AutoMation were used to refer to different things. The former referred to a used car store in its entirety, and the latter to a computerized inventory system that was "a relatively minor aspect of the CarMax operation"

(Shuy 2002:134). Shuy viewed this as Butters's strongest evidence of the absence of confusing similarity.

In their reports and depositions, the two experts went back and forth on these and other technical points. When the trial finally came, the two were sequestered in different hotels by their lawyers for eight days and told little about what was going on. In the end, neither testified. Shuy, who in hindsight regretted having taken the case, found out about the result only much later (a recurrent irritant in both his civil and criminal cases). What can we learn about forensic linguistics, and linguistics generally, from Shuy's accounts of cases like this? Five significant points emerge.

First, the linguistic analyses are of very high quality. The issues in such cases are close, and there is indeed much to be said on both sides. Shuy and Butters applied well-accepted linguistic theories and methods to the facts at hand and produced persuasive reports. If we were teaching linguistics, Shuy's cases would be an excellent source of illustrative materials on a range of topics. It is not surprising that courts routinely find that such analyses meet the standard of scientific reliability.

Second, at least in the instance of Shuy and Butters, the experts seem to succeed in walking the fine line between science and advocacy. As Shuy acknowledges in his writings, he understands that he is participating in an adversary process and that the lawyers may ignore an answer that does not advance their case. He stresses, though, that he is absolutely impartial in performing his work. As he puts it, "I do *not* call myself a forensic linguist . . . I consider myself a linguist who, in this instance, happens to be carrying out his analysis on data that grows out of a court case . . . the linguist analyzes the language evidence from a position of neutrality" (Shuy 1993:200).

Third, the participation of Shuy and other linguists in such cases raises some questions about equal access to justice, although they are not as troubling as in the criminal context. These are purely commercial disputes, with both sides paying their experts as part of the cost of maintaining their trademarks. It would be a rare trademark case in which linguists refused to appear on some sort of political grounds.[9] It would be an equally rare trademark case, however, in which language experts volunteered their services. Consequently, there are likely to be cases in which only one side can afford linguistic assistance. Losing a trademark is obviously not as serious a matter as going to jail, but the problem is still worth noting.

A fourth point concerns the ability of the expert witness to publish. In our experience, the lawyer and client effectively *own* the expert's work (see Conley and Peterson 1996). One cannot disclose the results of an investigation without permission. Some lawyers would argue that an expert is bound by a more far-reaching duty of loyalty, amounting to an implied agreement to not even comment on the case in a way that might be detrimental to the client's interest. Shuy's writings suggest that, at least for him, permission to disclose and comment is regularly forthcoming. But it is a matter of concern that many linguists appear to spend much, or most, of their time on work that is not automatically part of the scholarly public domain.

The fifth point involves the implications of the experts' work for linguistics itself. Shuy is correct, as we have noted, that he and others are applying established linguistic techniques to interesting problems. Once again, however, linguistics is answering questions posed by the law. This is very different from using the law as an arena for investigating questions raised by linguistics itself on theoretical grounds. A comment by Shuy is revealing. After describing his work in a case involving the trademark "doctrine of foreign equivalents" (it is possible to infringe an English-language trademark by using a foreign translation or a similar foreign word), Shuy writes, "I was never informed about the conclusion of this case. . . . Like other linguists, I am still anxiously awaiting the outcome of a salient case" (2002:149). In his expert role, Shuy would be understandably anxious to learn the outcome of the case. But why should he and other linguists, *as linguists*, care about who won? How would a court's decision affect the progress of linguistics? Is the legal tail wagging the scientific dog?

A final comment concerns a forensic linguist's review of the work on powerless language that we did in the 1970s. A 2002 issue of *Forensic Linguistics: The International Journal of Speech, Language and the Law* (the journal of the International Association of Forensic Linguists, now called simply *The International Journal of Speech, Language and the Law*) includes an essay by Joanna Kerr Thompson (2002) entitled "'Powerful/Powerless' Language in Court: A Critical Re-evaluation of the Duke Language and Law Programme." Thompson makes many excellent points. She argues, for example, that too many researchers who have used and built on our work have failed to appreciate its methodological limitations (which we readily acknowledge), and that we should have been more engaged in the critical reappraisal of the work (a fair comment). Her concern, however, seems to be less with improving the theoretical model than with "proffering advice on so sensitive a topic [witness credibility]," in particular to "ensure an adequate 'duty of care' to those potentially on the receiving end of linguistic counsel" (Thompson 2002:153–54). Elsewhere she writes that "the 'duty of care' owed by linguists to their 'clients' must be more closely defined" (Thompson 2002:153).

At this point we are puzzled. We have no clients; we have not given linguistic counsel, whatever that is; and we do not proffer advice. We asked questions that interested us as linguistic anthropologists. We published our findings in several academic journals and presented them before all kinds of legal and social science audiences. Whether we were right or wrong is a valid and important question, but its importance in no way depends on or derives from the use that experts may choose to make of our work.

Forensic Linguistics and Power

Much of the work that forensic linguists do is clearly on behalf of the powerless. The appearances of people like Loftus and Shuy in criminal cases have helped to redress the power imbalance that typically obtains between the state and the accused (the occasional celebrity felon notwithstanding). In Australia, the linguist Diana Eades (1995) has long worked to minimize the language barriers that Aborigines must overcome in dealing with the legal system. In this and many other countries, Susan Berk-Seligson (1990, reissued 2002) and others have labored to improve court interpretation, to the benefit of immigrants and other litigants who do not speak the national language. A great deal of other work in the field can be characterized as at least power-neutral. See, for example, Shuy's trademark cases, where two relatively powerful litigants seek to protect their investments. Neither side is inherently favored by forensic linguistics, and competent testimony should help the courts get it right.

In fact, it is hard to identify any instance in which forensic linguistics seems to be advancing the interests of the powerful in any overt and direct way. The potential problem, we believe, lies in the law's agenda-setting role. If forensic linguistics spends most of its time answering questions of interest to the law, then its contribution to promoting justice will necessarily be incremental. Consider, for example, the issue of gender bias in the courtroom, which was a major implication of our research on powerless language style. In her critique of our work, Thompson (2002) worries about "linguistic counselors," who presumably would help women and other powerless speakers to become better-received witnesses (compare the dialect interpreters recommended by some of the linguists whose work we discuss in chapter 10). The legal system defines a problem, and forensic experts bring social science to bear to ameliorate it.

Contrast this approach with that of Gregory Matoesian, whose work we reviewed at length in chapter 2. Matoesian dealt with the most powerless of all situations confronted by women in court: testifying as rape victims. Matoesian, however, did not begin with the law's assumptions. Instead, he used theory and methods developed elsewhere to examine rape victim testimony as a linguistic event. Far from discovering possibilities for incremental improvement, he delivered the radical message that the rape trial, with all the gender-based cultural baggage it carries, is structured in such a way as to make justice almost impossible. This is not a message that could have emerged if the law had set the agenda. This is bleak news, but is it the job of science to be hopeful and helpful?

Matoesian challenged the law's premises in a fundamental way. Much of the ad hoc work in forensic linguistics does not. As we have repeatedly argued throughout this book, the law reflects and reproduces society's power relations. Research such as Matoesian's unsettles those relations in a way that responding to the law's agenda cannot. Moreover, encouraging linguistics to become, in effect, an agent of the law may be a positive distraction from pursuing deeper questions. In this subtle and indirect way, then, contemporary forensic linguistics, even as it strives to promote just outcomes in individual cases, may be working to strengthen the structures that create injustice in the first place.

Going Forward: A Linguistically Driven Forensic Linguistics

We conclude this chapter with the book with which we began: Solan and Tiersma's *Speaking of Crime* (2005). After examining the vast and growing body of literature that now appears under the heading of forensic linguistics, we believe that Solan and Tiersma's work offers the best model for the future of the field. Rather than being linguists working for the law, they are linguists looking at the law, in ways that are determined by linguistics. They answer many questions that are of interest to the law, but, more importantly, they also ask many questions that would not have occurred to the law.

Solan and Tiersma deal with a range of situations in which the law appears to be practicing linguistics — as, for example, when courts interpret speech acts. In determining the legality of police conduct, judges must regularly decide, for instance, whether a suspect *asked for* a lawyer. Once the suspect does so, the police must stop the questioning until a lawyer is on the scene. In everyday interactions, we often ask for things in very indirect ways. A restaurant patron might say to the server, "I'd like the salmon special," or even, "I'm in the mood for the salmon." Although ostensibly mere expressions of desire, these utterances function as requests in the pragmatic context of the restaurant service encounter. But what about when a suspect under interrogation by the police says such things as "when I talk to my lawyer I'll [answer questions]," "I will get a lawyer," "maybe I need a lawyer," or "I'd like to have one [a lawyer] but you know it would be hard to get hold of one right now" (Solan and Tiersma 2005:57, 58)? Courts have refused to recognize these nonliteral requests, permitting police officers to ignore the suspect's obvious intent and continue the questioning.

The law's handling of expressions of *consent* is exactly the opposite, according to Solan and Tiersma. Whereas suspects must make explicit and literal requests for counsel, police officers have been permitted to obtain consent to search a suspect's property in the most roundabout way. For example, the US Supreme Court has found consent to search the trunk of a car where the officer asked, "Does the trunk open?" and the suspect responded in the affirmative. The problem is broader than merely the words used, as the pragmatic context of the encounter must be taken into account. Indeed, Solan and Tiersma (2005:59) conclude that when someone in a position of power or authority asks or requests us to do something, we will normally interpret it as a command.

Many of the issues they cover are also discussed in Shuy's *Language Crimes* (1993). Many of the same linguistic points are also made in both books. What is different is the intellectual approach. It may seem to be a fine distinction, but it is, we believe, a significant one. Shuy's book is a set of stories about linguistic analyses that he performed when lawyers presented him with particular cases. Solan and Tiersma began with a set of linguistic concerns and sought out legal contexts in which to explore them. Their answers involve both concrete suggestions for law reform and more basic critiques of the law's working assumptions. But their work is, in every case, linguistics applied to law, not linguistics responding to law. Any biases that may be present in their selection of issues have not been imposed by the law and thus do not reflect the power hierarchies that are embedded in it. Also, their findings are accessible to all, never the property of any particular client.

Testimony by forensic linguists in individual cases is both necessary and desirable. When courts confront linguistic issues (whether they are aware of them or not), competent experts must appear, to offer guidance. But case-by-case work should not be the driving force in the field of forensic linguistics (or the predominant activity of forensic linguists), nor should case reports comprise the bulk of its literature. "Theory" should not be merely the sum of what can be inferred from individual cases. Solan and Tiersma's work is, we believe, the model for a far more effective forensic linguistics, one in which linguistics challenges the primacy of the law rather than simply serving needs that the law defines.

CHAPTER NINE

Multimodal Communication
in the Courtroom

A s the title of this book suggests, law has usually been treated as a matter of words. Studies of language in general have historically focused on the verbal components of communication (spoken and written words), often treating the vast array of other phenomena that contribute to meaning-making in interaction as separable from or irrelevant to language. In legal contexts, this tendency is exacerbated by ideologies that privilege verbal and written language in legal procedures. Riner's (R. Conley 2015) work with death penalty juries, for instance, has shown that even though jurors rely in part on the embodied actions they experience in the courtroom — such as defendants' facial expressions and body postures — when making their decisions, they often state emphatically that consideration of these embodied actions should be barred from legal decision-making. The reliance on a written record (which generally excludes notation of nonverbal action) in legal appeal procedures exacerbates the tendency to view legal language only in terms of words.

The issue resides in part in how one defines language. In linguistics, multimodal components of interaction have traditionally been labeled "nonverbal" or "paralinguistic,"[1] thus positioning them as secondary or subordinate to language proper (Norris 2004). The majority of conversation and discourse analysis similarly prioritizes verbal aspects of interaction. This is partially due to the fact that conversation analysis (CA) originated as a system for analyzing phone calls, so visual analysis of embodied action was not possible at first. This bias is evident in the fact that while there are rigid guidelines for transcribing talk in both CA and discourse analysis, there are no consistent guidelines for how to depict nonverbal actions in a transcript (Luff and Heath 2015).

Despite these trends in language research, there is evidence that multimodal aspects of interaction, including eye gaze, gesture, body posture, facial expressions, and manipulation of material objects, can in fact contribute as much if not more than verbal language to interactional meaning (Norris 2004:x). There have been significant developments in the understanding of interaction as a multimodal system in fields such as CA, gesture studies, and linguistics (e.g., Goodwin 2003; Kendon 2004; Streeck, Goodwin, and LeBaron 2011). Legal discourse analysis, however, has lagged far behind.

This is somewhat puzzling, as legal trials are undoubtedly theatrical, visual, embodied affairs, both in reality and in the American imagination. Especially as depicted on television, lawyers are famous for their dramatic gesticulations and striking intonation patterns. Material objects and people's orientations to them garner significant focus in trials—just think of the infamous gloves in the O. J. Simpson trial. Jurors invariably attend to defendants' facial expressions during trial when evaluating their credibility and blameworthiness. Yet scholars and practitioners alike still tend to treat these aspects of trials as extralegal and thus irrelevant to law and its practice.

This chapter will highlight some work that has taken multimodal action seriously in legal contexts. Given the increasing tendency to video-record and broadcast trials, scholars have been able to closely analyze the embodied aspects of legal interaction. The chapter will review three such projects to reveal some of the most valuable lessons we can gain from looking beyond legal words to view legal practices as embodied, multimodal communicative events.

Defining Multimodality

As alluded to above, the multimodal aspects of interaction have been variously categorized within diverse fields of language studies. Traditionally, paralinguistic behavior (e.g., Trager 1958) referred to any aspect of verbal communication that did not contribute directly to the content of speech. This included voice quality, prosody (patterns of sound and rhythm), and pitch, as well as gasps and sighs. The broader category of "nonverbal language" (Duncan 1969) was then defined to include additional visual features of communication, such as body motions and body positioning in space. Gesture, or "visible bodily action that is seen as intimately involved in the activity of speaking" (Kendon 2004:ii), has generally been included in the latter category. Researchers continue to debate whether these "nonverbal" features of communication contribute to meaning to the same degree that words do, as well as whether they can be classified as part of the same communicative process.[2]

In the last few decades, efforts have been made to decentralize verbal language in studies of communication and instead theorize verbal and nonverbal behaviors as part of the same communicative process, with both contributing equally to meaning-making. Charles Goodwin has been a pioneer of such work. Expanding on the methods of conversation analysis, he and others (see Streeck,

Goodwin, and LeBaron 2011) have established a framework for analyzing the ways in which people coordinate language and embodied action in the course of face-to-face communication. This framework accounts for how multiple modes of interaction — including speaking, other embodied actions (such as gestures, eye gaze, and body positioning), and the material and visual aspects of the interactional context (such as objects and the space in which the interaction takes place) — mutually contribute to meaning. Actors may be attuned to all of these channels at once and often highlight one or more of them during an interaction. In alignment with such research, this chapter will use the terms *multimodal* and *embodied* to describe "nonverbal" aspects of interaction in order to emphasize their parity with verbal language.

Multimodal Aspects of Legal Interaction

Legal scholarship that does address multimodal aspects of communication tends to focus on how embodied actions, such as facial expressions and gesture, illuminate the affective components of law, such as judgments about credibility and state of mind. This coincides with the common ideology that feelings are conveyed more frequently and truthfully through nonverbal modes of communication than verbal ones (Remland 1994:6; Salekin et al. 1995). For instance, Susan Bandes (2014) writes about the centrality of facial expressions and body language to interpretations of demeanor in the courtroom. She argues that in capital cases the defendant's remorse — which is one of the primary factors in jurors' decisions to sentence defendants to life or death (Eisenberg et al. 1998) — is read in large part through his or her embodied actions while sitting, often silent, during trial. While work such as this is laudable for expanding the notion of law to include embodied communication, linking embodied actions to affect can be misleading, as it suggests that emotional states are the only or at least the primary information communicated through embodied action.

   The studies outlined below, in contrast, treat multimodal aspects of legal interaction as central to legal work, including trial strategy and jury decision-making. Goodwin's intricate analysis of the Rodney King trial illustrates how the prosecution's or defense's theory of a case is filtered through multimodal discursive practices, including attorneys' and witnesses' use of their own bodies in trial as well as videotape of others' embodied actions. Matoesian, in his further analysis of the William Kennedy Smith rape trial, argues that witnesses' embodied actions resist the traditionally assumed power structure of the attorney-witness interaction and therefore promote conflicting interpretations of evidence. And in her analysis of Texas death penalty trials, Riner (R. Conley 2015) reveals that capital jurors' attention to the physical arrangement of the courtroom and to defendants' embodied displays during trial has a significant impact on their decisions.

Charles Goodwin: Ways of Seeing in the Rodney King Trial

Perhaps because of its publication in an anthropological journal and the fact that the article analyzes a legal trial as well as interaction among archaeologists, Goodwin's innovative essay "Professional Vision" (1994)[3] received virtually no uptake among legal scholars. Despite its lack of visibility, the article provides a fruitful model for analyzing embodied legal interaction in almost any legal context.

Goodwin (1994:606) begins by stating the simple but important point that each profession uses specific discursive practices to shape "objects of knowledge" that distinguish it from other professions — not a novel concept to most language and law scholars. His real contribution lies in identifying three specific, embodied practices through which this knowledge-shaping occurs. The first, which he terms "coding," refers to the transformation of observed phenomena into objects of knowledge that are specific to a profession. The second, "highlighting," is a practice whereby a speaker marks specific perceived phenomena as salient in some way. The third practice is the orientation to and use of material objects within the interactional context. By utilizing these three practices, participants in an interaction build "professional vision," which "consists of socially organized ways of seeing and understanding events that are answerable to the distinctive interests of a particular social group" (Goodwin 1994:606). In the legal context, this social group could refer to the profession as a whole or to the particular interests of the prosecution or defense in a given case.

An analysis of videotaped testimony in the Rodney King trial illustrates how these embodied practices shape particular ways of seeing events central to the case. In March 1991, an African American man, Rodney King, was involved in a high-speed car chase with the Los Angeles Police. Following the chase, King was cornered, and police officers ordered him and his two passengers out of their car. King was tased multiple times and struck repeatedly with batons by the officers, who continued to beat him after he was subdued. The beating was captured on video by a bystander watching from his nearby apartment balcony. In addition to being aired on news media, this video became the central piece of evidence in the trial of the officers, all but one of whom were initially acquitted.[4] On April 29, 1992, hours after the acquittals were announced, riots broke out in Los Angeles, spurred by African Americans who were enraged by the trial's outcome.

Goodwin closely examines how, during the trial, the prosecution and the defense differently frame the bystander's videotape of the beating in order to support their respective versions of what happened. This analysis emphasizes that "the ability to see a meaningful event is not a transparent, psychological process but instead a socially situated activity accomplished through the deployment of a range of historically constituted discursive practices" (Goodwin 1994:606). That is, how a juror or judge sees and thus understands an event depicted in a trial is filtered through legal participants' actions, which promote a particular way of seeing. Goodwin asserts, however, that this is not merely legal trickery. All vision is perspectival and situated within particular communities of practice (Goodwin 1994:606). He notes, for instance, that in his writing of the article he engages in the exact same practices he is analyzing (Goodwin 1994:607).

Goodwin's use of the Rodney King trial to illustrate these phenomena is especially compelling, as he points out that the violence seen in the videotape of King's beating was so graphic that many assumed a conviction was inevitable (Goodwin 1994:615).[5] The officers' acquittal thus reveals (among other things) the power of professional vision. As Goodwin's analysis shows, the officers' attorneys were able to get jurors to "see" the videotape as something other than a depiction of egregious violence. And while Goodwin could not have foreseen this in 1994, his account of professional vision is perhaps even more salient now, at a time in which videos of similar acts have been widely spread across the internet and other media. Cell phone videos displayed on news media and on sites such as Facebook purport to depict unedited "real life" events, thus masking the specific and strategic frameworks that in fact shape their consumption.

In the King trial, the defense's presentation of the tape centered on the assertion that the tape was not simply "a record that spoke for itself" (Goodwin 1994:616). Instead, they argued, the events depicted could only be understood within the context of a particular profession: police work. The defense provided a coding scheme by which the jury could view the videotape in light of police officers' own professional vision. This coding scheme, given additional authority through its presentation by an expert witness, was offered so that jurors could see King's bodily movements as aggressive and threatening, thus justifying the officers' use of force. The coding scheme included the following:

1) If a suspect is aggressive, the proper police response is escalation of force in order to subdue him;

2) When the suspect cooperates, then force is de-escalated. (Goodwin 1994:616)

Using this scheme, an expert witness identified ten distinct uses of force in the videotape. The impact of filtering the videotape through this scheme is that the "massive beating" was transformed into ten individual events:

TEXT 9.1 (Goodwin 1994:617)[6]

EXPERT: There were ten distinct (1.0) uses of force. Rather than one single use of force . . . In each of those uses of force there was an

escalation and a de-escalation, (0.8) an assessment period, (1.5)
and then an escalation and a de-escalation again. (0.7) And another
5   assessment period.

This coding scheme made it possible for the defense to transform images that
initially appear to be out-of-control violence into demonstrations of stages of
carefully controlled police work. This included classifying kicks — what the
prosecution referred to as "cowardly stomps" — and baton strikes as tools required for such work (Goodwin 1994:618). A point in the tape at which the
prosecution claimed the officers were "beating a suspect into submission," for
instance, was transformed into evidence that a "period of de-escalation has
ceased" (Goodwin 1994:617).

Text 9.2 (Goodwin 1994:617)

DEFENSE: Four oh five, oh one. We see a blow being delivered. Is that
correct.
EXPERT: That's correct. The force has been again escalated (0.3)
to the level it had been previously, (0.4) and the de-escalation has
5   ceased.
. . .
DEFENSE: And at- at this point which is, for the record four thirteen
twenty nine, (0.4) We see a blow being struck and thus the end of the
period of de-escalation? Is that correct Captain.
10   EXPERT: That's correct. Force has now been elevated to the previous
level, (0.6) after this period of de-escalation.

This scheme of stages of escalation, combined with the deletion of human
agents from descriptions of acts of violence ("a blow being delivered," "a blow
being struck"), equips the jury with a "far from neutral" framework for seeing
the events depicted on the video (Goodwin 1994:617).
A second coding scheme was provided in order to interpret King's bodily
actions and determine whether each was aggressive or cooperative. The former
designation was used to justify the officers continuing to hit him. This way of
seeing the videotaped events depicts King, rather than the officers, as in control
of the situation (Goodwin 1994:618). Sergeant Charles Duke of the LAPD,
called as an expert for the defense, describes a point at which King seemingly
moves into a position to be handcuffed:

Text 9.3 (Goodwin 1994:619)

PROSECUTOR: So uh would you, again consider this to be a nonaggres-
sive movement by Mr. King?

SGT. DUKE: At this time no I wouldn't. (1.1)
PROSECUTOR: It is aggressive.
5   SGT. DUKE: Yes. It's starting to be. (0.9) This foot, is laying flat, (0.8)
There's starting to be a bend in uh (0.6) this leg (0.4) in his butt (0.4)
The buttocks area has started to rise, (0.7) which would put us at the
beginning of our spectrum again.

The prosecution argued that these movements by King were cooperative, but
the defense's coding scheme renders them aggressive, justifying, in their view,
the officers' continued beating. This is accomplished, in part, through language
that highlights King's movements as the beginning of an escalating scale of
action: "It's *starting* to be"; "There's *starting* to be a bend"; "The buttocks
area has *started* to rise." This semantic highlighting is amplified by images of
the witness's physical movements, as Sergeant Duke points on the screen to
the parts of King's body that are purportedly displaying aggression (Goodwin
1994:620).

At another point in the trial, a defense attorney presented printed frame grabs
of a part of the videotape in which King is running and very hard to see. The
photographs were enlarged and placed on an easel. Large white-line overlays
outlining King's body were added to the images, thus highlighting King as the
object of the attorney's argument: a "large, violent, charging African-American
man" (Goodwin 1994:622). Another effect of these printed photos is to eliminate the ephemeral nature of a videotape. With the enlarged photos, each image
remains visible indefinitely and is able to be scrutinized at length.

Goodwin argues that these processes of highlighting "[organize] the per-
ceptual field provided by the videotape into a salient figure, the aggressive
suspect, who is highlighted against an amorphous background containing non-
focal participants, the officers doing the beating" (Goodwin 1994:620). The
defense's establishment of this particular vision of the videotape was crucial
to the eventual acquittal of the officers. This was especially the case given the
prosecution's failure to provide a counterframework to the defense's for view-
ing the tape. Once the jury members accepted the defense's coding scheme as
a "relevant framework," their interpretation of the tape was transformed from a
"lay person's reaction to a man lying on the ground being beaten" to a "microanalysis" of movements made by a potential aggressor (Goodwin 1994:621).
In the second trial, which led to convictions, the prosecution provided a clear
counterframework by which to interpret King's movements.

Significantly, Goodwin's analysis of the King trial sees legal language as
much more than the words recorded on a court transcript. The coding and highlighting processes that provided the defense's view of the videotape were enhanced by the simultaneous engagement of verbal, visual, and embodied signs.
Without this mutual articulation of visual and embodied actions and material

artifacts used in the case, the defense's successful establishment of a particular professional vision would not have been possible. Goodwin's overall point is that when studying language in any context, we need to attend to verbal signs, embodied actions, and the material world as equally relevant components of a single system of communication.

Goodwin's analysis also has important implications for recognizing the power structures entailed in institutional interaction. Different professions, Goodwin asserts, "have the power to legitimately see, constitute, and articulate alternative kinds of events" (Goodwin 1994:627). Treating legal discourse as a way of seeing allows us to scrutinize the practices through which particular, authoritative versions of events and types of knowledge get constituted. This type of analysis also allows us to recognize the contingent nature of legal categories. Their meaning is not solidified until they are mobilized in a specific context in relation to specific phenomena, thereby providing opportunities for change (Goodwin 1994:627).

Gregory Matoesian: Reproducing Rape through Multimodal Interaction

In the past several years, Gregory Matoesian (2013, 2008a, 2008b, 2005) has refocused his extensive work on language in the William Kennedy Smith rape trial (discussed in chapter 2) to address the role of embodied action in courtroom discourse. This section will focus on his 2008 article "You Might Win the Battle but Lose the War: Multimodal, Interactive, and Extralinguistic Aspects of Witness Resistance" (Matoesian 2008a). Again, because this work was published in an obscure (to nonacademics) linguistics journal and is rife with arcane, discipline-specific terminology, it may remain largely off the radar of legal scholars. His analysis has significant implications, however, for one of the more thoroughly researched forms of legal language: lawyer-witness interaction. Matoesian argues that attending to multimodal actions in the courtroom can reconfigure how we think about the typical asymmetry of the lawyer-witness interaction. Specifically, he challenges the prototypical model of attorney control and witness passivity (Matoesian 2008a:195–96) by analyzing a case in which, through embodied actions, a witness gains a degree of control during her testimony. He argues, like Goodwin, that witnesses and other participants in a trial strategically rely on visual, embodied, and material resources when "confronting their legal realities in the courtroom" (Matoesian 2008a:196).

As explained in chapter 2, researchers have looked to language to illuminate the power dynamics at play in sexual assault cases. Specifically, some have focused on the witness cross-examination process as a revictimization and further disempowering of the assault victim (often along gender lines) (Mateosian 1993, 2001; Ehrlich 2001). Matoesian asserts, however, that we should look beyond the linguistic details of questioning sequences to other means by which a witness may destabilize the power dynamics in a trial (Matoesian 2008a:197). To more thoroughly interrogate institutional power structures in the courtroom, he argues, we need (1) a more interactive understanding of language, (2) to move beyond a bias toward the questioner as the controller of the interaction, and (3) to take seriously the role of visual and multimodal aspects of courtroom interaction in subverting asymmetries in participation (Matoesian 2008a:197).

As a form of institutional discourse, courtroom language is highly regulated. The traditional model of attorney-witness interaction is generally reduced to the powerful attorney, who holds the institutional authority to ask questions, and the disempowered witness, who is restricted merely to answering the questions posed (Matoesian 2008a:196). This model assumes that question control — the intricacies of which have been copiously examined by conversation analysts — is a real and consequential way in which attorneys wield power in the courtroom. While this point is well taken, this model, Matoesian contends, relegates the witness to a "passive answering space" (2008a:198), rather than permitting her to be an active participant in the interaction. He proposes that looking beyond the linguistic details of question-and-answer sequences to the variety of multimodal actions performed by both attorneys and witnesses can reveal interactional practices through which witnesses may empower themselves and challenge the dominant narrative of a case.

Matoesian analyzes the testimony of prosecution witness Ann Mercer, the victim's friend, in the William Kennedy Smith trial. Mercer saw the victim directly before and after the rape incident. (The incident, the trial — in which Smith was acquitted — and the surrounding media circus are described in chapter 2.) Matoesian specifically examines an excerpt of testimony in which Mercer attempts to amend her answer to a question she was asked the previous day about whether Senator Kennedy, the defendant's uncle, had "watched" the incident (Matoesian 2008a:198). Merely by making such a request, Mercer is already beginning to invert the typical attorney/witness turn-taking sequence. The attorney, not surprisingly, responds with skepticism, suggesting to the jury that Mercer is asking to change her answer to a question after "thinking about it overnight" (Matoesian 2008a:200). Mercer makes her request after an extremely long (in conversational terms) 7.3 second pause:

TEXT 9.4 (Matoesian 2008a:199–200)

DA: You knew that you were going to be asked questions only twelve hours ago. It was only twelve hours isn't that right?
(1.1)
AM [MERCER]: Yes.
5   (7.3)
((slight head tilt forward and back at 7.0))

*((lip smack/alveolar click and head movement forward toward
microphone with thinking face display at 7.3))*
AM: I would like to complete my answer on uh the question (.) about
10   (.) saying that Senat[or Kennedy was watching.
                         [*((gaze moves to DA))*
     (0.9)
     *((raised and sustained eyebrow flash with mouth open-close co-
     occurring with three micro vertical head nods))*
15   (3.3)
     DA: Uh (.) which question are you answering now miss
                                        [
     AM: You had asked me uh (.) yesterday
     (0.5) n'you also asked me this morning (0.5) about my statement to the
20   police
                            [   ]
     DA: You want to-
     AM: saying that she told me that Senator Kennedy was watching. *I
     would like to complete that answer for the jury please.*
25   (0.9)
     DA: *You mean* this is an answer that I asked you yesterday you now
     after thinking about it overnight want to complete the ah answer.
                    [   ]
     AM: Ah No. I didn't have the opportunity to *answer your*
30   *question yesterday ((staccato delivery))* I [believe=
                                        [*((slight gaze movement from DA
     to Judge and back))*
     =we had stopped [at that point.
                     [*((45 degree turn to Judge and back to DA))*
35   (1.2)
     DA: I'm sorry I thought you had uh completed your answer. If you
     want to say something to the jury that you've had time to think about
     (.) please go ((lower volume))
                                        [
40   AM: No- it- *I haven't had time to*
     think about it. I would have said the same thing yesterday when you
     asked me. ((Sped up))

Matoesian closely examines the sequence and character of the embodied
actions Mercer employs to support her departure from the institutionally sanctioned interactional order. She displays contemplation of and perhaps hesitancy
about making such a move at the start of her turn by first leaning toward the
microphone and then pulling back (Matoesian 2008a:202–3). She then turns her

gaze to the attorney, only to retract it to assume a "thinking face" (Matoesian 2008a:203). In a potential show of confidence in her move, she then regains a mutual gaze with the attorney. She holds this gaze, raising her eyebrows when she does not at first receive a response from him. After a continued lack of response (4.2 seconds total), she nods her head three times, indicating her preference that he grant her the request (Matoesian 2008a:203).

While these embodied details may seem superfluous in a discussion of legal language, their significance can be revealed by imagining the interaction (any interaction, for that matter) without such embodied communicative moves. Had Mercer kept her gaze down throughout the sequence, never engaging the attorney visually, her request might have been entirely ignored. Instead, through nonverbal means, she essentially challenges the attorney to grant her request and thus to participate with her in the inversion of the institutional interactional order. Though her request is reframed slightly by the attorney into an appeal to recant previous testimony, her success in creating a turn for herself in which she may address testimony that she chooses is undeniable.

The totality of these embodied actions as they are built over the course of a trial constitute, in Matoesian's words, "the interactional architecture of the courtroom" (2008a:204), shaping the institutional order that analysts tend to treat as a predetermined reality. Paying attention to such multimodal resources is therefore "a basic, not tangential, requirement for specifying how witness resistance emerges" in the courtroom (Matoesian 2008a:204). This perspective underlines the point made above: to understand how law in fact works, it must be understood as a sequence of unfolding — and thus contingent — actions, rather than as merely a "system of formal rationality" (Matoesian 2008a:206).

Robin Conley Riner: Multimodality and Capital Jury Decision-Making

A final example of the importance of incorporating a multimodal perspective into language and law studies comes from one of our projects (Riner), which investigated the language of death penalty trials and the effect that trial language has on jurors' decisions (R. Conley 2013, 2015). For this research I conducted fifteen months of ethnographic fieldwork in various counties across Texas, which included attending capital trials and interacting closely with defense teams. I then interviewed twenty-one jurors after their verdicts were rendered; they had served on nine different cases. The analysis consisted of comparing my interview data with trial transcripts in order to identify specific communicative practices from the trials that resonated with jurors during their interviews and may have played a role in their decision-making. One of the more poignant findings of the analysis was that jurors struggled with confronting defendants face-to-face during trial and then having to "distort, diminish, or negate these interactions in order to sentence those same defendants to death" (R. Conley

2015:45). Jurors' and defendants' engagement in embodied communication during trial thus emerged as a salient aspect of jurors' decision-making.

Evaluating the significance of embodied communication for jurors' understanding of a case is especially tricky, as jurors, along with many legal practitioners and scholars, operate within the ideology explicated at the beginning of this chapter: actions that lie outside the traditional purview of "language" (understood as written and spoken words) are thought to be outside the purview of law as well. Thus capital jurors do not merely struggle to reconcile their face-to-face encounters with defendants with their decisions to sentence them to death. This difficulty is compounded by jurors' belief that they must somehow eradicate these embodied encounters from their deliberations and rely only on the content of what is said on the witness stand. According to such "paralinguistic ideologies" (R. Conley 2015:85), jurors assume that their instructions to remain "objective" require that they ignore embodied experiences during trial in their decision-making. What makes this belief especially problematic is that, according to the interviews I conducted, jurors' judgments of defendants were in fact based in large part on embodied communication during trial.

As one jury foreman explained,

TEXT 9.5 (R. Conley 2015:72)

> JUROR: The charge said that we would only let evidence guide us . . . So you must try to put your emotion aside as much as you can and only go on what is presented as evidence, either from the stand or physical evidence.

According to this juror, anything that was not presented through witness testimony or physical evidence was not to be included in his decision-making. And while this coincides with rules of evidence for most criminal trials, capital sentencing verdicts are qualitatively different. They have been characterized as acts of mercy (*Kansas v. Carr*, 136 S. Ct. 633 (2016)), and capital jurors have been told to make individual "moral judgments" (*U.S. v. Wilson*, 967 F. Supp. 2d 673 (2013)) when sentencing capital defendants. Among the jurors I interviewed, however, this "death is different" perspective was not taken up. Rather, jurors' ideas about decision-making were based on the notion that nothing outside of the content of testimony should be allowed to impact their decisions.

Empathy between jurors and defendant, something capital defendants have a constitutional right to seek and thus something defense attorneys strive to promote, may in fact require certain forms of embodied communication. Justice William Brennan, among others, addressed the limiting nature of a legal ideology that occludes such experiences, proposing that legal judgment should be expanded to "reflect the 'subjective, experiential, and emotional' influences of decision-making" (R. Conley 2015:87; Henderson 1998:123). The real difficulty lies in how to fit aspects of multimodal interaction into a workable legal conception of evidence.

Juror interviews reveal that despite their expressed belief (albeit ill-founded, legally) that their verdicts should be based only on what is said and presented from the witness stand, jurors in fact attend to two particular multimodal aspects of trial interaction when making their decisions: the positioning of bodies in the courtroom, which affects with whom jurors may engage in face-to-face interaction, and defendants' embodied displays of emotion during trial (R. Conley 2015:88). In regards to the first, US legal policy acknowledges the import of having a defendant and jury copresent in the courtroom, as the physical presence of both is required for trials to proceed (Levenson 2008). The defendant's presence is thus expected but taken for granted and rarely examined from an academic perspective (R. Conley 2015:93). Though the spatial aspect of a courtroom is typically considered to be a "depoliticized surface" (Mulcahy 2007:384), the layout of a courtroom, including where specific people are positioned within it, is institutionally determined and is integral to how power relations are structured within the US trial system (R. Conley 2015:94). Our courtrooms are designed to encourage participatory justice, for instance, by allowing the public and press to take up a majority of the space (R. Conley 2015:94; Mulcahy 2007:385).

The Texas courtrooms where I conducted my fieldwork are fairly typical of US courtrooms. One of these was set up as follows: On entering the courtroom through the main door in the rear, you came first to the large gallery area where the public sat. Just beyond the gallery was the bar—a physical bar, and the source of the legal profession being called "the bar," since lawyers can cross it. Forward of the bar were two tables that seated the prosecution and defense teams, respectively. Directly in front of the tables was the elevated judge's seat, or bench. The witness stand was directly to the left of the bench when facing it from the gallery, and the jury box directly to the left of that against the left wall of the room.

Because the defendant was seated in front of the bar at one of the attorney tables, this arrangement necessitated that the jurors walk in front of the defendant as they enter or exit the courtroom. This made a number of the jurors I spoke with uncomfortable; they remarked at the defendant's ready ability to catch their gaze as they walked in and out. Some of them actively avoided making eye contact with defendants. Many of the jurors talked about eye contact—or lack thereof—with defendants as a meaningful experience for them, even though it is "not caught on record and certainly not part of the 'evidence'" (R. Conley 2015:96). Any way in which jurors' access to the defendant's face is limited by the setup of the courtroom or by jurors' own evasions serves to help jurors distance themselves from the defendant and thus to stymie empathy with him or her.

Observing multiple capital trials revealed that defendants went to great lengths to perform the "rational legal subject" in the courtroom (R. Conley 2015:101). Defendants did not physically stand out in their trials: they dressed like attorneys, they were not visibly restrained at all, and most stayed quiet, did not testify, and maintained a consistently flat demeanor throughout the trial. My interviews with jurors revealed that they relied a great deal on defendants' embodied displays during trial as a way to try to read their emotions. Because the majority of defendants did not testify, this reliance on defendants' actions that were not part of the presentation of evidence became even more salient. For many jurors, the defendant's apparent lack of emotion, read through these embodied cues (which were in large part directed by attorney coaching), served as evidence that the defendant lacked remorse or lacked a degree of humanity, and thus deserved a death sentence.

Similar to Bandes's work discussed above, this research shows that jurors especially relied on embodied displays to measure a defendant's remorse. This reliance rests on additional paralinguistic ideologies common to legal practice: that someone can "look" remorseful, and that one's outer countenance accurately reflects one's inner state (R. Conley 2015:103). A female juror I spoke with expresses this common expectation regarding the defendant's emotional displays during trial:

Text 9.6 (R. Conley 2015:104)

> Juror: When he cried a couple times, we did talk about that. You
> know, when he showed some kind of emotion and it only happened a
> few times, you know. We did talk about that.
> Robin: And you think that had any impact on [the decision]?
> 5 Juror: On the jur- on the verdict? It probably made us think a little
> more about, you know, someone who's just going to sit back in
> his chair the whole time and not react will- you'd probably think
> wasn't conflicted about it. Or, you know, wasn't remorseful about it.
> Whereas he seemed like he was, you know, and I think we took away
> 10 from the, the couple of times he showed emotion.

In describing an atypical defendant who did show emotion through a nonverbal action — crying — this juror reveals that performing the rational legal subject during trial may in fact work against a defendant. Another juror describes the emotionless demeanor of a different defendant and the negative impact it had on his verdict:

Text 9.7 (R. Conley 2015:104–5)

> Juror: But during that whole trial, he, if you were there, you too saw
> it: he had no emotion whatsoever. He was cold as a snake. Now if

someone was sitting in a jury box [*witness stand*] telling the world
what a horrible person I was, I think I would have at least been a
5   little bit interested in what they were saying . . . at least show an
interest in what's going on. And he showed none whatsoever . . . he
was just completely cold . . . I mean, you know, did he show any
human feeling?

This interview excerpt exposes a juror's desire to see what he deems to be
human reactions from a defendant during the course of the trial. It illustrates that
jurors rely on much more than the words spoken from the witness stand when
judging defendants. It also reveals, importantly, that seeing a trial only through
the lens of a transcript—that is, as only a collection of words—dehumanizes
the participants. Each trial participant is attuned to others as acting, embodied
subjects, and thus an understanding of trials must proceed from a perspective
that includes these embodied components.

Law, Language, and Multimodality

While these findings might simply seem to reflect the fallacy outlined above—
that it is misleading to consider embodied actions only for the affective information they convey—their true import is that they reveal that jurors themselves
espouse this fallacy. Both jury instructions (and other procedural aspects of law)
and law and language scholarship often treat jurors as "disembodied finders
of fact" (R. Conley 2015:115). By reseeing legal language as a multimodal
endeavor, however, we can start to humanize legal actors and see jurors as some
of the many embodied actors whose interactions constitute a legal proceeding.

The tendency to confine the understanding of legal interaction to verbal components alone has been guided in part by methodological limitations. The lack
of access to video-recorded trials, or to video recordings as part of the official
record of a case, is one such limitation. Even when video is available, factors
such as camera angles and the inability of a single camera to capture everything
going on in a trial further restrict the recording of multimodal interaction (Matoesian 2008a). In addition, disciplinary methods for recording and analyzing
nonverbal communication have lagged behind those for studying verbal language. But as more and more courts are moving to include up-to-date recording
technology to monitor their proceedings, scholars are suddenly well-positioned
to reenvision (literally and figuratively) legal communication.

CHAPTER TEN

Language and Race in the Courtroom

In previous editions of this book, we had little to say about race and the microdiscourses of the law. This was not because we thought the topic un-important; on the contrary, its significance was self-evident in 1998, when we wrote the first edition, and even more so in 2005, the date of the second edition. The problem was that there was little primary linguistic research to report. Although there has been a great deal of research on the racial dimensions of language generally (see Rickford and King 2016), we found little on the racial dimensions of *legal* language specifically. In fact, as late as 2010, the Australian forensic linguist Diana Eades commented accurately that there was "almost no linguistic research which examines African American interactions in the legal process" (2010:89). That was beginning to change by the time that Eades made her comment, and the change is accelerating. Eades herself, for example, has done extensive work at the microdiscourse level on the reception of Aboriginal English in the Australian legal system, and the impact of language on the treatment of Aboriginal people (see Eades 2012).

Some of the best recent work on race and legal language in the United States has been motivated by the tragic death of Trayvon Martin, an African American teenager. In 2012, the unarmed Martin was shot and killed by George Zimmerman, a white member of a "neighborhood watch" in the Florida gated community where Martin was staying with his father's fiancée. In a 911 call during the encounter, Zimmerman reported that Martin was "suspicious," and that he "looks like he is up to no good or he is on drugs or something." He further commented, "These assholes they always get away" (Slobe 2016:617). Ignoring the police dispatcher, Zimmerman followed Martin and shot him during an ensuing altercation. Zimmerman later told the local police that he had not followed Martin, but that Martin had jumped out of the bushes and attacked him with physical violence and verbal threats to his life. Zimmerman claimed a right of self-defense under Florida's "Stand Your Ground" law, which provides that someone behaving lawfully who is attacked by another need not retreat but can defend himself even to the point of using deadly force.

The initial decision by local law enforcement not to arrest or prosecute Zimmerman led to weeks of nationwide protest. The authorities then changed their mind and prosecuted Zimmerman for second-degree murder. His 2013 acquittal led to more protests, and the ensuing controversy merged into the metastasizing national controversy over police officers' use of lethal force against African American civilians.

In this chapter we will examine two detailed analyses of the pivotal role of race-related language in Zimmerman's trial. Both focus on the testimony of prosecution witness Rachel Jeantel, another African American teenager who was on the phone with Martin in the moments leading up to the shooting. John R. Rickford and Sharese King (2016:249) argue for "the central role" that Jeantel's particular dialect — African American Vernacular English (AAVE) — played in the jury's decision to discount her testimony. Significantly, Rickford has been a leading scholar of AAVE and its sociolinguistic effects for more than forty years. He also has a compelling personal perspective on dialect and vernacular, having been born in the former British colony of Guyana.

The second linguistic analysis of the Zimmerman trial is by a younger linguistic anthropologist, Tyanna Slobe (2016). Slobe also discusses the impact of Jeantel's AAVE on the reception of her testimony, but her specific focus is on some of the lexical usages that Jeantel attributed to Trayvon Martin in their final phone conversation — particularly his reported description of Zimmerman as a "creepy-ass cracker."

The Relationship between Race and Language

One possible answer to the question, What is the relationship between language and race? is "none." This is true in the sense that a person of any race can speak any language, whether by growing up as a native speaker or by learning it later in life. The same is true of dialects within a language. It is all a matter of geography and social environment — up to a point.

To introduce the complex relationship between language and race, permit one of the authors (JMC) to offer a personal anecdote:

> I grew up in the 1950s in Dorchester, a working-class section of Boston. Everyone in the neighborhood was white. In fact, almost everyone I knew there was Irish Catholic. And we all shared a dialect — an extreme version of the Boston accent featured (fairly accurately) in the movie *The Departed*. It is characterized by dropped post-vocalic *r*s

(as in "*The Depahted*"), hyper-rounded short *o*s (as in "Red Sawx"), and some ubiquitous lexical items used as an adjective or intensifying adverb, such as *wicked* and the cruder but wonderful word *pisser* (pronounced "pissah"), which carries a range of connotations from praise to ironic deprecation.

I've gone back to my neighborhood a few times over the years. All the original houses, including mine, are still there and occupied. The people *look* different from when I was growing up, reflecting changed immigration patterns. I've encountered people who had come — or whose parents or grandparents had come — from Southeast Asia, Cape Verde, and the Azores. In media terms, the "racial makeup" of the neighborhood had changed. But people have *sounded* the same, at least if they had learned English in the Boston speech community. This reality has been, at some level, surprising to me.

At a superficial level, this example shows that a language or dialect is not the exclusive or inherent property of any racial group. But at another level, it also illustrates an association between race and speech. The author apparently harbored some expectations about how people *should* talk. These expectations made the continuity of dialect in the face of ethnic change somehow surprising. While the author hopes that his reaction was nothing more than benign curiosity, the analyses of the Zimmerman trial we discuss here show that the impact of the race-language relationship can take a more sinister turn. We must confront Rickford and King's claim that "race is language and language race" (2016:981).

Before exploring this relationship further, it is necessary to say something about the meaning of race. This is a huge and contentious topic that is far beyond the scope of this book, but a few definitional comments are in order. If you look up the definition of race in a biology textbook, you will find something along the lines of an informal taxonomic category, a genetically distinct, geographically isolated, interbreeding population within a single species, whose members share some traits at a higher frequency than members of other groups. Accordingly, a bird-watching guide might identify the western and eastern "races" of a single species by their distinguishing color patterns.

Though it may work for birds, this definition does not translate well to human beings. All humans have been members of a single species, *Homo sapiens*, for at least the last twelve thousand years, and probably longer. But humans' mobility and enthusiasm for intergroup mating — aided and abetted by language, by the way — have drastically reduced geographic and reproductive isolation, especially in recent centuries. It is possible to use the biological concept of race to make some crude inferences about geography and history. People who have more melanin (i.e., darker complexions) are probably at least descended from people from equatorial regions, where melanin has a sunscreen-like protective function. Conversely, those with the lightest complexions are probably descended from people who lost their melanin when they migrated into high latitudes with less direct sunlight, where melanin would inhibit the synthesis of vitamin D. Other trivial physical characteristics sometimes associated with race, like hair texture and nose structure, have no apparent connection with natural selection in the evolutionary past.

Beyond these obvious inferences, the biological concept of race has little or no applicability to *Homo sapiens* — in fact, some critics have argued that biological race is a category that does not even exist in the case of our species (e.g., Zack 2001). Human race is instead a social construct, an idea invented more than two hundred years ago to emphasize differences among people and to justify inequality. In the words of a statement issued twenty years ago by the American Anthropological Association (1998),

> Racial beliefs constitute myths about the diversity in the human species and about the abilities and behavior of people homogenized into "racial" categories. The myths fused behavior and physical features together in the public mind, impeding our comprehension of both biological variations and cultural behavior, implying that both are genetically determined. Racial myths bear no relationship to the reality of human capabilities or behavior.

There is a vast (and also contentious) literature dealing with the biological aspects of language, but most of it involves the origins of human language, the neurological processes by which language is learned and produced, and the nature and extent of the differences in linguistic capacity between the human species and our animal relations. Significantly, this language and biology literature focuses on language (singular), not languages (plural), and thus stresses the unity of *Homo sapiens*. There is general agreement that humans all share (excepting only individual disabilities) a hardwired capacity to acquire language, which for most people works at peak efficiency in early childhood. Accordingly, exposure to any particular language (including sign language) during the first few years of life will trigger this capacity automatically; thereafter, language acquisition usually requires a conscious effort.

Beyond these few points, language is entirely cultural. The branching of languages, evolution and change within individual languages, the expansion and extinction of languages, and the rise and fall of the influence of particular languages are all reflective of — and have played a critical role in — historical cultural processes. Thus, English originally spread around the world as a "soft" component of the military and economic power of the British Empire, and its current status as the language of global capitalism is a manifestation of late-twentieth-century American economic hegemony. Whether the economic and military rise of China will have a similar linguistic aspect is an interesting question in the current century.

These things are also true for dialects, defined as distinctive variants within a language that are characteristic of regions or social groups. If anything, dialects (or vernaculars, as they are sometimes called) may carry even more cultural significance. In chapter 7 we discussed language ideology, which we defined there as a "'a body of ideas about language,' with a particular focus on political contexts." We stress that language ideologies are rarely neutral and can thus play a significant role in both asserting and challenging social, political, and economic power. The examples that follow in this chapter provide a vivid illustration of these principles. Among those who speak it, the use of a dialect may be a source of identity and in-group solidarity. But its reception by those outside the community of speakers may reflect deeply held biases; indeed, the mere use of a dialect may be invoked to justify those biases. In a legal context, this interplay of ideologies can have profound real-world consequences.

AAVE in the Zimmerman Trial: The Prosecution's Case (Rickford and King 2016)

John Rickford was one of the first linguistic scholars to identify AAVE as a distinctive dialect (e.g., Rickford 1975, 1999). To many speakers of Standard American English (including, Rickford and King (2016:970) stress, some African Americans), AAVE is simply "bad English," an unsystematically degraded version of the standard form. Such hearers may interpret the use of AAVE as evidence of the speakers' low intelligence or lack of education. But in fact, like a dazzling array of other nonstandard vernaculars, AAVE is a thoroughly systematic language variety with a distinctive lexicon and rules of phonology and grammar.

As Rickford and King point out, nineteen-year-old Rachel Jeantel was the "star witness" for the prosecution in the Zimmerman trial (2016:950). She was as close to an eyewitness as there was (other than Zimmerman), since she was on the phone just before Martin's death and was able to report what he was telling her about the situation. Yet the jurors — according to what they said in post-trial interviews — ignored her testimony. Moreover, "her vernacular speech was pilloried" (Rickford and King 2016:950) on television and in social media. These adverse reactions were largely attributable to her use of AAVE, Rickford and King argue.

They support their argument by specific trial-transcript references that illustrate many of the defining features of AAVE. Text 10.1, for example, is taken from the court reporter's transcript of Jeantel's direct examination by the prosecutor — in other words, it is supposed to be a friendly, not hostile, examination. The intended point of the testimony is that Trayvon Martin, per his comments to Jeantel on the phone, was running away from Zimmerman, not toward him, when he was shot.

TEXT 10.1 (Adapted from Rickford and King 2016:956)[1]

> RJ [JEANTEL]: He said he from — he — I asked him where he at. And he told me he at the back of his daddy fiancée house, like in the area where his daddy fiancée — by his daddy fiancée house. Like — I said, "Oh, you better keep running." He said, naw, he lost him.

Note several features of this brief, uninterrupted excerpt. First, the content is entirely supportive of the prosecution's case. Martin reports that he is someplace he has a right to be: at the back of the house where he is a guest. Then, Jeantel advises him to keep running. Martin responds that he has no need to because "he lost him." If this account is believed, there can be no doubt that Martin was running *away* from Zimmerman, not *toward* or *after* him.

The other significant features are stylistic and involve some defining attributes of AAVE. In the first two lines, for example, Jeantel deletes three *copulas*, or linking verbs: the *was* that would, in Standard American English, have been inserted in the middle of "he from" and (twice) "he at." The inclusion of the preposition "at" in the indirect question "where he at" is also characteristic of, though not exclusive to, AAVE. The second and third lines then contain multiple instances of deletion of the possessive marker (or token, as linguists often call it) -*s* (or, phonetically, -*z*): "his daddy fiancée" in place of the Standard American English "his daddy*'s* fiancée," and "fiancée house" rather than the standard "fiancée's house." This deletion is also characteristic of — and highly regular in — AAVE.

The prosecutor (BR) immediately interrupts (Text 10.2). It is clear that he is concerned about the intelligibility of Jeantel's speech, but he does not articulate precisely why (note "you make sure you're — "). The only plausible interpretation, of course, is that he is concerned that her use of AAVE will detract from the reception of her testimony in some way. The prosecutor's ostensible concern for the quality of the transcript seems a pretext, one that the practicing lawyer among us (JMC) can recall using.

TEXT 10.2 (Adapted from Rickford and King 2016:956)

> BR: Okay. Let me stop you a second. This — this lady [*the Court Reporter*] has got to take everything down, so you make sure you're — Okay. So after he said he lost him, what happened then?

In the remainder of the exchange, Jeantel continues to employ these AAVE usages as well as others, and both the prosecutor and the court reporter react in ways that mark those usages as deviating from Standard American English:

Text 10.3 (Adapted from Rickford and King 2016:956)

RJ: And he say he — he by — um — the area that his daddy house is, his daddy fiancée house is, and I told him "Keep running." He — and he said, "Naw," he'll just walk faster. I'm like, "Oh oh." And I — I ain't complain, 'cause he was breathing hard, so I understand why.
5   Soo.
BR: What — what happened after that?
RJ: And then, second later — ah — Trayvon come and say, "Oh, shit!"
CR: "Second later?"
RJ: A couple second later, Trayvon come and say, "Oh, shit!"
10   BR: Okay. Let me interrupt you a second. When you say, the words, "Oh, shit," pardon my language, who said that?
RJ: Trayvon.
BR: He said it to YOU?
RJ: Yes.
15   BR: Okay. And after he used, pardon my language, he said, "Oh, shit," what happened then?
RJ: The nigga behind me
CR: I'm sorry, what?
RJ: The nigga's behind — the nigga behind me.
20   BR: Okay. He used the N word again and said the nigger is behind me?

   Rickford and King emphasize multiple aspects of this critical stretch of testimony — critical because Martin reports with shock that Zimmerman, whom he had been trying to evade, had come up behind him. Hardly the spontaneous reaction we would expect if Martin had been chasing or stalking Zimmerman, as the latter claimed in his conversation with the police dispatcher. Moreover, Martin's decision to stop running when he reached what he thought was a safe place seems entirely rational. Had he kept running, Zimmerman almost certainly would have characterized it as suspicious flight and, as Martin feared, intensified his pursuit.

   As in the previous texts, there are multiple copula deletions: "he by" in the first line, rather than the standard "he was by," and two instances of "the nigga [is] behind me" toward the end (although those instances are separated by the same phrase with the contracted copula). There are also multiple deletions of the token -s, whether as a possessive marker (e.g., "his daddy fiancée house") or a marker of the plural (as in "second later" and "a couple second later"). The court reporter directly questions the latter usage, and Jeantel clarifies it not by adding the -s token but by adding the quantitative modifier "couple," which apparently satisfies the reporter. Nonetheless, the interjection clearly marks the usage as nonstandard. Jeantel also uses several distinctive verb forms: "I ain't complain" as a past tense form; "Trayvon come" for, perhaps, the Standard American English "Trayvon came back"; and "say" (twice) as a past tense form.

But probably the most striking aspects of Text 10.3 are two lexical items—"oh, shit" and "nigga"—and the prosecutor's responses to them. (We emphasize again that the prosecutor has called Jeantel as a witness, so he is the nominally friendly lawyer in this examination.) In the former instance, Jeantel says (twice), "Trayvon come and say, 'Oh, shit!'" After she says it the second time, the prosecutor immediately interrupts (his characterization). Two aspects of his interruption seem significant to us. The first is his twofold apology ("pardon my language") for repeating the profanity ("Oh, shit"), an apology presumably directed at the jury and everyone else in the courtroom. Saying "Oh, shit" has nothing to do with AAVE, nor is it remarkable in the context of a person discovering that an armed pursuer has caught up with him—many people could probably imagine themselves saying the same thing in similar circumstances. But the prosecutor's double apology does tend to emphasize that, yet again, Jeantel has said something that violates the norms of "standard" linguistic behavior.

The second noteworthy aspect of the prosecutor's interruption is that he follows his first apology by asking what seems to be an unnecessary question: "Who said that?" Reading the transcript, it seems obvious that only Martin could have said, "Oh, shit!" To the extent that the prosecutor really was confused (or feared that other listeners would be), that probably relates to difficulty in processing in real time the nonstandard usage "Trayvon come and say." The interruption thus calls attention to that usage. The net effect is that, at the pivotal evidentiary point in Jeantel's testimony, two official actors interrupt her to call into question the intelligibility of her vernacular speech.

The final point involves Jeantel's reporting of Martin's use of the word "nigga." Rickford and King explain that "this was not the 'old school' use of the N-word for a person of African descent, but the 'new school' use . . . in which *nigga* (with that spelling) is unspecified for ethnicity and can 'refer to anyone of any race or ethnicity'" (2016:968, citing Spears 1998:241). By this interpretation, it is, from an AAVE speaker's perspective, the equivalent of a Standard American English speaker having said something like "the guy's behind me."

Both of Jeantel's interlocutors quickly interrupt. First, after Jeantel initially says, "The nigga behind me," the court reporter interjects, "I'm sorry, what?" Although the effect is probably to draw attention to the word "nigga," the interruption may have been prompted by the copula deletion between "nigga" and "behind." Jeantel apparently takes it that way, restating the phrase with the copula inserted ("The nigga's behind") before repeating her original phrasing. The prosecutor then jumps in to tie down the fact that the intended statement was "the nigger is behind me." In doing so, however, he first indirectly apologizes for Jeantel's use of "nigga" by referring to it as "the N word." One can understand a non–African American's reluctance to use that word in public (the prosecutor, Bernardo de la Rionda, is a Cuban American of Caucasian appearance). Ironically, though, he then goes ahead and uses it. The transcript renders his word as "nigger," suggesting that he, unlike Jeantel, pronounced the final *r*. We cannot know whether he did so because of a lack of familiarity with the new-school AAVE term or in a deliberate effort to distance himself from that usage. In either case, the effect can only be, yet again, to underscore the nonstandard nature of Jeantel's vernacular.

Rickford and King also do an exhaustive quantitative analysis of Jeantel's speech, comparing it to the speech of numerous other speakers of AAVE and Caribbean English previously documented by Rickford and others. They find her speech to be entirely typical of such communities: "Jeantel's variation is systematic and essentially follows the same patterns found in Black vernacular or Creole English-speaking communities in the New World" (Rickford and King 2016:963). This fact — that Jeantel's speech is not idiosyncratic but reflective of her speech community — will become especially significant as we consider their next point, the effect of her vernacular on listeners.

Rickford and King adduce evidence from multiple sources, including juror interviews, social media, and empirical research unrelated to the case, to show that Jeantel's vernacular had a severely adverse impact on the reception of her testimony in the courtroom and beyond. In considering the effect on her immediate and most important audience, the six jurors, it is critical that there was not a single African American among them, no one "who might have been more familiar with AAVE and less likely to stigmatize it" (Rickford and King 2016:963). According to a Puerto Rican juror (referred to as Maddy) interviewed on CNN, Jeantel's speech was "hard to understand" and her testimony "not credible." Astonishingly, Maddy reported, this factually pivotal testimony was never discussed in more than sixteen hours of deliberations and "played no role whatsoever" in the verdict (Rickford and King 2016:950).

Social media responses to Jeantel's speech were even more negative. Examples quoted by Rickford and King include "She is a dullard, and idiot, an individual who can barely speak in coherent sentences"; "a perfect example of uneducated urban ignorance"; "she speaks Haitian hood rat"; "inarticulate, fat drughead"; and — consistent with the comment of Maddy the juror — "I couldn't understand 75% of what she was saying" (2016:957). In reviewing such comments, Rickford and King observe that "some African Americans were as trenchant in their critiques of Jeantel as anyone else" (2016:970).

Rickford and King also cite an array of academic studies that demonstrate that such reactions to AAVE and other dialects are typical. Among the examples they cite (Rickford and King 2016:976–78) are surveys and experiments showing lower comprehension and negative evaluation of lower-status African languages by speakers of high-status languages; of accented, nonnative English by native speakers of Standard American English; and of AAVE-speaking students by white, Standard American English–speaking elementary school teachers. In courtroom-simulation experiments, speakers with regional or ethnically associated accents have been evaluated as less credible and more likely to be guilty than standard speakers. All this adds up to what John Baugh (2003) has called "linguistic profiling." Rickford and King stress that it "should not necessarily be attributed to racial prejudice at the individual level, but to institutional racism at the societal level" (2016:978). We will return to linguistic profiling and its potential remedies at the end of the chapter. But first we review another linguist's analysis of Rachel Jeantel's testimony in the Zimmerman trial.

AAVE in the Zimmerman Trial: The Defense's Cross-Examination (Slobe 2016)

Anthropologist Tyanna Slobe published a contemporaneous linguistic analysis of the Zimmerman trial. She focuses on Trayvon Martin's characterization of George Zimmerman — as reported by Rachel Jeantel — as a "creepy-ass cracker," and the ways in which other courtroom actors use and respond to this phrase. Specifically, she argues that Don West, Zimmerman's lawyer, "attempted to socialize the jury into a specific way of 'hearing' *creepy-ass cracker* as violent language" in order to support the claim that Zimmerman reasonably feared for his safety (Slobe 216:616). Rickford and King also comment on this issue.

By way of background, Rickford and King, following the *Dictionary of American Regional English* (Cassidy and Hall 1985), define *cracker* as a rustic or backwoodsman; more generally, a poor, rural white person, especially in the South Atlantic region; and, by extension, a white racist. The term is described as especially derogatory among black speakers. The -*ass* suffix is also interesting. Among African American speakers, "ass-words" are common and generally neutral (Spears 1998). Affixing *ass* to a noun or adjective can serve as an emphatic intensifier, as seems to be the case here. (For a benign example, think of the comedian Cedric the Entertainer's signature line, "I am a grown-ass man.") But more often, ass-words simply mark a conversation as being conducted in an uncensored, in-group environment — certainly true of Martin's final phone conversation with Jeantel. But there is no doubt here that both sides viewed the phrase *creepy-ass cracker* as deviant and potentially dangerous. For the prosecution, it was something that needed to be explained away; for the defense, it was an opportunity to be exploited.

Defense counsel West apparently introduces the phrase into the trial during his cross-examination of Jeantel. In Text 10.4, West (DW) is challenging Jeantel's (RJ) claim that Zimmerman's actions were racially motivated. Instead, West suggests, it was Martin, as reported by Jeantel, who injected race into the confrontation. West has just asked, in two different ways, "What makes that racial?":

TEXT 10.4 (Adapted from Slobe 2016:622–23; Rickford and King 2016:969)

RJ: Describing the person that was watchin' him and following
him—
DW: I see.
RJ: —sir.
5   DW: Describing the person is what made you think it was racial?
(0.6)
RJ: Yes.
(0.9)
DW: And that's because he described him (1.0) as a creepy-ass
10   cracker?
RJ: Yes.
DW: So it was racial (0.5) because Trayvon Martin put race in this.
RJ: Mm no.
DW: You don't think that's a racial comment?
15   RJ: No.
(3.7)
DW: You don't think that creepy-ass cracker (0.5) is a racial com-
ment?
RJ: No.

Following this exchange, prosecutor Bernardo de la Rionda attempts to neu-
tralize Jeantel's language by having her confirm that creepy-ass cracker simply
reflects "the way people speak in your culture, in your age group." But, as Slobe
(2016:625) points out, this explanation sets up an obvious counterargument that
West is quick to exploit: that "Jeantel's language, which she shares with her
peer group, indicates that her peer group is rife with racial animus, particularly
against white people."

West presses the point in a series of slowly articulated (Slobe describes his
style as "hyper-articulated" Standard American English) questions with many
pauses. For example, "What culture is that where people describe other people
as creepy-ass crackers?" and "Do people that you live around and with call white
people, um, creepy-ass crackers?" Jeantel's only response to the onslaught is
to interject, "a pervert." West initially brushes past this ("I'm sorry?"), but then
observes that this accounts for *creepy*, but not *cracker* ("So the creepy is the
pervert part that you were talking about?").

West then brings his exercise in linguistic profiling to a climax:

TEXT 10.5 (Adapted from Slobe 2016:627)

DW: So forget that [*the pervert part*] for a second. You're saying that
in the culture that you live in, in your community, uh, people call,
people there call white people crackers?

RJ: Yes sir.
5   (1.0)
DW: And do they use the n-word regularly?
(0.5)
RJ: Yes sir.
DW: And you're saying so did Trayvon Martin?
10   (7.4)
Trayvon Martin referred to white people as crackers? (1.5) Correct?
(8.3)
RJ: I don't recall sir.
(3.3)
15   DW: OK thank you nothing else.

Slobe's analysis of this interaction stresses several microlinguistic strategies that West employs, including *pauses* and *deixis*. We will consider each in turn.

Pauses and Silence

As background to Slobe's analysis, read Texts 10.4 and 10.5 aloud with a stopwatch in hand, pausing as West did. Against the expectations of normal conversation, the half-second pause is noticeable. The full-second pause is dramatic. And each of the multi-second pauses seems like an eternity.

Slobe (216:628) contends that the pauses "are exploited as a means of signaling discomfort on behalf of the speaker" — that is, West means to suggest to the jury that he is so uncomfortable with Martin's reported racially charged language that he has to pause before and after repeating it. The pauses thus create distance — literally and figuratively — between the polite, Standard American English–speaking community that West presumes to represent and the caricature of Martin and Jeantel's "culture" that he has just created. West leaves no doubt as to which one enjoys moral superiority.

We agree with Slobe but would add two additional points. The first is that pauses, whatever they may signal about a speaker's real or feigned discomfort, are also uncomfortable for listeners. Here again, readers should draw on their experience with everyday conversation. One speaking turn usually follows directly on another, to the point where overlapping speech is common. A noticeable silence suggests a breakdown: the current topic has been exhausted; the last utterance before the silence has been difficult to understand or process; or perhaps something about what the last speaker said has left others literally speechless — they might be surprised, offended, or disbelieving. Because silence is uncomfortable, another speaker may jump in with a follow-up question, a topic change, or an apology for the previous speaker (*we know you meant no offense, but . . .*).

Since jurors cannot speak in situations like this, however, they must simply remain silent in the face of silence, processing it however they will. At a minimum, an unnatural (in terms of the expectations of natural conversation) silence would seem likely to emphasize the speech that immediately precedes it, and perhaps that which follows it as well. Applying this logic to West's statement in lines 9 and 10 of Text 10.4 ("he described him (1.0) as a creepy-ass cracker"), the jury might have perceived an emphasis on the source of the description (*he*, meaning Trayvon Martin) and the content of the description ("creepy-ass cracker").

This leads to our second point: that silence may also lead jurors to think about its source and purpose. Experience with conversation suggests that jurors might ask themselves such questions as, Why is no one talking?, Who *should* be talking?, and Why is that person *not* talking? The silences in Text 10.4 all result from West pausing during or before his own speaking turn. The longest one (3.7) comes between Jeantel's answer, denying that "creepy-ass cracker" is a racial comment, and West's next question. It is difficult to interpret West's silence as anything other than an adverse, disbelieving comment on Jeantel's denial and an invitation to the jurors to share in that view.

In Text 10.5, however, the two longest pauses (7.4 and 8.3 seconds) result from Jeantel's failure to begin an expected speaking turn by answering a pending question. In each case, West lets the silence linger for what is, by courtroom standards, an exceedingly long time. In the first instance, he ends the silence by rephrasing the question; in the second, Jeantel finally gives a noncommittal answer—which West leaves hanging for 3.3 seconds before ending the interaction. Here again, the interpretation seems obvious: by acquiescing in Jeantel's failure to speak when expected, West is tacitly passing judgment on her silence and inviting the jury to do the same.

We would emphasize that the strategic use of silence need not have anything to do with race. Lawyers use this strategy—quite intentionally—all the time in cases that do not involve race in any way. Its purpose is, as it apparently was here, to emphasize, to pass unspoken judgments, and to encourage jurors to react in particular ways. But the strategy does take on special salience in the intensely racial context of the Zimmerman case. The effect is not simply to comment on an individual witness's testimony but to mark Martin and Jeantel's speech—and thus them, their speech community, and their "culture"—as "deviant" relative to the Standard American English community that West represents. In a cruel irony, West's strategy serves to shift the onus of racism from Zimmerman to Martin and Jeantel by "positioning [the standard-speaker community] as morally superior because of its assumed colorblind orientation" (Slobe 2016:626).

Deixis

West further underscores the distance between his supposedly colorblind speech community and that of Martin and Jeantel through the use of *deixis*. Deixis is linguistic pointing, using words and phrases called *deictic markers*.

Common deictic markers include such binary pairs as *this* and *that*, and *here* and *there*. Linguists have demonstrated in many contexts that speakers routinely use deixis to affiliate themselves with or distance themselves from other people, practices, and circumstances. Although people use deixis constantly in everyday speech, few of them are likely to have any awareness of the practice or its potential effects.

Recall the beginning of Text 10.5, in particular West's reference to Martin and Jeantel's community: "the culture that *you* live in, in *your* community, uh, people call, people *there* call white people crackers." The italicized words have deictic effect and contrast starkly with their implied binary opposites. Thus, *you* live in a different culture than *we* do; people use racially offensive terms like cracker in *your* culture but not in *our* culture; and they use such language *there* but not *here*. The implicit *we*, *our*, and *here* presumably reference the idealized colorblind community that includes West and his courtroom audience. Each binary pair suggests not only physical distance between speaker and referent but social and moral distance as well.

As in the case of strategic silence, there is no inherent relationship between deixis and race. Moreover, it is extremely unlikely that Don West had any awareness of his deictic tactics. Here again, though, a commonplace language practice takes on a particular poignancy in the context of a case that seems to be entirely about race. As documented above, both the prosecutor (by perceived necessity) and the defense counsel (as a matter of tactics) draw attention to the distinctive phonology, syntax, and lexicon of Jeantel's AAVE. Defense counsel West then imparts a value-laden spin to what might otherwise be a matter of simple language variation. Through his use of silence, deixis, and other linguistic strategies that Slobe documents, West repeatedly — whether consciously or not — drives home the arguments that language reflects culture and cultures differ in their moral worth.

Linguistic Profiling

Virtually everything surrounding Rachel Jeantel's testimony fits into Baugh's concept of *linguistic profiling*. Even during direct examination by the ostensibly friendly prosecutor, Jeantel's language takes on a profile as different, hard to understand, and sometimes shocking. By pausing, questioning, and sometimes distancing himself — and, by implication, the jurors — from the distinctive features of her speech, the prosecutor calls attention to them. The court reporter's interruptions compound the effect. On cross-examination, the prosecutor focuses specifically on some of the aspects of Jeantel's speech that he can characterize as racial, if not racist.

The effect of all this — particularly at the end of the cross-examination — is to invert the role of racism in the trial. Most of the pretrial publicity and protests amounted to debate about *Zimmerman's* alleged racism and the role it might have played in the killing and the official response. But the prosecutor (presumably by inadvertence) and the defense lawyer (more likely as a matter of strategy) managed to put *Trayvon Martin's* racial attitudes on trial.

There are two compelling analogies between the Zimmerman trial and the issues and evidence we discussed in other chapters. The first concerns *language ideology*, which we defined in chapter 7 as a set of shared beliefs about language. The portrayal of Jeantel (and, through her, of Martin) as a linguistic "other" raises an obvious question: By comparison to what? There must be some assumed norm against which her otherness can be marked.

In both direct and cross-examination, the lawyers repeatedly suggest that Jeantel and Martin deviate in various ways from a linguistic ideal that they and the jurors share. In that ideal version of English, speakers use standard grammar and vocabulary. Importantly, they do not use — for any purpose — terms that could be construed as racial slurs. Another way to say this is that the lawyers are invoking an ideology about what constitutes standard, normal, and proper linguistic behavior.

The prosecutor's questions and statements seem to acknowledge that deviant speakers are, at a minimum, hard to understand. His dancing around the use of *nigga* further suggests that deviant speech has the capacity to offend adherents of the standard ideology. The defense lawyer upgrades this suggestion to a virtual accusation that violators of the standard ideology are members of a racist community, if not actively racist themselves.

This leads to the second analogy. Recall chapter 2's discussion of the *sexual double bind* that defense lawyers exploit during their cross-examination of the alleged victim in acquaintance rape cases. The pattern of questioning gives the woman two bad choices. One is to acquiesce in the suggestion that she is powerless and unobservant, which will lead to an argument that she lacks credibility as a witness. Alternatively, if she takes a strong and assertive stance, the defense will argue that she could not have fallen prey to an acquaintance.

The cross-examination of Rachel Jeantel put her (and Trayvon Martin) into a *racial double bind*. In commenting on the use of "creepy-ass cracker," one inference that the defense lawyer sets up is that Jeantel and Martin were actively biased against white people. The other is that, regardless of their own racial views, in "the culture that [they] live in, in [their] community," anti-white racial slurs are used and tolerated. Whichever direction Jeantel chooses, the unstated conclusion is that Martin was the kind of person who might contemplate violence against white people.

Conclusion: Can Anything Be Done?

In considering the practical impact of vernacular in the courtroom, it is important to note that there are two distinct if related problems: comprehension and bias. Anyone — biased or not — can have difficulty understanding an unfamiliar vernacular. At first glance, that is no different from a monolingual English speaker being unable to understand Spanish.

But the mere inability to understand a vernacular of one's own language may trigger a chain of reasoning that can either expose underlying language-based biases or create them: *She can't speak English that I can understand, so there must be something wrong with her. Because I can't understand her, I won't believe her.* In sociolinguistic terms, the hearer invokes a language ideology that holds that vernacular speakers of the hearer's language are not just *non*standard but *sub*standard. As we documented in chapter 7, there are comparably pejorative language ideologies about speakers of different languages. However, monolingual speakers are more likely to understand and respond to the differences between languages in a value-neutral way than they are with vernaculars.

In addition, there is the problem of preexisting bias against the group associated with either a language or a vernacular. A general anti-immigrant bias may be activated by hearing someone speak any language other than English in an American courtroom; similarly, hearing Spanish in that context may trigger a particular bias against Latino immigrants. As the social media reactions to Rachel Jeantel's testimony illustrate so vividly, simply hearing AAVE can lead some to outbursts of raw racism.

Rickford and King acknowledge the dual problems of comprehension and bias, noting that Jeantel's "AAVE, though systematic, was misheard and maligned" (2016:980). They conclude their analysis of the Zimmerman trial with a "call to action" to linguists, suggesting several specific steps that their colleagues can take to promote justice for "vulnerable" vernacular speakers (Rickford and King 2016:980). Many of the efforts they recommend amount to long-term attacks on fundamental problems: linguists should, for example, do more research on cross-dialect comprehension and evaluation, do more work in individual legal cases, and help vernacular speakers learn Standard American English — but only if they want such help.

Three of their suggestions, however, are recommendations for immediate change in the way vernaculars are treated in court. First, linguists are urged to "advocate for the use of interpreters as an option for deep AAVE and other vernacular speakers, recognizing that in some cases witnesses or plaintiffs/defendants may not want that option" (Rickford and King 2016:981). We might extend this recommendation to include expert witnesses who would explain to the jury what vernacular speech does and does not mean.

While this is a good idea in principle — effectively treating vernaculars in the same way that courts treat different languages — Rickford and King's own analysis of the prosecutor's direct examination of Jeantel raises serious questions about whether it might do more harm than good. In that theoretically friendly examination, the prosecutor repeatedly tried to explain Jeantel's vernacular. Whatever else they did, these interventions surely marked her speech as nonstandard. Rickford and King persuasively argue that that marking contributed significantly to the jury's negative reaction to her critical testimony.

Would the use of an interpreter for a vernacular speaker diminish that sort of reaction? Or, by further emphasizing the vernacular's nonstandard qualities, would it make the problem worse? The reaction of the jurors was along the lines of *this person speaks English, but badly.* An interpreter would presumably have helped with the basic problem of understanding Jeantel's syntax and lexicon. But would an interpreter or expert witness have helped to clear up the jurors' normative misconceptions about vernacular, or have strengthened them through simple emphasis? Rickford and King recognize this dilemma when they note that some parties might decline the help. The most difficult issue may be to discern when the help should be accepted.

Their second suggestion is meant to promote the representation of AAVE speakers on juries: eliminating the use of peremptory challenges against African American jurors. Lawyers can challenge prospective jurors for cause, as when there is an admission of bias against either side. But they also have a number (which will vary by state) of peremptory challenges, which they can use to remove a prospective juror without stating a reason. The Supreme Court has forbidden the exercise of peremptory challenges for purposes of racial discrimination; showing that usually involves proof of a pattern. The Court has not, however, gone so far as to prohibit the use of individual challenges against members of a racial group without a showing of discriminatory intent. Thus, while Rickford and King's recommendation might well be effective, it would require a significant extension of current law.

Their third recommendation is that linguists be allowed to check court reporters' transcripts of vernacular speakers' testimony, and that jurors then be given those transcripts to review during their deliberations. As they acknowledge, this suggestion — eminently sensible as it may seem — has not been adopted in any English-speaking country. Moreover, there is a curious reluctance in many jurisdictions to allow jurors to receive *any* transcripts, out of fear that they will give undue weight to the evidence thus highlighted. Despite these practical impediments, this reform could possibly come about through court rulemaking or mere changes to judges' practices, without the need for legislation or Supreme Court intervention.

We would make the further point that solutions to the problem of linguistic profiling should *not* include urging lawyers to avoid doing what the defense lawyer did in the Zimmerman case. Criminal defendants have a constitutional right to the effective assistance of counsel. In turn, all lawyers have an ethical duty of zealous advocacy of their client's position, within the bounds of the law. Criminal defense lawyers have a particular duty to force the prosecution to prove all elements of its case beyond a reasonable doubt. Carrying out this duty has always involved probing and exploiting the weaknesses of prosecution witnesses on cross-examination. This is exactly what Don West did in cross-examining Rachel Jeantel. He likely believed that not only was he allowed to do so, he was duty-bound to do so. This belief is widely if not universally shared among the criminal defense bar. Thus, dissuading lawyers from this sort of linguistic profiling would require a fundamental change in law and legal ethics.

On balance, we are pessimistic that linguistic profiling will disappear from courtrooms in the foreseeable future. As the analysis of the prosecutor's direct examination of Rachel Jeantel reveals, linguistic profiling can happen even when the lawyer doing it is the sponsor of the vernacular testimony. Hostile profiling is easier to condemn from a moral perspective. But every proposed reform faces significant practical and legal hurdles to its adoption, and identifying change as "reform" is far from a straightforward exercise.

CHAPTER ELEVEN

Conclusion

If we were to state the arguments of the previous chapters in a single sentence, it would be this: the details of legal discourse matter. First and foremost, the details of legal discourse matter because language is the essential mechanism through which the power of the law is realized, exercised, reproduced, and occasionally challenged and subverted. Most of the time, law is talk: the talk between disputants; the talk between lawyers and clients; the courtroom talk between lawyers, parties, judges, and witnesses; the legal talk that gets reduced to writing as statutes and judicial opinions; and the commentary on all of this other talk that people like us engage in. Therefore, if one wants to find particular, concrete manifestations of the law's power, it makes sense to sift through the microdiscourse that is the law's defining element. If the objectives are to understand the nature of the law's power, to see how that power is exercised over real people, to identify points at which it might be challenged, and to assess which challenges are likely to work, then microdiscourse is the place to look.

In this book, we have argued that the details of legal discourse matter from a series of different empirical perspectives. In chapter 2, we presented evidence that the law's power to revictimize rape victims is not an abstraction but a concrete linguistic reality. The feeling of revictimization seems to emerge from a limited number of things that lawyers routinely say to and about rape victims during trial. Ironically, and tellingly, they are not the things that advocates for rape victims' rights have usually focused on.

In chapter 3, we examined the language of mediation, particularly as it is used in divorce. Our first objective was to document how mediation "works," in the sense of providing an environment in which hostile parties begin talking again in an effort to agree on a solution to a dispute. The key seems to be a set of linguistic strategies that mediators use to steer the parties away from the conversational structure of argument. We then considered whether mediation — which is usually advertised as a balanced, value-neutral, participant-controlled process — is subject to bias. That is, are there ways in which certain kinds of disputants, with the at-least-implicit connivance of the legal system, can exert power and pursue their own agendas? The answer is clearly yes; the subtle but convincing evidence lies in the linguistic details of mediation practice.

In chapter 4, we sought linguistic evidence for the widespread claim that Anglo-American law is patriarchal. We found it on at least two levels: in the legal system's preference for a speech style that is used preponderantly by males and in its parallel devaluing of account structures and forms of argument that derive primarily from the social experiences of girls and women.

In chapter 5, we took a microlinguistic look at the natural history of disputes. We developed a descriptive typology that accounts for the different kinds of linguistic events that can occur over the life of a dispute. By examining these various linguistic events in detail, we argued, it is possible to understand more fully the ways in which disputants, their representatives, and the decision makers before whom they appear can exercise and contest for power.

Then, in chapter 6, we examined the portability of legal discourse analysis, reporting on the effort to use linguistic analysis to resolve some longstanding questions about the jurisprudence of societies far removed from our own. We reemphasized a point made repeatedly throughout the book: that claims about the nature and purpose of law — its macrodiscourse — are highly suspect unless grounded in a thorough understanding of the microlinguistic realities of legal practice.

In chapter 7, we explored the concept of language ideology, or shared beliefs about language and its use. After introducing the concept, we considered two examples — one from an American criminal trial and the other from Islamic divorce courts in Kenya — of how language ideology influences the workings of the law at the microdiscourse level. In chapter 8 we reviewed the work of contemporary forensic linguists who are connecting language and law in a very direct way, by using the methods of linguistics in an effort to influence and improve law and legal proceedings.

In chapter 9 we argued that the analysis of legal microdiscourse must also take into account the nonverbal, multimodal aspects of communication in legal settings. Finally, chapter 10 shows how language and language ideologies can be used to manipulate jurors' reactions to race in a criminal trial. Here again, a new understanding of a critical, higher-order legal issue has emerged from a line-by-line analysis of legal language.

In making these varied claims for the indispensability of legal discourse analysis, we have also intended to connect the historically distinct research traditions of sociolegal scholarship and sociolinguistics. As we discussed in chapter 1, the core claim of sociolegal scholarship is that the law in practice does not live up to the ideal of fairness. Justice is contingent, and the critical contingencies are such categories as gender, race, and class. What has been missing from much sociolegal research, in our view, is a detailed explication of what injustice looks like as it happens.

Sociolinguistics, on the other hand, has a rich tradition of showing precisely how linguistic events—stories about troubles, requests for help, collaborative searches for blame, and so on—unfold. However, the sociolinguistic lens has not always been focused on events that "count" in the legal and political world. Throughout our respective teaching careers, we have often heard the complaint that sociolinguistics "sometimes seems to be learning more and more about less and less" as it has catalogued and described innumerable instances of the social conditioning of language.

A significant theoretical motive in writing this book is to highlight some important connections between the sociolegal and the sociolinguistic traditions and thereby to suggest the potential for future collaborations in law and language. In this concluding chapter, we discuss several areas of incipient collaboration that offer particularly exciting prospects: the search for the origins of legal language, the cross-cultural analysis of legal discourse, and the use of law and language to influence political and legal reform.

Where Does Legal Language Come From?

As sociolinguistics probes ever deeper into the details of disputing language, a recurrent theme is how elegantly patterned that language seems to be. Members of every society appear to have vast stores of cultural knowledge about disputing, as well as an elaborate sense of how to conduct themselves and interpret the behavior of others in a variety of legal and quasi-legal contexts. But where do they get this knowledge? Aside from its inherent intellectual interest, this question is of vital practical importance to those interested in reforming some problematic aspects of disputing behavior. Consider, for example, the evidence presented in chapter 3 that many women end up having their disputing styles turned against them by divorce mediators. In order to provide equal access to justice for everyone, reformers must understand how the women as well as the mediators acquire their respective approaches to disputing.

In a society such as this one, with a complex, professionalized dispute resolution system, the question of origins has at least two parts. The first is, Where do the lay members of society learn how to conduct themselves in disputes? The second part asks how legal professionals learn the particular discourse styles and strategies that have been in evidence throughout the book. These styles and strategies are very different from their everyday counterparts; how are they acquired? Promising beginnings have been made in answering these questions.

Learning How to Argue

When seeking the origins of any social behavior, a logical place to start is with
children. A good deal of research has now been done on the disputing language
of children.[1] Some of the most interesting work has been done by Amy Sheldon,
Diane Johnson (Sheldon and Johnson 1994; see also Sheldon 1993), and Marjorie Goodwin (e.g., 2011; M. Goodwin and C. Goodwin 1987). Sheldon's and
Johnson's inquiries have focused on gender differences in disputing language
among preschool children. They have identified two distinct styles of disputing
discourse. *Single-voice discourse* is characterized by unmitigated self-assertion.
It involves direct, confrontational speech acts in which the speaker pursues his
or her own goals without regard to the dispute's effect on the other party. In
double-voice discourse, by contrast, "self-assertion is accomplished with linguistic mitigation" (Sheldon and Johnson 1994:42). That is, while the speaker
is oriented primarily toward the self, double-voice discourse also evidences
sensitivity to and a feeling of responsibility for the well-being of the other
disputant. Sheldon and Johnson stop short of characterizing these two styles
as, respectively, masculine and feminine. They argue instead that double-voice
discourse is typical of interactions in the "solidarity-based" groups in which
young girls usually play. Single-voice discourse, on the other hand, is a defining
characteristic of the "dominance-based" groups in which young boys typically
play. Although the gender correlation is apparent, it is the norms of the two
kinds of groups that select one or the other discourse style rather than the gender
of each group's members per se.

Although Sheldon and Johnson are restrained in drawing implications from
their studies, the possibilities are provocative. They note, for example, the obvious connection between dominance-based disputing discourse and patriarchy.
Elsewhere, Sheldon (1993) has elaborated on the connection between the affiliative, relationship-focused conflict style of little girls and Carol Gilligan's
(1982) theory that women's moral reasoning derives from an ethic of care,
whereas men's moral reasoning grows out of an ethic of rights. We have argued throughout this book that Anglo-American law expresses a preference
for linguistic practices that are more typical of men than of women. Sheldon
and Johnson may have discovered some of the earliest manifestations of these
preferences in the lives of individual men and women.

Sheldon and Johnson also comment on the ways in which women and girls
may be disadvantaged in various dispute settings. Clearly girls' (and women's)
double-voicing is well-suited to the social norms that govern self-assertion in
all-female, solidarity-based groups. However, double-voice discourse may
not serve girls as well in mixed-sex conversations, because dominance-based
norms are often operating there (Sheldon and Johnson 1994:61).

These findings have potentially profound implications. They can help us understand, for example, the source of many of the problems that women experience in divorce mediation. If in their earliest social disputes girls learn to temper their pursuit of self-interest with concern for the needs of the opponent, while boys learn precisely the opposite, then it should come as no surprise that women would at once like mediation and fare badly in it. We might expect women to prefer mediation because it is designed to be nonconfrontational, relational, and affiliative. At the same time, we would expect women to be disadvantaged because men are likely to ignore these aspects of the process and devote all their attention to the single-minded pursuit of a favorable outcome for themselves.

How Do Lawyers Learn Legal Discourse?

As we have repeatedly seen, the discourse of legal professionals is distinctive on multiple levels. The most superficial level is legal jargon. Lawyers and judges regularly use words and phrases such as *directed verdict*, *j.n.o.v.*, and *mens rea*, which are not part of the everyday vocabulary of laypeople, as well as common words and phrases that have specialized legal meanings, such as *consideration*, *pleading*, and *complaint*. The source of legal jargon in the practice of the law is obvious: law students are required to learn it in law school.

Other aspects of the law's professional discourse are far subtler, however. We saw in chapter 3, for example, that divorce lawyers transform their clients' stories in regular and predictable ways. They do so by imposing a particular discourse structure on those stories. Similarly, we argued in chapter 4 that the legal system prefers certain kinds of story structures and logical frameworks. The source of these preferences is far from obvious. Law school does teach a process that law professors often refer to as "thinking like a lawyer." This means knowing how to infer rules of law from the comparative analysis of judges' written decisions in particular cases. Especially in the first year, law students read large numbers of cases and study the relationship between facts and outcomes. Their objective is twofold: to become familiar with the paradigm cases that have yielded rules of wide applicability and to learn how to predict the reactions of courts to novel situations. Almost every law school exam question presents the students with an original (and often bizarre) fact pattern and demands that they predict the likely legal response. The theory of this kind of testing is that this is just what lawyers do when clients appear in their offices and tell them about their problems.

This approach to legal education selects rather ruthlessly for a particular style of analysis. Students who get high grades usually read quickly through complex fact patterns, zeroing in on "relevant" facts — that is, facts that judges and law professors will see as having a bearing on legal rights and remedies — and immediately discarding everything else. Students who go to their professors to ask about low exam grades are often told that they "got bogged down in irrelevancies" or "never got to the point."

The demand that students learn how to think like a lawyer has both positive and negative consequences. On the positive side, it seems clear that judges often *do* think in precisely this way. Thus, the predictive skill that traditional legal education seeks to impart is a real and significant aspect of professional competence. On the negative side, it seems equally clear from the evidence presented throughout this book that the consumers of the law *rarely* analyze their problems in the same way. Accordingly, by its exclusive focus on the professional mode of analysis, legal education may be sending the message that the thought processes of the people the profession purports to serve are irrelevant and inadequate.

Until recently, legal education has paid virtually no attention to this problem. The analysis of legal education's contribution to the lawyer-client communication gap is just beginning to progress beyond the kinds of general observations made in the preceding paragraphs. Some of the most significant work to date has been done by Elizabeth Mertz (2007, 1996, n.d.), a law professor trained as both an anthropologist and a lawyer. Mertz has asked what it is about legal education that so transforms the discourse practices of law students that they seem to lose touch with their own society. She and her colleagues have recorded, transcribed, and analyzed first-year classes in eight US law schools that vary significantly in location, mission, and prestige.

Mertz's observations include the following:

1. *The social context of disputes is treated differently than in the everyday world.* When ordinary people talk about their troubles, social context is always very important; often it is everything. Yet when law professors lead their students through discussions of cases, a common tactic is to abstract the disputants from their social context, to conceive of them almost as *acontextual.* When law professors propose hypotheticals (as they often do), Mertz (2007:113–14) observes, the characters are "stereotypic, abstract individual[s]" — "average" farmers or "average" home buyers with a standard set of attributes and apparently no social connections. The characters also tend to be rational wealth-maximizers with few moral concerns. While some degree of abstracting is undoubtedly necessary in order to simplify the rule-deducing process for beginning students, an obvious question is whether at some point the students begin to adopt the unreal worldview that such decontextualized discourse embodies.

2. *The discourse practices of law professors appear to be influenced by their backgrounds.* While law professors generally treat context as something that is relevant only in exceptional cases (as, for example, when a "bad" judge may act on some sort of bias), such commentary may be more common in classes taught by women and by men of color. Interestingly, it is not always the professors themselves who are injecting these factors: students seem more willing to raise issues of context in classes taught by professors who are not white men. Perhaps these professors have had more occasion to think about the importance of context in their own lives than have their white male colleagues, and they

thus are more inclined to see it as relevant to legal outcomes. In any event, Mertz's preliminary findings suggest that "thinking like a lawyer" may come more naturally to people with particular social experiences.

3. *The language of law professors fosters an "us/them" divide between law and society.* Mertz identifies the propensity of law professors to use a collective *we* to refer to the professor, the student being questioned, and the court that heard the case, as in "Where are we in the case? We're in Wisconsin." The regular use of this collective-professional *we*, Mertz argues, has several significant effects. It unites the professor and the student as professionals who are reading the legal text from a perspective that is different from that of the ordinary people who are engaged in the dispute. Likewise, it transports the student and the professor, together, into the case. When they arrive, their vantage point is that of the court rather than that of the disputants.

The effect of these various discourse practices is to perpetuate "a universalist language capable of translating almost any conceivable event or issue into a common rhetoric" (Mertz n.d.:23). Law schools inculcate both a way of talking about problems and the logic that lies behind that way of talking. Because such logic is an essential tool of current legal practice, law schools could not give up teaching it even if they wanted to do so. What Mertz reminds us, however, is that the discourse of legal education has other consequences that have not been identified or thought through with sufficient care. As law professors use language to socialize their students, they are simultaneously distancing the students from the social contexts from which they emerged, the same social contexts that their future clients will inhabit.

Mertz's work has demonstrated convincingly that legal education is fundamentally a linguistic process. Law professors do not conspire to strip students of their social consciousness; on the contrary, the vast majority of American law professors are card-carrying social progressives. What seems to be happening is that law professors are insufficiently attentive to the relationship between discourse and power. As law students emulate the ways that law professors talk about people and their problems, they also begin to take for granted the patterns of thinking that such talk embodies. If legal education is interested in understanding and dealing with the consequences of its classroom discourse practices, then much more work of the sort that Mertz has undertaken will be essential.[2]

Comparative Legal Discourse

We included chapter 6 in an effort to show the comparative potential of legal discourse analysis. Using the work of Laurence Goldman, Joel Kuipers, and Larry Nesper, we attempted to relate the methods of discourse analysis to the traditions of legal anthropology. Goldman, in a polemical way, shows how to use discourse analysis to challenge the conventional wisdom of legal anthropology, whereas Kuipers's work is an elegant demonstration of how to analyze legal discourse in another culture. The overall point of the chapter was that traditional legal anthropology, as a result of inadequate attention to the details of discourse, has sometimes missed the point in studying comparative law. Indeed, as Goldman's work illustrates, it has on occasion gotten things backwards.

In earlier editions, we argued for the development of a new, discourse-based legal anthropology. It is now clear that this development is well underway. This discipline shares legal anthropology's traditional concern with the comparative study of systems for resolving disputes and maintaining order, but adds a concern for the subtleties of legal reasoning that can be appreciated only at the microlinguistic level. It enables us, for example, to analyze the natural history of disputes in other societies at the same level of detail at which Gail Jefferson, Anita Pomerantz, and others have analyzed Western disputes. This new legal anthropology no longer simply reports that the Azande attribute the collapse of a granary to witchcraft or summarizes facts and outcomes of Barotse tribal court cases in the manner of Western case reports. Rather, it uses the details of how the members of a particular society talk their way through disputes in an effort to illuminate their legal process and its power dynamics.

An increasing number of legal anthropologists are trying to practice just this sort of approach. An exemplar of the benefits of merging the traditional concerns of legal anthropology and the power of discourse analysis in a single ethnographic project is Susan Hirsch's (1998) study of family law among the Muslim inhabitants of coastal Kenya, discussed in detail in chapter 7. Rather than simply reporting that Islamic law is an instrument of patriarchy, Hirsch asks what patriarchy means in terms of the law's everyday linguistic practices. Rather than simply asking what the law *is*, she examines how it *works* at a level of detail unavailable in traditional legal ethnography. The result is not only a sharper picture of the particular legal system with which she is concerned but also an original perspective on the general question of how gender is inscribed in law. Her work is, we believe, an appropriate model for future legal anthropology, as well as a blueprint for the cross-cultural study of sociolegal issues.[3]

A more recent example, also cited in chapter 7, is Justin Richland's (2008) ethnography of Hopi tribal courts. Like Nesper, Richland seeks to connect an evolving culture of tribal law with a new sense of tribal sovereignty. By focusing on the details of discourse, he shows how participants in tribal litigation invoke tradition — nominally part of the past — to bring about cultural change and shape the future of Hopi justice. He also reveals how the Hopi system is exporting its values to the US legal system in unexpected ways.

Deconstructing Law Reform

Legal audiences in particular often ask whether law and language research has any practical significance. The answer is an unqualified, if not always obvious, yes. One area where the merger of traditional sociolinguistic and sociolegal concerns can make a particularly significant contribution is the evaluation of legal reform efforts. Gregory Matoesian's analysis of rape shield laws, reviewed in chapter 2, illustrates this potential. Advocates of rape shield laws have long argued that prohibiting defense lawyers from inquiring into a woman's prior sexual history will significantly alleviate the feeling of revictimization that dissuades many rape victims from going ahead with prosecution. Matoesian demonstrates, however, that defense lawyers do not need to exploit prior sexual history in order to humiliate and demoralize the victim. Instead, ordinary and hitherto noncontroversial cross-examination techniques can be used to the same effect. If he is right, the reform efforts have missed the point because of their proponents' failure to understand the linguistic reality of revictimization.

In parallel ways, the work on mediation that we reviewed in chapter 3 reflects the law of unintended consequences at work in the legal reform process. The widespread adoption of divorce mediation was celebrated as the most progressive kind of reform. It was (and for the most part still is) widely seen as promoting the psychological well-being of the divorcing spouses and their children; responding to the prevailing desire of women for a more supportive, nonconfrontational forum; and saving money for everyone. But it is now suspected that in material terms women may be worse off in mediation than in traditional adjudication. Linguistic evidence is reinforcing these suspicions by identifying some of the pathways through which gender bias might operate.

Chapter 10 offers a comparable perspective on law, language, and race. The claim that there is racial bias in the criminal justice system is neither new nor controversial. But the work of John Rickford, Sharese King, Tyanna Slobe, and others who have studied the language of the Trayvon Martin case reveals that there is a powerful *linguistic* component in that racial bias. In the trial of Martin's killer, speakers of American Standard English reacted to an unfamiliar dialect that correlates with race, with apparently grave consequences for justice. Perhaps most perniciously, the injustice manifests itself in the course of lawyers simply doing what they perceive to be their duty. It is thus an especially intractable problem, with no obvious legal fix. Nonetheless, as in the case of rape trials and mediation, we can benefit from the deeper understanding of bias that sociolinguistics can provide, if only to understand how daunting the task of law reform is.

Sociolinguists in the Legal World

By this point, we hope that we have amply demonstrated that microlinguistic analysis is an extraordinary tool for studying social problems. Political concepts such as power, domination, and bias come vividly to life when the linguistic processes through which they are enacted are revealed. We believe that this potential to illuminate and influence the law imposes some responsibilities on those who work in the various traditions of microlinguistic analysis.

In earlier editions, we criticized sociolinguists, conversation analysts, and other scholars of language for a lingering reluctance to deal with questions of power. For example, when reading the works of Jefferson, Pomerantz, and other seminal conversation analysts, one sometimes sensed an unwillingness in the author to go beyond the discovery of the rules of interaction to a consideration of what their social consequences might be. Even then, there were some exceptions to this rule. For example, in *Order in Court*, a conversation analysis of judicial proceedings, Max Atkinson and Paul Drew (1979:228) acknowledge that their work is "suggestive of ways in which certain features of court-room interaction that may have organizational advantages in facilitating the accomplishment of a court's work simultaneously provide a basis for moral assessments to be made about particular speakers." In a different vein, much of Deborah Tannen's initial work on gender differences in conversational style (e.g., Tannen 1993) revolves around questions of power, as does the work collected in Allen Grimshaw's (1990) *Conflict Talk*. Nonetheless, there was in our judgment a need for a more explicit recognition of the fact that the rules of linguistic interaction, especially in legal contexts, have profound implications for the distribution of power in our society.

This is another area where scholarship has developed in the direction we advocated. An entire subfield, *critical discourse analysis*, now focuses on "the way social power abuse, dominance, and inequality are enacted, reproduced, and resisted by text and talk" (Van Dijk 2003:353). Multiple volumes now feature the textual microanalysis of questions of law and power—for example, Ehrlich, Eades, and Ainsworth (2016) on issues of legal consent; Heffer, Rock, and Conley (2013) on lay-legal communication; and Solan and Tiersma's (2012) wide-ranging collection on language and law, which contains summaries of much of their own excellent work from the past twenty-five years.

A second critical point that we made in earlier editions remains a problem in the present: people who do this kind of work need to write more clearly. With some exceptions, work in conversation and discourse analysis—whether done by conversation analysts, linguists, or anthropologists—is virtually impenetrable to the nonspecialist. A certain amount of jargon may be defensible. There is no justification, however, for the convoluted constructions, odd in-group usages, and apparently intentional obscurity that plague the writing in the field. In our experience, people in the legal world are eager to know the kinds of things that law and language scholars can tell them. Often, however, they find the form of the presentation so opaque and off-putting that they give up before understanding the content. This is regrettable, since it is vitally important that lawyers, judges, and legal educators come to appreciate the significance of their discourse practices. Much of the important research in law and language is truly elegant, and there is no reason that it cannot be described in straightforward language.

We also urged those of us who do law and language research to rethink our transcription conventions, and this concern remains. Since the early work of Jefferson, the goal of conversation analysis has been to transcribe conversation in a way that captures as much of the original sound pattern as possible. This remains an appropriate practice for scholarly discourse among specialists. Such transcripts are extremely difficult for nonspecialists to work with, however. Researchers might consider publishing parallel transcripts, one designed to meet the needs of their professional linguistic audience, the other the needs of legal readers without a linguistic background. (To illustrate the difference, compare the transcription styles in Matoesian 1993 and Matoesian 1995.) The objection that the former is somehow "purer" than the latter is unpersuasive. Since no transcript can ever capture fully the sounds of a conversation, every set of conventions necessarily involves a number of judgments and choices driven by the needs and interests of the audience (Bucholtz 2007).

Law and Society, Law and Language

The ultimate objective of each of these recommendations is to continue to promote a fuller integration of law and language into law and society scholarship. The two fields have shared a similar focal point: the failure of the law to live up to its ideal of equal treatment. They have, however, approached the issue from opposite poles. Law and society has attacked the problem from the top down, combining political claims with empirical research that has often been conducted at a fairly high level of abstraction from daily practice. Law and language has worked from the bottom up, beginning with descriptions of linguistic practices and working gradually toward a capacity to test political claims. In carrying out their respective research programs, both have emphasized the effect of variation, especially in such dimensions as race, class, and gender. Law and society has argued that these kinds of variation have affected access to justice. Law and language has documented how such variation manifests itself in the linguistic practice of the legal system, inviting — although rarely making — judgments about political significance. If this book succeeds, it will remind each of these research traditions of its need for the other. It will also remind a broader audience that a meaningful appreciation of justice requires understanding both the concept of power and the mechanisms through which it is applied.

NOTES

Chapter One

1. Danet studied a Massachusetts trial in which a doctor who had performed an abortion was prosecuted for manslaughter. Danet analyzed the different ways in which prosecution and defense categorized the entity that had been aborted: "baby" and "little baby boy" by the prosecution, "fetus" and "products of procreation" by the defense.

2. We mean two things by *linguistic analysis*. First, we mean it in the narrow, technical sense of analysis that draws explicitly on linguistic theory and methods. We also use it in a broader sense to refer to any kind of analysis, whether or not formally linguistic, that focuses on language in an intensive way.

3. The term *utterance* is also difficult to define. We have in mind something akin to what conversation analysts mean when they describe a complete turn at talk. Harvey Sacks, Emanuel Schegloff, and Gail Jefferson (1974) noted that speakers in conversational exchanges normally get to speak until they reach a *turn relevance place*. A person usually speaks until a turn is syntactically complete — the turn relevance place is reached — at which point that speaker or another must negotiate who gets the next turn. An utterance, as we use the term, is very much like the *turn* Sacks, Schegloff, and Jefferson have described. For readers not familiar with this literature, it might be useful to think of *utterance* as referring to a simple sentence or something that works like a simple sentence.

4. R. A. Hudson, in his early and influential textbook *Sociolinguistics* (1980:4), characterizes the difference between sociolinguistics and the various forms of structural linguistics as a matter of emphasis: "I shall refer throughout to 'sociolinguists' and 'linguists' as though they were separate individuals, but these terms can simply be used to reflect the relative amount of attention given to the social side of language, without taking the distinction too seriously." He also points out that, while most linguists recognize that one *should* pay attention to the social contexts of language, sociolinguists dedicate themselves to determining *how* to do so.

As Hudson's comments suggest, many language-oriented scholars who are not usually thought of as sociolinguists have also attempted to incorporate the social context of language into their theorizing. John Searle's (1969) speech act theory and H. Paul Grice's (1975) work on conversation are examples. Many of the issues we discuss in this book could be profitably examined from such perspectives, but that is beyond the scope of the sociolinguistic analysis that we are undertaking.

5. Perfectly formed utterances are those that follow the rules of formal (written) English grammar. It was typical for linguistics texts to devote their primary attention to explaining the structure of sentences such as "John hit the ball" or "Lions love meat and gravy" rather than the messier and more complex sentences that actually occur in everyday contexts. For illustrations, see Bloomfield 1933:17–77 and Chomsky 1964: 61–84.

6. Nonideal utterances are those real-world utterances that are problematic from the perspective of a strict grammarian. For example, one commonly hears sentences such as "My mother, no I mean my aunt, lived, no well that isn't quite right, she didn't really live there, she thought about living there. Anyway . . ."

7. See generally Fasold 1990:39–64. We discuss some examples of linguistically oriented legal anthropology in chapters 6 and 8.

8. Representative work appears in Tannen 1993.

9. Some of the most important papers on conversation analysis in institutional contexts have been collected by Paul Drew and John Heritage (1992) in *Talk at Work*. A comment in the paper by Emanuel Schegloff (1992:106) illustrates our point: "The issue I mean to address is *not* 'Is there such a thing as gender/class/power/status/organization/ etc.?' or 'Does it effect anything in the world?'"

10. This question is suggested by Marc Galanter's classic article "Why the 'Haves' Come Out Ahead" (1974), which proposes a number of structural answers.

Chapter Two

1. In North Carolina, for example, the marital defense to rape was not fully abolished until 1993. See N.C. General Statutes §14-27.8; see also Koss 1994:223–24; Bohmer 1991:327–29.

2. To illustrate again with North Carolina law, the crime of first-degree rape (N.C. General Statutes §14-27.2) against an adult victim requires the use of a deadly weapon, serious personal injury, or multiple perpetrators. Most acquaintance rapes will therefore fall into the less serious second-degree category (§14-27.3).

3. We consider later in the chapter whether these tactics and their effects are unique to rape trials or are simply generic cross-examination strategies that may be especially problematic in the rape context.

4. Van Pearlberg, Jimmy D. Berry, Julie L. Miller, and Linda A. Goldman (1995: 53A-4 to 53A-7) offer an example of a "how to" manual for defense lawyers on exploiting the victim's lifestyle and prior sexual history. Such advice is conventional wisdom among criminal lawyers.

5. North Carolina, for example, has created an Office of Coordinator of Services for Victims of Sexual Assault, the purpose of which is "to establish a network of coordinated public and private services for victims of sexual assault." See N.C. General Statutes §§143B-394.1 to 143B-394.3.

6. North Carolina (N.C. General Statutes §15-166) allows the trial judge to exclude "bystanders" (persons other than those directly involved in the trial) from the courtroom during rape trials. Efforts to restrict what the press may disclose have proved to be of dubious constitutionality. In *The Florida Star v. B.J.F.*, 491 U.S. 524 (1989), the Supreme Court struck down a Florida law that imposed penalties on a newspaper that published the identity of a sexual assault victim.

7. Federal Rule of Evidence 412 provides a model that has been widely adopted by the states. See Pearlberg et al. 1995:53A-10 to 53A-12 for examples.

8. Before proceeding with the analysis, one further comment is in order. Most of the social science writing about rape that we have discussed, including Matoesian's, seems to assume that rape defendants are guilty and that the proper task of legal reform is to eliminate barriers to convicting them. Readers may note, for example, that Matoesian's analyses of trial transcripts rarely mention one particular class of possible explanations: that the complaining witness is not telling the truth and that the defendant is not guilty. We do some of this as well, as when, for reasons of clarity, we refer to the complaining witness in a rape case as the "victim." We, too, are convinced that rape is a problem of epidemic proportions, that acquaintance rape is not taken seriously enough, and that the prosecution of rape puts extraordinary and unfair burdens on the victim. However, we want to respect the fundamental legal values of the presumption of innocence and the right to due process. In our judgment, undermining these values in any context, even one as compelling as rape, is a risky undertaking. Readers will reach their own conclusions about these matters, of course, but they should give the issue their thoughtful attention.

9. These postulates are perhaps most appropriately limited to American and/or British English and the societies in which they are spoken, since most conversation analysis studies have been based there. We note, however, that anthropologists have often objected to the implicit assumption within conversation analysis that generalizations about how conversation works in the United States or Britain might apply elsewhere. For example, Robert Hayden (1987) noted different practices with respect to interruption in Indian *panchayats* (councils), and Elinor Ochs Keenan (1976) questioned the applicability of Grice's conversational maxims in Malagasy language and society.

10. All of the data presented here are drawn from transcripts of the cross-examination of female rape victims by male defense lawyers. This is not the result of any selection on our part. In all of Matoesian's published transcripts and in all of the rape cases we have studied, the male defendant has been represented by a male lawyer. There are still few female criminal-defense lawyers, and even fewer who represent men charged with rape. Why this is so is an interesting and complex question that is beyond the scope of this book. By contrast, female prosecutors are common, and many of them specialize in rape cases. Moira Lasch, the prosecutor in the William Kennedy Smith trial, which we discuss at the end of this chapter, is such a specialist.

11. Matoesian (1993:148) identifies a dozen distinct question forms.

12. In lines 1–2, the lawyer starts to ask an open-ended WH question but then switches to a yes/no question about the witness's age before the witness has a chance to answer the WH question.

13. The colloquy in lines 29–33 can also be seen as a single tag question. The witness's first "Mmhmm" in line 31 interrupts the question, and the lawyer then completes it by adding the tag "Correct?" in line 32.

14. After all the witnesses for both sides have testified, the lawyers are allowed to make closing arguments to the jury. The law gives the lawyers wide latitude to summarize and comment on any aspect of the evidence.

15. Witnesses are sometimes "rescued" during cross-examination by the friendly lawyer (the district attorney, in this context) or the judge. The lawyer might object to the line of questioning and ask the judge to rule that the witness be given a chance to explain her answers. Alternatively, or in addition, the lawyer can go back over the same ground on redirect examination and give the witness a chance to explain or elaborate on the answers she gave on cross-examination. These possibilities do not fundamentally alter the power imbalance we have described, however, because the witness is entirely dependent on the intervention of others.

16. This is an instance where the district attorney might have attempted a rescue by insisting to the judge that the witness be allowed to complete her answer. The fact that no rescue ensues affirms the dependency and ultimate powerlessness of the witness.

17. By focusing our analysis on the rape *trial*, we do not mean to diminish the significance of the pretrial process, during which the police and the prosecutor examine the victim to determine whether to go forward with the case. This process undoubtedly contributes to the feeling of revictimization. Indeed, in evaluating the victim as a prospective witness, the prosecutor — whether male or female — may employ some of the same discourse strategies that defense lawyers use on cross-examination.

18. The discovery that revictimization is an artifact of the adversary system would have some interesting implications for efforts to reform the prosecution of rape. If the adversary system itself dooms the complaining witness to a process of domination, thereby denying her a fair hearing for her story, then the only remedy would seem to be to divert rape cases into another kind of system. But such radical change would be beyond the power of a legislature because the right of a criminal defendant to confront his accuser publicly, and with the assistance of counsel, is guaranteed by the Sixth Amendment to the Constitution. It might be possible to evade these constitutional imperatives by handling at least acquaintance rape through a noncriminal process. Some colleges have tried to do so through their student conduct codes, in apparent recognition of the problems of dealing with rape through traditional adversary procedures. This, however, has brought criticism from all quarters: from defense lawyers screaming for due process and from victims' rights advocates decrying the trivialization of a violent crime. See, for example, Ruth Sheehan, "Campus Courts on Trial," *Raleigh News & Observer*, Sept. 29, 1996, p. 1.

19. Our colleague Marion Crain has raised the possibility of analogizing rape to robbery. Both involve the appropriation of something (sex or money), and, in both cases, it is necessary to determine whether the thing appropriated was freely given or taken by force or threat. It would seem, at least a priori, that both classes of cases would present frequent instances of ambiguity about the nature of the appropriation. But we know that the question of domination comes up all the time in rape cases and almost never in robbery cases. Why? Crain asks. The answer, she suggests, lies in the cultural presumptions that we bring to bear. In economic matters, we presume self-interest; thus, we find it hard to believe that a person who claims to have been forced to turn over his or her money really meant to give it away. With rape, though, we

may begin from a premise of consent because we assume that women who do certain things, wear certain clothes, or have certain kinds of friends are making themselves sexually available.

20. This comment assumes that the defense lawyer is male, which is almost invariably the case. See note 10 above.

21. Louis Bilionis has observed to us that Smith's final answer is a kind of announced silence. It is a silence that stands in ironic contrast to the silences of the female victims that we discussed earlier in the chapter, however, because Smith's silence is a powerful rather than helpless one.

Chapter Three

1. In interviews with a large number of divorce lawyers in Maine, sociologist Craig McEwen and political scientists Lynn Mather and Richard Maiman (1994) found them to be generally supportive of mediation. One reason that lawyers like divorce mediation is that it allows for face-to-face settlement negotiations between the parties in an atmosphere of civility. Settling cases without bringing the parties together is difficult, the lawyers report. Lawyer-to-lawyer negotiations are inefficient, with the lawyers shuttling proposals to and from their clients. Miscommunications are also common. But face-to-face discussions, even with the lawyers present, frequently degenerate into shouting matches. Mediation represents the best of both worlds. The parties are brought together, but the norms of mediation, as enforced by the mediator, ensure that they will behave themselves.

The divorce lawyers also reported to McEwen, Mather, and Maiman (1994:166) that mediation helps them resolve a difficult professional conflict. Lawyers see themselves as obligated to serve simultaneously as "client advocate" and as "reality tester." The advocate is the loyal champion of the client's cause, pushing the client's position regardless of the odds. The reality tester assesses the case from a cool professional perspective, calculates the probabilities, and tells the client the truth, even if he or she does not want to hear it. Lawyers find it easy to be advocates. But advocates who let their clients become falsely optimistic are failing to provide competent legal service and may be inviting malpractice suits. The problem is that, when the reality tester delivers bad news, the client may lose faith in the advocate and look for a new one.

The great benefit of mediation is that someone else serves as the reality tester. A lawyer can walk into the mediation room as an advocate and then sit back while the opposing party and the mediator expose the weaknesses in the client's case. When the client perceives the problem and suggests that some concessions might be necessary, the lawyer can agree reluctantly without any hint of disloyalty to the cause.

2. This variability is well documented in the ethnographic work of Susan Silbey and Sally Merry (1986). They report that mediation, as they have seen it practiced, is not a consistent process. Rather, mediators typically adopt one of two styles: bargaining or therapy. Bargainers focus on concrete agreements. They ignore the emotional demands of the parties and concentrate instead on demands that can be traded off against each other. Bargainers emphasize their professional expertise in law and the legal process. They warn the parties of the dangers of failing to agree and ending up in the costly and capricious legal system. They exert considerable control over the process. They often

caucus with the parties individually and sometimes strike out on their own to draft agreements they think the parties will accept.

The therapeutic style, by contrast, "is a form of communication in which the parties are encouraged to engage in a full expression of their feelings and attitudes" (Silbey and Merry 1986:20). Therapeutic mediators stress their expertise in managing personal relationships. They, too, urge avoidance of the legal system, but their rationale is that the court will be inattentive to the parties' emotional needs. Whereas bargainers tend to dismiss feelings in pursuit of concrete objectives, therapists treat emotional concerns as paramount. Conflicts are characterized as misunderstandings or failures of communication. As a result, therapists are sometimes at an impasse when they find that the parties understand each other perfectly well but simply do not agree.

Each style has a distinctive language. Bargaining "converts the experiences and claims of the disputants into the language of negotiation and exchange." In asserting a quasi-legal kind of authority, "[t]he mediator wraps him or herself in the same mystical cloth as the jurist, the rabbi, or the priest." The language of therapy, conversely, "attempts to recast disputants' individual experiences into terms of mutually valued relationships." Therapy "seeks to cultivate a language of mutual recognition of the importance of [the parties'] relationship, shared rather than individual interests, and collective values rather than competitive demands" (Silbey and Merry 1986:26–27).

3. Many social scientists have criticized conversation analysis for avoiding questions of purpose and effect. A part of the response has always been that the publication of extremely detailed textual data allows interested readers to ask those questions themselves.

4. Garcia (1991:831n18) reports that 60 percent (191 out of 321) of the accusations or complaints made in the mediation sessions she studied contained such downgrading characteristics.

5. These terms, as well as the phrase "fifty percent a parent," are marvelously evocative of Fineman's (1991) characterization of therapeutic discourse, which we discuss in chapter 4.

6. Garcia (1995:39–41) does speculate about the possible social consequences of her linguistic findings. She suggests that the mediator activism she documents may decrease both the probability of reaching an agreement and the degree of compliance with any agreement that is reached.

7. For further discussion of this question, see Conley and O'Barr 1990:181–85.

8. Much of this work was inspired by Robin Lakoff's *Language and Woman's Place* (1975). Examples include the contributions in Tannen 1993, Philips et al. 1987, and Thorne et al. 1983. Deborah Tannen's (1986, 1990) best sellers have been enormously successful in popularizing the analysis of language and gender.

Chapter Four

1. See chapter 3 for a detailed review of this argument with respect to divorce.

2. A case study in this approach is the campaign of Catharine MacKinnon and Andrea Dworkin for the enactment and enforcement of a restrictive anti-pornography ordinance in Indianapolis. The city ultimately adopted an ordinance they had drafted, but the courts found it unconstitutional (MacKinnon 1989:206).

3. We discuss these developments in linguistics in chapter 1.

4. This work is reported in O'Barr 1982 and Conley et al. 1978.

5. These findings were presented initially in Conley et al. 1978 and in a revised form in O'Barr 1982.

6. Subsequent studies of powerless language have confirmed the existence and significance of the phenomenon. They have also refined the definition of powerless language and developed a more precise understanding of its effects in a variety of contexts. For a review of more-recent research trends, see Morrill and Facciola 1992.

7. We pointedly used the past tense in the discussion in the text. One might reasonably question the continuing validity of our findings in light of the educational and career gains that women have made over the past several decades. Perhaps powerless language has become less prevalent, or at least has lost the strong gender correlation it seemed to have had in the 1970s. More recent research on powerless language continues to demonstrate its impact on listener perceptions, although the strength of the association between powerless speech and gender is unclear (Hosman 1989; Wright and Hosman 1983; Morrill and Facciola 1992).

8. A standard formulation is this: "In determining the weight to be given to the testimony of each witness as to whether he or she is to be believed, you should apply the same test of truthfulness that you would in your everyday affairs" (O'Barr 1982:95).

9. It is not clear that the law could do anything even if it wanted to. In the 1970s, we conducted an experimental test of whether jurors' assessments of credibility are affected by instruction from the judge to disregard powerless language and found that they are not (O'Barr 1982:94–96).

10. *Eisenstadt v. Baird*, 405 U.S. 438 (1972).

11. To take a single example, consider the increasingly strict limits on a lawyer's right to exercise peremptory challenges to dismiss prospective jurors during the jury selection process. Historically, lawyers were allowed to dismiss a certain number of jurors peremptorily, meaning for any reason or no reason at all. In 1986, in *Batson v. Kentucky*, 476 U.S. 79, the Supreme Court held that prosecutors could not dismiss prospective jurors for reasons of race. (Prosecutors had often dismissed jurors of the same minority group as the defendant; defense lawyers employed an opposite strategy.) In a series of post-*Batson* cases, courts have extended the racial prohibition to criminal defense lawyers and to both sides in civil trials, and gender and religion have been added to the list of forbidden bases for dismissal.

12. See, for example, the papers collected in Briggs 1996, all of which are based on narrative studies done in the 1980s.

13. As we explained in our earlier report (Conley and O'Barr 1990:181–85), there is a further complication. When we describe a litigant as rule- or relationally oriented, we are referring to his or her central tendency. Most litigants, through the accounts they give, display at least some elements of both orientations. "Rules versus relationships" is thus more accurately described as a continuum than as a dichotomy.

14. As law teachers, we are often struck by how this process of linguistic co-optation affects female law students. Many of them (as well as significant numbers of men) come to their first-year classes with a Gilliganesque approach to analyzing trouble situations, only to abandon it in pursuit of the ability to "think like a lawyer." We are left wondering what is happening to their thought processes outside the classroom. We deal more fully with the topic of legal education in chapter 8.

Chapter Five

1. Although interest in the developmental stages of disputes has a long history in anthropology, we are indebted to June Starr, who made a strong case for the importance of attempting to find ways to study it in a seminar she presented at Duke University in the 1970s.

2. Although many people have found the model useful, others have criticized it from the outset. For example, in the very issue of *Law & Society Review* in which it first appeared, sociologist Robert Kidder (1980–81) questioned its applicability beyond the Western individual-rights-based idea of a dispute.

3. The term *naming* may obscure an important distinction. Numerous anthropological and linguistic studies have pointed out the power associated with naming things. In a memorable paper, Brenda Danet (1980b) analyzed a trial in which a doctor who performed an abortion was charged with homicide. She found that the prosecution named the aborted entity a "baby" or even a "little baby boy," whereas the defense chose names such as "fetus" and "products of conception."

The Felstiner-Abel-Sarat model seems to lump under the heading of *naming* two conceptually distinct phases: articulating the problem, and giving it a name. Pomerantz's data are about the process of articulating the problem. Giving it a name — that is, saying that this occurrence is a specific example of a particular thing, as, for example, calling it "sexual harassment" or "rape" or "robbery" — is very different from describing what happened.

4. It is, of course, possible that the initial mentioning of the problem may fix responsibility and thus obviate the interactive work. An example might be "Sam's kid hit my car with his baseball." However, the empirical data presented by Pomerantz and Gail Jefferson (1980, 1985, 1988) suggest that the announcement is more likely to take the form of "My car got hit with a baseball," followed by an interactional sequence that leads to the responsible party. An intriguing possibility is that some people tend to make the link earlier than others. If there are such differences, it would be interesting to investigate whether they correlate with gender or other social variables.

5. The extent to which people attribute responsibility to human versus nonhuman (i.e., supernatural, accidental, etc.) causes varies across cultures, according to anthropological sources. We take up this problem more fully in chapter 6.

6. This realization reminds us that stories do not exist apart from their various tellings. It is in one sense meaningless to ask what the "real" story is, or what the "facts" are, because stories, trouble-tellings, and accounts of problems are deeply conditioned by the linguistic and interactional environments in which they are told. Receptive, encouraging listeners help us elaborate stories. By their responses, they help us produce these accounts, becoming coauthors of what we tell. If they demur, if they resist, if they turn a deaf ear, the stories may never emerge or may lose much of their potential complexity. All this flies in the face of how the law treats disputes. By conceiving of cases as being made up of core "facts" that stay the same from retelling to retelling, the law seems to presume the existence of an authoritative version of the story that can be discovered and preserved.

7. The Felstiner-Abel-Sarat model merges the processes of articulating the problem to the blamed party and requesting a remedy. The conversation analysis evidence just

reviewed would suggest that in real situations articulating and requesting may occur as separate interactions, with the details largely dependent on the response of the blamed party.

8. Conversation analysts take care to point out that the word *preferred* is not intended to imply anything about the speakers' actual feelings or intentions (Atkinson and Drew 1979:59). It refers only to the linguistic structure of the exchange, in particular the way in which the speakers "attend" to the alternative second parts.

9. As evidence, they cite the fact that accusers often structure their accusations so as to preclude a simple flat denial. They also point to the legal principle that sometimes allows silence in the face of an accusation (i.e., nondenial, the unanticipated response) to be interpreted as an admission.

10. By focusing on legal channels for disputing, we do not mean to deny the possibility that disputants will resort to extra- or illegal methods. In the real world, of course, people sometimes resolve problems by threatened or actual violence (shooting a trespassing animal, for example) or by various other "self-help" remedies (such as seizing a disputed piece of property when the other side is not looking). What these methods all have in common is that they involve, or at least contemplate, physical action beyond talk. Those who are unwilling to do more than talk about their dispute must give up or resort to the legal system.

11. Material in this section is drawn from our own research on small claims courts, as reported in Conley and O'Barr 1990.

12. Variation in judicial styles among small claims judges is described in detail in chapter 5 of Conley and O'Barr 1990.

13. There is no effective appellate mechanism to prevent such things from happening. In some jurisdictions, a defendant can remove a case from small claims to formal court at the time it is filed, but there is no appeal if it is allowed to stay in small claims court. In other places, a defendant who is dissatisfied with the judgment of the small claims court can demand a retrial in a formal court. When this happens, however, the higher court usually starts all over from the beginning, rather than reviewing the proceedings in the small claims court.

14. For a discussion of the relationship between lawyers' talk and jurisprudential theories, see Conley and O'Barr 1988.

15. An interview with a litigant after the case is an artificial context for talking about the dispute in the sense that it is a far different environment than a conversation that the litigant might have with a family member or friend. But since it is virtually impossible for researchers to position themselves as overhearers of such discussions in the real world, post-trial interviews are the best available sources of information on the further transformation that disputes may undergo after the legal case is concluded.

16. We have borrowed the natural history theme from Michael Silverstein and Greg Urban (1996), who have adapted it to the study of discourse.

Chapter Six

1. For a short overview of the field of legal anthropology, see Conley and O'Barr 1993.

2. One of Nader's chapters does provide an extended transcript of an interview with

a judge (1990:97–104). Her case descriptions, however, are reminiscent of Gluckman's and Bohannan's.

3. It also suggests that in the moots "discriminatory and coercive intentions," if present, would probably be manifest in subtler forms than confrontational questioning (Goldman 1986:374).

4. Goldman translates *piaga* literally as "go" in the sense of "happen" or "occur." Goldman's idiomatic translations indicate that it acquires further meaning from its subject. Thus, his literal translation of line (5) is "water goes (habitual)," which he then renders as "people used to drown." Similarly, line (9) is literally "trees misadventures go (habitual)," while line (13) is "holes go (habitual)."

5. Habit is sometimes expressed through other grammatical constructions in English, as in *Hardwood burns slowly* and *The men burn brush on Wednesdays*.

6. However, English does have ways of distinguishing events that happen with and without agents. Compare *The house burned* with *I burned the house*.

7. A shorter report appears in an important collection of essays edited by anthropologists Jane Hill and Judith Irvine (1992). This volume, entitled *Responsibility and Evidence in Oral Discourse*, contains a series of papers on the general topic of "the relationship between the devices that manage responsibility, the local cultural understanding of responsibility and evidence, and the nature of social identity revealed by their management" (Hill and Irvine 1992:20). The papers are remarkably diverse, covering such issues as evidentiary standards in American courts (Philips 1992), verbal abuse in a Senegalese village (Irvine 1992), and the production of meaning in rituals of divination (Du Bois 1992). Since accepting or rejecting the concept of accident is a means of managing responsibility, these papers shed significant, if sometimes indirect, light on the issue that Goldman has raised.

8. The word *li'i* is central to Kuipers's analysis. He translates it as "word" or "voice" and then explains that it connotes two rather different things: a promise that creates a prolonged moral duty and an immediate performance. It thus evokes simultaneously the permanence of tradition and the ephemeral individuality of particular oral performances (Kuipers 1990:2).

9. A related piece of work is Peter Just's (1990) study of liability and equity in Indonesian Dou Donggo law. Just finds that the Dou Donggo impose "stricter than strict" liability on people for wrongs that "might have" been committed regardless of whether or not the particular accused has actually caused any damage. On the other hand, they have a very precise system for determining moral culpability for a wrong. He concludes that Western and Dou Donggo notions of liability are at once comparable and distinguishable.

Chapter Seven

1. Michael Silverstein (1998:123–24) dates this pejorative term to the Napoleonic reaction against an Enlightenment effort to establish *idéologie* as the science of "human nature." "Mere ideologue" became a dismissive epithet used against those who dealt in speculative abstractions.

2. The oldest versions of the second-person singular pronouns were *thu* and *the*.

3. As this point suggests, linguistics has its own language ideologies. For a discussion of the issue see Errington (2003) and England (2003).

4. We thank University of North Carolina colleague John Orth, a legal historian, for reminding us of this language.

5. On the former point, for example, the website of the Lincoln Bicentennial Commission states that "[b]efore Lincoln's presidency . . . [t]hose referring to this country used the plural: 'the United States are.' After Lincoln's presidency . . . the United States became a singular noun: 'the United States is'" (Bishop 2003). On the latter point, Carl Sandburg (1939:38–39) reports in his famous biography of Lincoln that the president-elect, stopping in Indianapolis en route from Illinois to Washington for his inauguration, used the phrase "*these* United States" in addressing a crowd, then told the governor and legislature what would happen if "the United States should merely hold and retake *its* forts and other property."

6. For a case study of a national-language ideology (Indonesia), see Errington (2000).

7. Susan Berk-Seligson (1990:217) has long argued for preserving a recording of all non-English testimony in order to allow for the possibility of challenging and improving on the original trial transcript. This is a self-evidently excellent idea. It does not address Haviland's concern, however, since, as a practical matter, the legal system will still insist on a single "official" transcript as the basis for appeals.

8. Haviland discusses "the evolving 'linguistic ideologies' of anthropology itself" (2003:765), citing Duranti's (2001) critical analysis. For other examples see Whitely (2003) and Errington (2003).

9. Although Hirsch (1998:293n19) acknowledges that "[s]cholars disagree on the utility of 'Swahili' as an ethnic category," she uses Swahili as an adjective "to refer to those coastal Muslims of African, Arab, Asian, or mixed ancestry who would agree that 'Mswahili' is one term that *could* be used to identify them in at least *some* contexts." Their language is Kiswahili.

10. They have, survived, however, in essentially the same form. The 2010 Constitution of Kenya (article 170) ratifies Kadhi's Courts as "subordinate courts" with jurisdiction "limited to the determination of questions of Muslim law relating to personal status, marriage, divorce or inheritance in proceedings in which all the parties profess the Muslim religion and submit to the jurisdiction of the Kadhi's courts."

11. More recent examples of ethnographic work with a strong focus on language ideology include Richland (2008), discussed in chapter 6, and Mertz (2007), discussed in chapter 11.

Chapter Eight

1. We base the inference that the letter was unsolicited on its contents. It is available on the website www.acandyrose.com/donaldfoster.htm.

2. *Daubert v. Merrell Dow Pharmaceuticals, Inc.*, 509 U.S. 579 (1993).

3. *Kumho Tire Co. v. Carmichael*, 526 U.S. 137 (1999).

4. Gibbons's broader definition draws on a definition promulgated by AILA (Association Internationale de Linguistique Appliquée).

5. For an illustrative transcript of Loftus giving expert testimony in 1978, see Loftus (1979:217).

6. *United States v. Smithers*, 212 F. 3d 306, 311 (6th Cir. 2000).

7. For an example of a case in which Loftus was not permitted to testify, see *People v. Sanders*, 11 Cal. 4th. 475, 905 P. 2d 420 (1995).

8. Lawrence Rosen (1977) has argued that problems with the admission of social science testimony in court are related, in part, to the fact that different social scientists are likely to give variable testimony about the same issue. He contends that this is understandable because of the different theoretical frames and schools of thought in which they work. Such inconsistency, however, has led many judges to find social science unreliable when compared to the so-called hard sciences, where agreement at least appears to be more common among different specialists.

9. One can imagine academic language experts avoiding companies that had particularly notorious records as polluters, abusers of labor, etc.

Chapter Nine

1. "Paralinguistic" also refers to aspects of speech that do not contribute to its content, such as prosody and intonation (Trager 1958). This chapter, however, will not address these audible actions specifically.

2. For a review of these trends within the field of linguistics, see Karpiński 2012.

3. A version of this article that includes only the Rodney King analysis was later published by Charles and Marjorie Goodwin in *The Construction of Professional Discourse*, ed. Britt-Louise Gunnaarsson, Per Linell, and Bengt Nordberg (London: Longman, 1997).

4. The jurors were hung on the verdict of one of the four officers charged. Two of the officers were later found guilty of federal charges of violating King's civil rights. The other two officers were acquitted of the federal charges.

5. President George H. W. Bush even made a public comment to this effect.

6. As with other transcripts cited in this book, we have edited the transcripts excerpted in this chapter, omitting in many cases CA transcription conventions that denote intonation and other interactional details when they are not relevant to our discussion. Therefore the transcripts do not appear in a form identical to how they are presented in their original publication contexts.

Chapter Ten

1. In this and other texts that we adapt from Rickford and King (2016) or Slobe (2016), we have included the material from the court reporter's transcript, but not any of the editorial or explanatory comments added by those scholars. In some instances we have included their timed pauses and silences, indicated by numbers (seconds) in parentheses.

Chapter Eleven

1. One of the earliest examples of such work is a comparative study of children's insults in three different cultural settings by Laura Lein and Donald Brenneis (1978). Examining the language of insults used by black working-class American children, white middle-class American children, and Hindi-speaking Indian children, Lein and Brenneis conclude that some aspects of disputing behavior seem universal, whereas others are culture-specific. They have been subsequently criticized for studying artificial arguments

among children who were playing roles rather than naturally occurring arguments, although they did so for understandable logistical reasons.

2. Although Mertz has focused thus far on classroom discourse, this is only the tip of the iceberg. From the very first days of law school, law students mimic their class discussions in their study groups and lunchroom arguments. The classroom provides an authoritative model that they seem eager to practice at every opportunity.

3. Consistent with the practice in contemporary anthropology, Hirsch has also discussed her findings with the people she studied and has fed their comments back into her analysis.

REFERENCES

Abel, Richard L.
1989   *American lawyers*. New York: Oxford University Press.

Allison, Julie A., and Lawrence S. Wrightsman
1993   *Rape: The misunderstood crime*. Newbury Park, CA: Sage.

American Anthropological Association
1998   Statement on race. Available at http://www.americananthro.org/ConnectWith
        AAA/Content.aspx?ItemNumber=2583 (accessed January 19, 2018).

Anonymous
1996   *Primary colors: A novel of politics*. New York: Random House.

Atkinson, J. Maxwell, and Paul Drew
1979   *Order in court: The organization of verbal interaction in judicial settings*.
        Atlantic Highlands, NJ: Humanities Press.

Austin, J. L.
1962   *How to do things with words*. New York: Oxford University Press.

Bakhtin, Mikhail
1981   Discourse in the novel. In *The dialogic imagination: Four essays by
        M. M. Bakhtin*, edited by Michael Holquist, translated by Caryl Emerson and
        Michael Holquist. Austin: University of Texas Press (original 1935).

Bandes, Susan
2014   Remorse, demeanor, and the consequences of misinterpretation: The limits
        of law as a window into the soul. *Journal of Law, Religion and State* 3:
        170–99.

Bartlett, Katharine T.
1994   Feminist perspectives on the ideological impact of legal education upon the
        profession. *North Carolina Law Review* 72:1259–70.

Baugh, John
2003   Linguistic profiling. In *Black linguistics: Language, society, and politics in Africa and the Americas*, edited by Sinfree Makoni, Geneva Smitherman, Arnetha F. Ball, and Arthur K. Spears. Oxford: Routledge.

Bauman, Richard, and Charles L. Briggs
1990   Poetics and performance as critical perspectives on language and social life. *Annual Review of Anthropology* 19:59–88.
2000   Language philosophy as language ideology: John Locke and Johann Gottfried Herder. In *Regimes of language: Ideologies, polities, and identities*, edited by Paul V. Kroskrity. Santa Fe, NM: School of American Research Press.

Bennett, W. Lance, and Martha S. Feldman
1981   *Reconstructing reality in the courtroom: Justice and judgment in American culture.* New Brunswick, NJ: Rutgers University Press.

Berk-Seligson, Susan
1990   *The bilingual courtroom.* Chicago: University of Chicago Press. Reissued 2002.

Bishop, Michael F.
2003   Divided we fall: Would we still be a "United" States without Lincoln's legacy? www.lincolnbicentennial.gov/press-febr17.html.

Black, Donald J.
1971   The social organization of arrest. *Stanford Law Review* 23:1087–111.

Bloomfield, Leonard
1933   *Language.* New York: Holt, Rinehart & Winston.

Bohannan, Paul
1964   Anthropology and the law. In *Horizons of anthropology*, edited by Sol Tax. Chicago: Aldine.
1969   Ethnography and comparison in legal anthropology. In *Law in culture and society*, edited by Laura Nader. Chicago: Aldine.
1989   *Justice and judgment among the Tiv.* 3rd ed. Prospect Heights, IL: Waveland Press (orig. 1957).

Bohmer, Carol
1991   Acquaintance rape and the law. In *Acquaintance rape: The hidden crime*, edited by Andrea Parrot and Laurie Bechhofer. New York: Wiley.

Bohmer, Carol, and Marilyn L. Ray
1994   Effects of different dispute resolution methods on women and children after divorce. *Family Law Quarterly* 28:223–45.

Brenneis, Donald
1988   Language and disputing. *Annual Review of Anthropology* 17:221–37.

Briere, John, and N. Malamuth
1983   Self-reported likelihood of sexually aggressive behavior: Attitudinal versus sexual explanations. *Journal of Research in Personality* 17:315–23.

Briggs, Charles, ed.
1996   *Disorderly discourse: Narrative, conflict, and inequality*. London: Oxford University Press.

Bryan, Penelope
1992   Killing us softly: Divorce mediation and the politics of power. *Buffalo Law Review* 40:441–523.

Bucholtz, Mary
2007   Variation in transcription. *Discourse Studies* 9:784–808.

Caputi, Jane, and Diana E. H. Russell
1992   Femicide: Sexist terrorism against women. In *Femicide: The politics of woman killing*, edited by Jill Radford and Diana E. H. Russell. New York: Twayne.

Carimico, Graceann, Thuy Huynh, and Shallyn Wells
2016   Rape and Sexual Assault. *Georgetown Journal of Gender and the Law* 17:359–406.

Cassidy, Frederic G., and Joan Houston Hall, eds.
1985   *Dictionary of American Regional English*. Cambridge, MA: Harvard University Press.

Chomsky, Noam
1964   *Current issues in linguistic theory*. The Hague: Mouton.

Clarke, Stevens H., Laura F. Donnelly, and Sara A. Grove
1989   *Court-ordered arbitration in North Carolina: An evaluation of its effects*. Chapel Hill: Institute of Government, University of North Carolina.

Comaroff, John L., and Simon Roberts
1981   *Rules and processes: The cultural logic of dispute in an African context*. Chicago: University of Chicago Press.

Conley, John M.
2016   Legal discourse. In *The Routledge handbook of linguistic anthropology*, edited by Nancy Bonvillain. New York: Routledge.

Conley, John M., and David W. Peterson
1996   When ethical systems collide: The social scientist and the adversary process. In *Recent developments in forensic linguistics*, edited by Hannes Kniffka. Frankfurt: Peter Lang.

Conley, John M., and William M. O'Barr
1988   Fundamentals of jurisprudence: An ethnography of judicial decision making in informal courts. *North Carolina Law Review* 66:467–507.
1990   *Rules versus relationships*. Chicago: University of Chicago Press.
1993   Legal anthropology comes home: A brief history of the ethnographic study of law. *Loyola of Los Angeles Law Review* 27:41–64.

Conley, John M., William M. O'Barr, and E. Allan Lind
1978   The power of language: Presentational style in the courtroom. *Duke Law Journal* 78:1375–99.

Conley, Robin
2008   "At the time she was a man": The temporal dimension of identity construc-
         tion. *Political and Legal Anthropology Review* 31(1):28–47.
2013   Living with the decision that someone will die: Linguistic distance and
         empathy in jurors' death penalty decisions. *Language in Society* 42(5):
         503–26.
2015   *Confronting the death penalty: How language influences jurors in capital
         cases.* Oxford: Oxford University Press.

Corsaro, William A., and Thomas Rizzo
1990   Disputes in the peer culture of American and Italian nursery-school children.
         In *Conflict talk*, edited by Allen D. Grimshaw. Cambridge: Cambridge
         University Press.

Cotterrell, Roger
1994   *Law and society.* Aldershot, England: Dartmouth Publishing.

Crawford, Sandra
2017   Collaborative law: A brief overview. *Illinois Bar Journal* 108:28–31.

Crook, J. A.
1995   *Legal advocacy in the Roman world.* Ithaca, NY: Cornell University Press.

Danet, Brenda
1980a   Language in the legal process. *Law & Society Review* 14:445–564.
1980b   "Baby" or "fetus"? Language and the construction of reality in a manslaugh-
         ter trial. *Semiotica* 32:187–219.

Davis, Natalie Zemon
1987   *Fiction in the archives: Pardon tales and their tellers in sixteenth-century
         France.* Palo Alto, CA: Stanford University Press.

Deeb, Hadi N.
2013   Boiling down to the m-word at the California Supreme Court. *Journal of
         Linguistic Anthropology* 23:41–64.

Dixon, R. M. W.
1979   Ergativity. *Language* 55:39–138.

Dole, Gertrude
1966   Anarchy without chaos: Alternatives to political authority among the Kui-
         kuru. In *Political anthropology*, edited by M. J. Swartz, V. W. Turner, and
         A. Tuden. Chicago: Aldine.

Drew, Paul, and John Heritage
1992   *Talk at work: Interaction in institutional settings.* Cambridge: Cambridge
         University Press.

Du Bois, John W.
1992   Meaning without intention: Lessons from divination. In *Responsibility
         and evidence in oral discourse*, edited by Jane H. Hill and Judith T. Irvine.
         Cambridge: Cambridge University Press.

Duncan, S.
1969   Nonverbal communication. *Psychological Bulletin* 72:118–37.

Duranti, Alessandro
2001   An historical perspective on contemporary linguistic anthropology. *Teaching Anthropology: SACC Notes* 7(2):20–24.

Eades, Diana
2012   The social consequences of language ideologies in courtroom cross-examination. *Language in Society* 41:471–97.
2016   *Sociolinguistics and the legal process.* Bristol, UK: Multilingual Matters.

Eades, Diana, ed.
1995   *Language in evidence: Issues confronting Aboriginal and multicultural Australia.* Sydney: University of New South Wales Press.

Edelman, Lauren B.
2016   *Working law: Courts, corporations, and symbolic civil rights.* Chicago: University of Chicago Press.

Eder, Donna
1990   Serious and playful disputes: Variation in conflict talk among female adolescents. In *Conflict talk*, edited by Allen D. Grimshaw. Cambridge: Cambridge University Press.

Ehrlich, Susan
2001   *Representing rape: Language and sexual consent.* New York: Routledge.
2016   Post-penetration rape: Coercion or freely given consent? In *Discursive constructions of consent in the legal process*, edited by Susan Ehrlich, Diana Eades, and Janet Ainsworth. Oxford: Oxford University Press.

Ehrlich, Susan, Diana Eades, and Janet Ainsworth, eds.
2016   *Discursive constructions of consent in the legal process.* Oxford: Oxford University Press.

Eisenberg, Theodore, Stephen P. Garvey, and Martin T. Wells
1998   But was he sorry?: The role of remorse in capital sentencing. *Cornell Law Review* 83:1599–645.

Eisenstein, Zillah R.
1988   *The female body and the law.* Berkeley: University of California Press.

England, Nora C.
2003   Mayan language revival and revitalization politics: Linguists and linguistic ideologies. *American Anthropologist* 105(4):733–43.

Epstein, A. L., ed.
1967   *The craft of social anthropology.* London: Social Science Paperbacks, in association with Tavistock.

Errington, Joseph
2000   Indonesian('s) authority. In *Regimes of language: Ideologies, polities, and identities*, edited by Paul V. Kroskrity. Santa Fe, NM: School of American Research Press.

220   References

2003   Getting language rights: The rhetorics of language endangerment and loss.
          American Anthropologist 105(4):723–32.

Estrich, S0p5.042usan
1987   *Real rape.* Cambridge, MA: Harvard University Press.

Evans Grubbs, Judith
1995   *Law and family in late antiquity: The Emperor Constantine's marriage
          legislation.* New York: Oxford University Press.
1996   Pietas and potestas: The family in Roman imperial law. Unpublished manu-
          script.

Evans-Pritchard, E. E.
1937   *Witchcraft, oracles, and magic among the Azande.* Oxford: Clarendon Press.

Fasold, Ralph
1990   *The sociolinguistics of language.* Oxford: Basil Blackwell.

Federal Bureau of Investigation
2016   Crime in the United States. Available at https://ucr.fbi.gov/crime-in-the-u.s
          /2016/crime-in-the-u.s.-2016 (accessed January 18, 2018).

Felstiner, William, Richard Abel, and Austin Sarat
1980–81 The emergence and transformation of disputes: Naming, blaming, claim-
          ing. . . . *Law & Society Review* 15:631–54.

Fineman, Martha Albertson
1991   *The illusion of equality: The rhetoric and reality of divorce reform.* Chicago:
          University of Chicago Press.

Foster, Donald W.
1989   *Elegy by W. S.: A study in attribution.* Newark: University of Delaware
          Press.
2000   *Author unknown: On the trail of anonymous.* New York: Henry Holt.

Foucault, Michel
1970   *The order of things: An archaeology of the human sciences.* London:
          Tavistock.
1972   *The archaeology of knowledge and the discourse of language.* London:
          Tavistock.
1977   *Discipline and punish: The birth of the prison.* London: Allen Lane; New
          York: Pantheon.
1978   *The history of sexuality.* Vol. 1, *An introduction.* New York: Random
          House.
1980   Two lectures. In *Power/knowledge: Selected interviews and other writings,
          1972–1977,* edited by Colin Gordon. Brighton, England: Harvester Press.
1985a   *The history of sexuality.* Vol. 2, *The use of pleasure.* New York: Viking.
1985b   *The history of sexuality.* Vol. 3, *The care of the self.* New York: Pantheon.

Frake, Charles O.
1969   Struck by speech. In *Law in culture and society,* edited by Laura Nader.
          Chicago: Aldine.

Galanter, Marc
1974   Why the "haves" come out ahead. *Law & Society Review* 9:95–160.

Garcia, Angela
1991   Dispute resolution without disputing: How the interactional organization
         of mediation hearings minimizes argument. *American Sociological Review*
         56:818–35.
1995   The problematics of representation in community mediation hearings:
         Implications for mediation practice. *Journal of Sociology & Social Welfare*
         22:23–46.

Gibbons, John
2003   *Forensic linguistics: An introduction to language in the justice system.*
         Oxford: Blackwell Publishing.

Gibbs, James L., Jr.
1962   Poro values and courtroom procedures in a Kpelle chiefdom. *Southwestern
         Journal of Anthropology* 18:341–50.
1967   The Kpelle moot. In *Law and warfare*, edited by Paul Bohannan. Garden
         City, NY: Natural History Press.

Gilligan, Carol
1982   *In a different voice: Psychological theory and women's development.* Cam-
         bridge, MA: Harvard University Press.

Gluckman, Max
1955   *The judicial process among the Barotse of Northern Rhodesia (Zambia).*
         Manchester, England: Manchester University Press.
1965   *The ideas in Barotse jurisprudence.* New Haven, CT: Yale University Press.
1969   Concepts in the comparative study of tribal law. In *Law in culture and
         society*, edited by Laura Nader. Chicago: Aldine.
1973   *Custom and conflict in Africa.* New York: Barnes and Noble.

Goffman, Erving
1959   *The presentation of self in everyday life.* Garden City, NY: Doubleday.
1963   *Behavior in public places: Notes on the social organization of gatherings.*
         New York: Free Press.
1967   *Interaction ritual: Essays in face-to-face behavior.* Garden City, NY: Anchor
         Books.

Goldberg-Ambrose, C.
1992   Unfinished business in rape law reform. *Journal of Social Issues* 48:
         173–86.

Goldman, Laurence
1986   A case of "questions" and the questions of "case." *Text* 6:345–92.
1993   *The culture of coincidence: Accident and absolute liability in Huli.* New
         York: Clarendon Press.

Goodale, Mark
2017   *Anthropology and law: A critical introduction.* New York: New York Uni-
         versity Press.

Goodwin, Charles
1994   Professional vision. *American Anthropologist* 96(3):606–33.
2003   The body in action. In *Discourse, the body, and identity*, edited by Justine Coupland and Richard Gwyn. New York: Palgrave/Macmillan.

Goodwin, Marjorie Harness
2011   Engendering children's play: Person reference in children's conflictual interaction. In *Conversation and gender*, edited by Susan A. Speer and Elizabeth Stokoe. Cambridge: Cambridge University Press.

Goodwin, Marjorie Harness, and Charles Goodwin
1987   Children's arguing. In *Language, gender, and sex in comparative perspective*, edited by Susan U. Philips, Susan Steele, and Christine Tanz. Cambridge: Cambridge University Press.

Greatbatch, David, and Robert Dingwall
1989   Selective facilitation: Some preliminary observations on a strategy used by divorce mediators. *Law & Society Review* 23:613–41.

Grice, H. Paul
1975   Logic and conversation. In *Syntax and semantics, Vol. 3: Speech acts*, edited by P. Cole and J. Morgan. London: Academic Press.

Grillo, Trina
1991   The mediation alternative: Process dangers for women. *Yale Law Journal* 100:1545–610.

Grimshaw, Allen D., ed.
1990   *Conflict talk: Sociolinguistic investigations of arguments in conversations.* Cambridge: Cambridge University Press.

Hall, Kermit, William M. Wiecek, and Paul Finkelman, eds.
1996   *American legal history: Cases and materials.* New York: Oxford University Press.

Haviland, John B.
2003   Ideologies of language: Some reflections on language and U.S. law. *American Anthropologist* 105(4):764–74.

Hayden, Robert M.
1987   Turn-taking, overlap, and the task at hand: Ordering speaking turns in legal settings. *American Ethnologist* 14:251–70.

Heffer, Chris, Frances Rock, and John Conley
2013   *Legal-lay communication: Textual travels in the law.* Oxford: Oxford University Press.

Hellinger, Marlis, and Hadumod Bußmann, eds.
2002   *Gender across languages: The linguistic representation of women and men.* Amsterdam: John Benjamins.

Henderson, Lynne
1991   Law's patriarchy. *Law & Society Review* 25:411–44.
1998   The dialogue of heart and head. *Cardozo Law Review* 10(1–2):123–48.

Heritage, John, and David Greatbatch
1986   Generating applause: A study of rhetoric and response at party political
        conferences. *American Journal of Sociology* 92:110–57.

Hill, Jane H., and Judith T. Irvine, eds.
1992   *Responsibility and evidence in oral discourse*. Cambridge: Cambridge
        University Press.

Hirsch, Susan
1998   *Pronouncing & persevering: Gender and the discourses of disputing in an
        African Islamic court*. Chicago: University of Chicago Press.

Hosman, Lawrence A.
1989   The evaluative consequences of hedges, hesitations, and intensifiers:
        Powerful and powerless speech styles. *Human Communications Research*
        15:383–406.

Hosman, Lawrence A., and Susan A. Siltanen
1994   The attributional and evaluative consequences of powerful and powerless
        speech styles: An examination of the "control over others" and "control of
        self" explanations. *Language & Communication* 14:287–98.

Hudson, R. A.
1980   *Sociolinguistics*. Cambridge: Cambridge University Press.

Hughes, Scott H.
1995   Elizabeth's story: Exploring power imbalances in divorce mediation.
        Georgetown Journal of Legal Ethics 8:553–96.

Hunt, Alan, and Gary Wickham
1994   *Foucault and law: Towards a sociology of law as governance*. London:
        Pluto Press.

Hymes, Dell
1968   The ethnography of speaking. In *Readings in the sociology of language*,
        edited by Joshua Fishman. The Hague: Mouton.

Irvine, Judith T.
1989   When talk isn't cheap: Language and political economy. *American Ethnolo-
        gist* 16:248–67.
1992   Insult and responsibility: Verbal abuse in a Wolof village. In *Responsibility
        and evidence in oral discourse*, edited by Jane H. Hill and Judith T. Irvine.
        Cambridge: Cambridge University Press.

Irvine, Judith T., and Susan Gal
2000   Language ideology and linguistic differentiation. In *Regimes of language:
        Ideologies, polities, and identities*, edited by Paul V. Kroskrity. Santa Fe,
        NM: School of American Research Press.

Izumi, Carol
2010   Implicit bias and the illusion of mediator neutrality. *Washington University
        Journal of Law and Policy* 34:71–155.

Jefferson, Gail
1980   On "trouble-premonitory" response to inquiry. *Sociological Inquiry* 50: 153–85.
1985   On the interactional unpackaging of a "gloss." *Language in Society* 14: 435–66.
1988   On the sequential organization of troubles-talk in ordinary conversation. *Social Problems* 35:418–41.

Just, Peter
1990   Dead goats and broken betrothals: Liability and equity in Dou Donggo law. *American Anthropologist* 17:75–90.

Karpiński, Maciej
2012   The boundaries of language: Dealing with paralinguistic features. *Lingua Posnaniensis* 2:37–54.

Keenan, Elinor Ochs
1976   The universality of conversational postulates. *Language in Society* 5: 67–80.

Kelly, Joan
1989   Mediated and adversarial divorce: Respondents' perception of their processes and outcomes. *Mediation Quarterly* Summer 1989:71–87.

Kendon, Adam
2004   *Gesture: Visible action as utterance.* Cambridge: Cambridge University Press.

Kidder, Robert L.
1980–81 The end of the road? Problems in the analysis of disputes. *Law & Society Review* 15:717–25.

Koss, Mary P.
1988   Hidden rape: Sexual aggression and victimization in a national sample of students in higher education. In *Rape and sexual assault*, edited by A. W. Burgess. New York: Garland.

Koss, Mary P., ed.
1994   *No safe haven: Male violence against women at home, at work, and in the community.* Washington, DC: American Psychological Association.

Kroskrity, Paul V.
2000   Regimenting languages: Language ideological perspectives. In *Regimes of language: Ideologies, polities, and identities*, edited by Paul V. Kroskrity. Santa Fe, NM: School of American Research Press.
2016   Language ideologies: Emergence, elaboration, and application. In *The Routledge handbook of linguistic anthropology*, edited by Nancy Bonvillain. New York: Routledge.

Kuipers, Joel
1990   *Power in performance: The creation of textual authority in Weyewa ritual speech.* Philadelphia: University of Pennsylvania Press.

Labov, William
1966   *The social stratification of English in New York City.* Washington, DC: Center for Applied Linguistics.
1972a   *Language in the inner city.* Philadelphia: University of Pennsylvania Press.
1972b   *Sociolinguistic patterns.* Philadelphia: University of Pennsylvania Press.
1979   Locating the frontier between social and psychological factors in linguistic variation. In *Individual differences in language ability and language behavior*, edited by Charles J. Fillmore, Daniel Kempler, and William S.-Y. Wang. New York: Academic Press.

Lakoff, Robin
1975   *Language and woman's place.* New York: Harper & Row.

Lasswell, Harold
1936   *Politics: Who gets what, when, how.* New York: McGraw-Hill.

Lein, Laura, and Donald Brenneis
1978   Children's disputes in three speech communities. *Language in Society* 7:299–323.

Levenson, Laurie L.
2008   Courtroom demeanor: The theater of the courtroom. *Minnesota Law Review* 92:573–633.

Levi, Judith N.
1994   *Language and law: A bibliographic guide to social sciences research in the U.S.A.* Chicago: American Bar Association.

Levi, Judith N., and Anne G. Walker, eds.
1990   *Language in the judicial process.* New York: Plenum Press.

Lévy-Bruhl, Lucien
1923   *Primitive mentality (La mentalité primitive)*, translated by Lilian A. Clare. New York: Macmillan Company.

Lind, E. Allan, and Tom R. Tyler
1988   *The social psychology of procedural justice.* New York: Plenum.

Litosseliti, Lia, and Jane Sunderland, eds.
2002   *Gender identity and discourse analysis.* Amsterdam: John Benjamins.

Llewellyn, Karl N., and E. Adamson Hoebel
1961   *The Cheyenne way.* Norman: University of Oklahoma Press (orig. 1941).

Loftus, Elizabeth F.
1979   *Eyewitness testimony.* Cambridge, MA: Harvard University Press.
1987   My turn. *Newsweek*, June 29, 10.

Loftus, Elizabeth F., and Katherine Ketcham
1991   *Witness for the defense: The accused, the eyewitness, and the expert who puts memory on trial.* New York: St. Martin's Press.
1994   *The myth of repressed memory.* New York: St. Martin's Press.

Luff, Paul, and Christian Heath
2015   Transcribing embodied action. In *The handbook of discourse analysis*, 2nd
        ed., edited by Deborah Tannen, Heidi E. Hamilton, and Deborah Schiffrin.
        West Sussex, UK: John Wiley & Sons.

Lyons, John
1968   *Introduction to theoretical linguistics*. Cambridge: Cambridge University
        Press.

MacKinnon, Catharine A.
1989   *Toward a feminist theory of the state*. Cambridge, MA: Harvard University
        Press.

Malinowski, Bronislaw
1985   *Crime and custom in savage society*. Totowa, NJ: Rowman & Allanheld
        (orig. 1926).

Matoesian, Gregory M.
1993   *Reproducing rape: Domination through talk in the courtroom*. Chicago:
        University of Chicago Press.
1995   Language, law, and society: Policy implications of the Kennedy Smith rape
        trial. *Law & Society Review* 29:669–701.
2001   *Law and the language of identity: Discourse in the William Kennedy Smith
        rape trial*. Oxford: Oxford University Press.
2005   Struck by speech revisited: Embodied stance in jurisdictional discourse.
        Journal of Sociolinguistics 9(2):167–94.
2008a   You might win the battle but lose the war: Multimodal, interactive, and
        extralinguistic aspects of witness resistance. *Journal of English Linguistics*
        36(3):195–219.
2008b   Role conflict as an interactional resource in the multimodal emergence of
        expert testimony. *Semiotica* 171:15–49.
2013   Language and material conduct in legal discourse. *Journal of Sociolinguistics* 17(5):634–60.

Mauet, Thomas A.
1992   *Fundamentals of trial techniques*. Boston: Little, Brown.

Maynard, Douglas W.
1984   *Inside plea bargaining: The language of negotiation*. New York: Plenum
        Press.

McCann, Michael W.
1994   *Rights at work: Pay equity reform and the politics of legal mobilization*.
        Chicago: University of Chicago Press.

McElhinny, Bonnie
2003   Three approaches to the study of language and gender. *American Anthropologist* 105(4):848–55.

McEwen, Craig, Lynn Mather, and Richard J. Maiman
1994   Lawyers, mediation, and the management of divorce practice. *Law & Society Review* 28:149–86.

McIlvenny, Paul, ed.
2002   *Talking gender and sexuality*. Amsterdam: John Benjamins.

Mellinkoff, David
1963   *The language of the law*. Boston: Little, Brown.

Merry, Sally Engle
1986   Everyday understandings of the law in working-class America. *American Ethnologist* 13:253–70.
1990   *Getting justice and getting even: Legal consciousness among working-class Americans*. Chicago: University of Chicago Press.

Mertz, Elizabeth
1985   Beyond symbolic anthropology: Introducing semiotic mediation. In *Semiotic mediation: Sociocultural and psychological perspectives*, edited by Elizabeth Mertz and Richard J. Parmentier. Orlando, FL: Academic Press.
1994   Legal language. In *Annual Review of Anthropology*. Vol. 23. Palo Alto, CA: Annual Reviews, Inc.
1996   Recontextualization as socialization: Text and pragmatics in the law school classroom. In *Natural histories of discourse*, edited by Michael Silverstein and Greg Urban. Chicago: University of Chicago Press.
2007   *The language of law school: Learning to "think like a lawyer."* Oxford: Oxford University Press.
n.d.   Linguistic constructions of differences and history in the U.S. law school classroom. American Bar Foundation Working Paper No. 9419.

Miller, Richard E., and Austin Sarat
1980–81 Grievances, claims, and disputes: Assessing the adversary culture. *Law & Society Review* 15:525–66.

Morgan, Rachel E., and Grace Kena
2017   Criminal victimization, 2016. Bureau of Justice Statistics Report, available at https://www.bjs.gov/index.cfm?ty=pbdetail&iid=6166 (accessed January 18, 2018).

Morrill, Calvin, and Peter C. Facciola
1992   The power of language in adjudication and mediation: Institutional contexts as predictors of social evaluation. *Law & Social Inquiry* 17:191–212.

Mulcahy, Linda
2007   Architects of justice: The politics of courtroom design. *Social and Legal Studies* 16(3):383–403.

Nader, Laura
1990   *Harmony ideology: Justice and control in a Zapotec mountain village*. Palo Alto, CA: Stanford University Press.

Nesper, Larry
2007   Negotiating jurisprudence in tribal court and the emergence of a tribal state: The Lac du Flambeau Ojibwe. *Current Anthropology* 48:675–99.

Norris, Sigrid
2004   *Analyzing multimodal interaction: A methodological framework.* New York: Routledge.

O'Barr, William M.
1982   *Linguistic evidence: Language, power, and strategy in the courtroom.* New York: Academic Press.

O'Barr, William M., and Bowman K. Atkins
1980   "Women's language" or "powerless language"? In *Women and language in literature and society*, edited by Sally McConnell-Ginet, Ruth Borker, and Nelly Furman. New York: Praeger.

Ochs, Elinor
1979   Transcription as theory. In *Developmental pragmatics*, edited by Elinor Ochs and Bambi B. Schieffelin. New York: Academic Press.

O'Donnell, Katherine
1990   Difference and dominance: How labor and management talk conflict. In *Conflict talk*, edited by Allen D. Grimshaw. Cambridge: Cambridge University Press.

Papke, David R., ed.
1991   *Narrative and the legal discourse.* Liverpool: Deborah Charles.

Pearlberg, Van, Jimmy D. Berry, Julie L. Miller, and Linda Goldman
1995   Defense of a rape case. In *Criminal defense techniques*, edited by Amanda J. Pisani and Elizabeth L. Englehart. New York: Matthew Bender.

Philips, Susan U.
1990   The judge as third party in American trial-court conflict talk. In *Conflict talk*, edited by Allen D. Grimshaw. Cambridge: Cambridge University Press.
1992   Evidentiary standards for American trials: Just the facts. In *Responsibility and evidence in oral discourse*, edited by Jane H. Hill and Judith T. Irvine. Cambridge: Cambridge University Press.

Philips, Susan U., Susan Steele, and Christine Tanz, eds.
1987   *Language, gender, and sex in comparative perspective.* Cambridge: Cambridge University Press.

Pomerantz, Anita
1978   Attributions of responsibility: Blamings. *Sociology* 12:115–21.

Rape, Abuse & Incest National Network
2018   Statistics. Available at https://www.rainn.org/statistics (accessed January 18, 2018).

Remland, Martin S.
1994   The importance of nonverbal communication in the courtroom. *New Jersey Journal of Communication* 2(2):124–45.

Richland, Justin B.
2008   *Arguing with tradition: The language of law in Hopi tribal court.* Chicago: University of Chicago Press.

Rickford, John R.
1975   Carrying the new wave into syntax: The case of Black English BIN. In *Analyzing variation in language*, edited by Ralph Fasold and Roger Shuy. Washington, DC: Georgetown University Press.
1999   *African American vernacular English*. Oxford: Blackwell.

Rickford, John R., and Sharese King
2016   Language and linguistics on trial: Hearing Rachel Jeantel (and other vernacular speakers) in the courtroom and beyond. *Language* 92:948–88.

Rosen, Lawrence
1977   The anthropologist as expert witness. *American Anthropologist* 79: 555–72.

Rumsey, Alan
1990   Wording, meaning, and linguistic ideology. *American Anthropologist* 92(2):346–61.

Russell, Diana E. H.
1984   *Sexual exploitation: Rape, child sexual abuse, and workplace harassment.* Beverly Hills, CA: Sage.

Sacks, H., E. Schegloff, and G. Jefferson
1974   A simplest systematics for the organization of turn-taking for conversation. *Language* 50:696–735.

Salekin, Randall T., James R. P. Ogloff, Cathy McFarland, and Richard Rogers
1995   Influencing jurors' perceptions of guilt: Expression of emotionality during testimony. *Behavioral Sciences and the Law* 13(2):293–305.

Sandburg, Carl
1939   *Abraham Lincoln: The war years.* New York: Harcourt, Brace & Co.

Sankoff, Gillian
1980   *The social life of language.* Philadelphia: University of Pennsylvania Press.

Sarat, Austin, and William Felstiner
1995   *Divorce lawyers and their clients.* London: Oxford University Press.

Schegloff, Emanuel
1992   On talk and its institutional occasions. In *Talk at work: Interaction in institutional settings*, edited by Paul Drew and John Heritage. Cambridge: Cambridge University Press.

Schwartz, Bernard
1993   *Main currents in American legal thought.* Durham, NC: Carolina Academic Press.

Searle, John
1969   *Speech acts.* Cambridge: Cambridge University Press.

Shearing, C., and R. Ericson
1991   Culture as figurative action. *British Journal of Sociology* 42:481–506.

Sheldon, Amy
1993   Pickle fights: Gendered talk in preschool disputes. In *Gender and conversational interaction*, edited by Deborah Tannen. New York: Oxford University Press.

Sheldon, Amy, and Diane Johnson
1994   Preschool negotiators: Linguistic differences in how girls and boys regulate the expression of dissent in same-sex groups. *Research on Negotiations in Organizations* 4:37–67.

Shuy, Roger W.
1993   *Language crimes: The use and abuse of language evidence in the courtroom.* Cambridge, MA: Blackwell Publishing.
2002   *Linguistic battles in trademark disputes.* New York: Palgrave MacMillan.

Silbey, Susan S., and Sally E. Merry
1986   Mediator settlement strategies. *Law & Policy* 8:7–31.

Silverstein, Michael
1979   Language structure and linguistic ideology. In *The elements: A parasession on linguistic units and levels*, edited by Paul R. Clyne, William F. Hanks, and Carol L. Hofbauer. Chicago: Chicago Linguistic Society.
1985   Language and the culture of gender: At the intersection of structure, usage, and ideology. In *Semiotic mediation: Sociocultural and psychological perspectives*, edited by Elizabeth Mertz and Richard J. Parmentier. Orlando, FL: Academic Press.
1998   The uses and utility of ideology: A commentary. In *Language ideologies: Practice and theory*, edited by Bambi B. Schieffelin, Kathryn A. Woolard, and Paul V. Kroskrity. New York: Oxford University Press.

Silverstein, Michael, and Greg Urban, eds.
1996   *Natural histories of discourse.* Chicago: University of Chicago Press.

Slobe, Tyanna
2016   Creepy-ass cracker in post-racial America: Don West's examination of Rachel Jeantel in the George Zimmerman murder trial. *Text & Talk* 36: 613–35.

Solan, Lawrence M., and Peter M. Tiersma
2005   *Speaking of crime.* Chicago: University of Chicago Press.

Solan, Lawrence M., and Peter M. Tiersma, eds.
2012   *The Oxford handbook of language and law.* Oxford: Oxford University Press.

Spears, Arthur K.
1998   African-American language use: Ideology and so-called obscenity. In *African-American English: Structure, history and use*, edited by Salikoko S. Mufwene, John R. Rickford, Guy Bailey, and John Baugh. London: Routledge.

Spohn, Cassia, and Julie Horney
1992   *Rape law reform: A grassroots revolution and its impact.* New York: Plenum Press.

Streeck, Jürgen, Charles Goodwin, and Curtis LeBaron, eds.
2011   *Embodied interaction: Language and body in the material world.* Cambridge: Cambridge University Press.

Sunshine, Jason, and Tom R. Tyler
2003   The role of procedural justice and legitimacy in shaping public support for policing. *Law and Society Review* 37:513–48.

Tannen, Deborah
1986   *That's not what I meant!: How conversational style makes or breaks your relations with others.* New York: Morrow.
1990   *You just don't understand: Women and men in conversation.* New York: Morrow.

Tannen, Deborah, ed.
1993   *Gender and conversational interaction.* New York: Oxford University Press.

Tannen, Deborah, Heidi E. Hamilton, and Deborah Schiffrin, eds.
2015   *The handbook of discourse analysis*, 2nd ed. West Sussex, UK: John Wiley & Sons.

Thompson, Joanna Kerr
2002   "Powerful/powerless" language in court: A critical re-evaluation of the Duke language and law programme. *International Journal of Speech Language and the Law* 9:153–67.

Thorne, Barrie, Cheris Kramarae, and Nancy Henley, eds.
1983   *Language, gender, and society.* Rowley, MA: Newbury House.

Trager, George L.
1958   Paralanguage: A first approximation. *Studies in Linguistics* 13:1–12.

Trinch, Shonna
2013   Recalling rape: Moving beyond what we know. In *Legal-lay communication: Textual travels in the law*, edited by Chris Heffer, Frances Rock, and John Conley. Oxford: Oxford University Press.

Trudgill, Peter
2003   Series editor's preface. In *Forensic linguistics: An introduction to language in the justice system*, by John Gibbons. Oxford: Blackwell Publishing.

Turton, David
1975   The relationship between oratory and the exercise of influence among the Mursi. In *Political language and oratory in traditional society*, edited by Maurice Bloch. New York: Academic Press.

Tyler, Tom R.
1990   *Why people obey the law.* New Haven, CT: Yale University Press.

INDEX

THE CHICAGO SERIES IN LAW AND SOCIETY
Edited by John M. Conley and Lynn Mather

Series titles, continued from front matter:

Everyday Law on the Street: City Governance in an Age of Diversity
by Mariana Valverde

Lawyers in Practice: Ethical Decision Making in Context
Edited by Leslie C. Levin and Lynn Mather

Collateral Knowledge: Legal Reasoning in the Global Financial Markets
by Annelise Riles

Specializing the Courts
by Lawrence Baum

Asian Legal Revivals: Lawyers in the Shadow of Empire
by Yves Dezalay and Bryant G. Garth

The Language of Statutes: Laws and Their Interpretation
by Lawrence M. Solan

Belonging in an Adopted World: Race, Identity, and Transnational Adoption
by Barbara Yngvesson

Making Rights Real: Activists, Bureaucrats, and the Creation of the Legalistic State
by Charles R. Epp

Lawyers of the Right: Professionalizing the Conservative Coalition
by Ann Southworth

Arguing with Tradition: The Language of Law in Hopi Tribal Court
by Justin B. Richland

Speaking of Crime: The Language of Criminal Justice
by Lawrence M. Solan and Peter M. Tiersma

Dealing in Virtue: International Commercial Arbitration and the Construction of a Transnational Legal Order
by Yves Dezalay and Bryant G. Garth

Rights at Work: Pay Equity Reform and the Politics of Legal Mobilization
by Michael W. McCann

The Language of Judges
by Lawrence M. Solan

Reproducing Rape: Domination through Talk in the Courtroom
by Gregory M. Matoesian

Getting Justice and Getting Even: Legal Consciousness among Working-Class Americans
by Sally Engle Merry

Rules versus Relationships: The Ethnography of Legal Discourse
by John M. Conley and William M. O'Barr

Lightning Source UK Ltd.
Milton Keynes UK
UKHW010608190719
346440UK00001B/1/P